Twelve Weeks to Change a Life

Twelve Weeks to Change a Life

AT-RISK YOUTH IN A FRACTURED STATE

Max A. Greenberg

UNIVERSITY OF CALIFORNIA PRESS

University of California Press, one of the most distinguished university presses in the United States, enriches lives around the world by advancing scholarship in the humanities, social sciences, and natural sciences. Its activities are supported by the UC Press Foundation and by philanthropic contributions from individuals and institutions. For more information, visit www.ucpress.edu.

University of California Press
Oakland, California

Library of Congress Cataloging-in-Publication Data

Names: Greenberg, Max A., author.
Title: Twelve weeks to change a life : at-risk youth in a fractured state / Max A. Greenberg.
Description: Oakland, California : University of California Press, [2018] | Includes bibliographical references and index. |
Identifiers: LCCN 2018038421 (print) | LCCN 2018042485 (ebook) | ISBN 9780520969988 (Epub) | ISBN 9780520297746 (cloth : alk. paper) | ISBN 9780520297760 (pbk. : alk. paper)
Subjects: LCSH: Problem youth—Services for—California—Los Angeles. | Problem youth—Counseling of—California—Los Angeles. | Youth and violence—California—Los Angeles.
Classification: LCC HV1437.L67 (ebook) | LCC HV1437.L67 G74 2018 (print) | DDC 362.71/60979494—dc23

LC record available at https://lccn.loc.gov/2018038421

28 27 26 25 24 23 22 21 20 19
10 9 8 7 6 5 4 3 2 1

For Kyra

Contents

Acknowledgments

I am indebted in a way I cannot repay to the young men and women who talked with me, who brought their bright eyes and eager words even after long days and hard weeks. It was a pleasure and it was a privilege to get to know you all, as fleeting as it was. I hope you see yourselves in this. Thank you to the people I met at Peace Over Violence and in the work of violence prevention across Los Angeles, who were relentlessly kind and passionate. I entered that world because I saw, and still see, a great deal to admire and be hopeful for in the endeavor, even as I turn it over in the light to explore how it works. In no small part, this is because the people who do this work have earned my respect and my admiration. Thank you for welcoming me into your lives.

This is a study in large part about the importance of connection and, for me, there has been one connection in particular that made this book possible. Mike Messner: your generosity and humanity are what I strive for as a scholar. This began as a project in graduate school at the University of Southern California and I am building with the tools I acquired there. Sharon Hays's fingerprints are pressed into the concrete foundation of my theory and writing. Pierrette Hondagneu-Sotelo set me on this path during my second year in graduate school and has seen it through to the end.

Shari Dworkin has been a guide in ways large and small all along the way. Graduate school is a team sport, the victories sweetened and defeats softened because they are done with friends at your side. Jeff Sacha showed me the value of saying kind things out loud and is, simply, family. Kit Myers and Brandy Jenner always show me we are in this together. Thank you: Brady Potts for getting excited when I was onto something. Megan Carroll for being thoughtful and noticing things I missed. Michela Musto for showing me how to be a pro. Kristen Barber for the well-placed words of confidence. Tal Peretz for being my counterpoint and coauthor. Freeden Oeur, Tristan Bridges, CJ Pascoe, for their confidence and trust in this project and in me. Mike's dissertation group for keeping me challenged, supported, and well fed. The Haynes Lindley Fellowship, which saw the possibility in my research and supported my writing.

Since I have returned east, this book has been nurtured by the incredible community of scholars at Boston University. Nazli Kibria gave me a chance and everyone there has welcomed me since day one. Jess Simes, Cati Connell, Ana Villarreal, Ashley Mears, Saida Grundy, Emily Barman: your generosity and sharp analytic insights have made me a better scholar.

All of the reviewers, some named and others not, thank you. Lynne Haney and Lucia Trimbur, who pushed me off my well-worn path toward ideas I had not considered; this project is immeasurably better for it. Naomi Schneider, who saw something in this project when it was ragged and the quotes were too long. Thank you, Naomi, and the entire team at University of California Press, for all of your hard work. This book is better because of Rebecca Steinitz, who took my desire to write a beautiful book seriously but never let me sacrifice clarity. Thank you to the reviewers and editorial support at Sociological Perspectives, where portions of this book appear, for all of your insight.

This is a book about disconnection and it is one I was able to write, in part, because I am so tied to other people. My safety net is large and well woven. I learned how to think constructively from my mother, Lisa Greenberg, over long conversations around our kitchen table. My father, Steve Greenberg, taught me an ethnographic mindset, that everyone is family, you just don't know it yet. Judy Norsigian opened her home and gave her support without hesitation. My Waban family has picked up my slack and kept me going: Elizabeth Cooper, Benoit Aubertin, Geneva

Cooper, Dan Emerson, Craig Norberg-Bohm. Sig Suchowicki, David Sayre, Debbie Sayre: thank you for being in my corner. Felix, you have been the best distraction I could hope for.

Kyra Norsigian has been my steady drum, my informant, my sounding board, and my heart when I was too pounded down by words and data to feel much. She reminds me why I do this. Thank you isn't enough, but it will have to do.

1 In Medias Res

THE LIVES WE MEANT TO LIVE

When we count over the resources which are at work "to make order out of casualty, beauty out of confusion, justice, kindliness and mercy out of cruelty and inconsiderate pressure," we find ourselves appealing to the confident spirit of youth. We know that it is crude and filled with conflicting hopes, some of them unworthy and most of them doomed to disappointment, yet these young people have the advantage of "morning in their hearts"; they have such power of direct action, such ability to stand free from fear, to break through life's trammelings, that in spite of ourselves we become convinced that "They to the disappointed earth shall give. The lives we meant to live."

Jane Addams, 1909

.   .   .   .   .

"Things come back like a flashback, like in a car accident," said Angel, 19 years old and wide eyed. I asked if he had ever heard of post-traumatic stress disorder.[1] He had not. I explained that when people go through something scary or painful, like a car crash, memories of it could come flooding back like they were in that moment again. Angel told me that when he gets angry with his ex, he can see in his mind a time that he "put hands on her" and ripped her dress. He wanted to control the flashbacks but didn't know how. "It's kind of hard getting over it, 'cause like, she always has, she always has that in her head, too, like in her mind." We were in an empty classroom at the small charter school he attended in South Los Angeles. On the walls around us were students' "dream collages" for a school assignment, pictures cut out of magazines and pasted onto construction paper showing images of what they wanted for their future. I saw one covered in expensive cars and a swimming pool, another with models in swimsuits, chopped out of their surroundings. Angel was remorseful about his past actions but also stuck, unable to figure out how to move on. He wanted to get back together with his ex.

> There's a couple of things that I did to her that she will never forget. Like it haunts me a lot. Like it bothers me that I even did that. Like there was once that we got in an argument and I ended up spitting in her face. It always bugs me, like she always brings it up, too. I'm trying to like, I don't know, like it happened out of anger, too, like I regret it so bad. But like I don't know how we get over that.

While the collages around Angel played out stories of the future, Angel and the person he loved couldn't get away from the past. As much as they tried, they couldn't begin in the middle. And it wasn't just his own violence that Angel couldn't get away from, but his home and community life also bore scars. He told me that there was "all this violence and I knew I was at that place, like I was doing violence, violence was going on in my life."[2] The violence surrounding Angel came with messages. Growing up, Angel was taught "that females were always less than us." It used to be that every time he got angry, it would "come down to violence" because he did not care about anything else at that moment. He would punch walls. One time, he punched glass and badly lacerated his hand.

Angel's father "works for a good company. He does like statues and things like that." His mother worked on a maintenance crew. Even with steady jobs, Angel's parents struggled to pay for their car and apartment. "It's pretty expensive rent: pretty expensive one-room house. That's for six people." This put pressure on him at home, where his family gave him a hard time for still being in school at 19 years old. Angel saw finishing high school as a path to supporting his family and was hurt that they wanted him to quit school and find a job.

Angel explained that the way he thought about women was changing "after a couple experiences and, like, getting my things together and moving out, and getting my head out the streets." He had started to gain control of his temper. "It's changing little by little," he told me. Still, his history would not let go easily. Angel told me that "certain mistakes from the past" meant that he had to be careful in his neighborhood. When I asked Angel if there was anything he did to stay safe, he answered, "Just stay in my house." The past had its own inertia beyond Angel's control. Even as he tried to change his life, the past pulled at him. His past, after all, was not his alone; it lived on in the stories of others: in tales of the street, in flash-backs and relationships.

Angel was at risk.[3] It was this fact that had brought me into his life through an interpersonal violence prevention program. The program had shown up in his classroom seemingly out of nowhere and was trying to change him and deter the dangers that loomed across his future. Programs like this one, in essence, started in the middle, *in medias res,* for a life that was ongoing. They dropped into lives and institutions already in progress. I had come to violence prevention looking for hope for the future; how-ever, in many ways, for most of the young people I met, violence was already a fact of biography. Angel and young people like him require us to ask: What does it mean to be at risk?[4]

Two years earlier, I had begun research into feminist violence preven-tion programs, interested in how they took the personal stories that emerged from consciousness-raising and turned them into evidence-based programs. Like most people, I assumed that programs worked in the ways described in the evaluation literature: as powerful and effective approaches toward changing attitudes and behaviors.[5] But on the ground, I found that they were far more fractured and temporary than anyone had described them. I looked to the sociological literature on the state and found that, though the programs had things in common with the policies analyzed by scholars of neoliberalism, in myriad ways they were distinct.[6] I came to see that prevention programs and at-risk youth were pieces of an underexplored shift in how the state deals with social problems. For three and a half years, I embedded myself in the world of violence preven-tion in Los Angeles, particularly in an organization, Peace Over Violence, that implemented multiple programs. I set out to understand how the system was organized and how it was experienced.

After a year and a half observing and participating in prevention pro-gramming, I had seen how young people were shuffled through the system, but I knew less about how they made sense of the programs that streaked across their lives. Which brings us back to Angel. When it came to the program, he was ambivalent: "I don't have no problem with you all," he told me. However, he believed that the outsiders who came into his class—and there were many of them, myself included—couldn't really understand what he had been through. He went on: "Everyone around here, like, it's just nothing but drama, violence. No love." This gap in understanding, I found, was at the heart of programs. Young people marked as at risk and the facilitators tasked with changing their lives—citizens and the state—grazed each other's lives, unable to understand one another.

After the interview ended I gave Angel the chance, as I did every young person, to ask me anything he wanted. Many young people took this as an opportunity to get my take on ideas from the prevention program, such as what I thought a healthy relationship looked like, or to ask me the same questions I had asked them. Others simply shrugged. A few asked me something similar to what Angel did, "What made you get into this?" by which he meant violence prevention. I told Angel that a friend of mine had been sexually assaulted and I had struggled to know what to do. I wanted to be able to support her, and myself, and to better understand why it happened. "Yeah. My, my ex been through that, too." He nodded. "Can I ask you a question? How can I help, like, somebody go through that?" Angel and I talked for another 20 minutes. He kept asking questions. My story had opened up a door. As I found repeatedly, personal stories made it possible to make a connection, to narrow social distance, at least for a while.[7]

This was not counseling, nor did Angel and I have any kind of lasting connection. In fact, I was acutely aware of the distance between my experience and his, as well as the force of race, class, and place in shaping how we ended up in that room. It was a rare chance—an opening in time and space—to talk about the reverberations of trauma, and to work through complex and compounding histories, something that I found was rare in the lives of youth marked as at risk. The young people I talked to spent a lot of time around adults, especially in schools, but those adults rarely if ever asked young people about their lives or talked about their own, especially when it came to harm and trauma. This book takes those stories—and their absence—seriously.

Harm lives twice. First in a flash, often away from view. And then a second life, long and searing, as trauma and memory. Violence prevention claims to undermine the first, and though it may, what it fails to reckon with is this second life of harm, where it is reconstructed and interpreted and felt far away from its physicality. This second life of harm exists in real and tangible ways, even in bright and quiet classrooms. Harm takes on its lingering weight after the act, when it comes flooding back during an exam or on a date and sends us spiraling; when we cannot focus at a job; when we tell stories about it and remedy it—or we don't.

I wish I could tell you that our conversation helped Angel. I wish I could say anything about what happened next for him, but I never saw him again. The program's time at that school was up, which meant it was time to move on the next day to a different school, a different batch of strangers, with new and yet familiar stories. And then again and again, over and over. This churn of intervention and change, of which violence prevention was just one part, is the manifestation of a collection of policies designed to be fleeting and distant that I call the ephemeral state.

INTO THE EPHEMERAL STATE

The students were gone and I looked around the room. The space resembled the public school architecture I saw across Los Angeles: flickering halogen lights, dense rows of desks, pale walls and windows carved up with metal grating. Posters called out to youth to get tested or wear protection or not bully, alongside skeletons and maps of the human brain. Other rooms had bright inspirational posters of college-ready culture, which cried out with the watchwords of youth empowerment: Motivation! Respect! Leadership! A sheet of paper with blue sky and clouds printed on it had been scotch-taped onto the window, which had a thick film and did not open. This was a fitting metaphor for the wide range of programs that try to change youth: a promise of hope within the bars and concrete of broken-down institutions.

Throughout my research, I found myself in pockets of ephemeral change, flecked through massive institutions. Public schools are just one example, but an apt one. These lumbering institutions are largely dedicated to the long, slow grind of people processing: sorting and converting individuals into one category or another, issuing labels and credentials, sometimes alongside economic assistance.[8] Think of the grinding days at a courthouse, hours of testing at school, or long waits for food stamps and you will have a feel for these institutions. I call this the slow state. In these places, the apparatus of government seems to be saying: You must learn to wait.[9]

These traditional arrangements of time and space in social policy are inverted in the ephemeral state. Rather than a slow-moving institution, the state acts through a multiplied field of fleeting interventions into institutions and daily life that encourage rapid transformation. Policy blinks into existence for a short time and then vanishes. At one level, grants and contracts reshuffle economic pressures every few years, and on another level, short-term programs flash by in days. Unlike the slow state, which keeps track of every personal detail, programs set out to accumulate masses of depersonalized data.[10] If the file cabinet is the symbolic distillation of the slow state, a messenger bag full of worksheets, pre- and post-surveys, sign-in sheets, and a tattered curriculum, all wiped of identifying data, represents the ephemeral state. These two temporal dimensions of the state—slow and ephemeral—produce a kind of social whiplash.[11]

This is what it was like in the ephemeral state: A security guard led Anne, a young white facilitator, through a keycarded door, past a maze of cubicles and attorney-client meeting rooms, and into the dim basement of the Children's Court of Los Angeles. Beyond a long table with five adults doing paperwork, the room opened up and about 30 young people, mostly Latino and Black, sat in rows of thin plastic chairs or stretched out on floormats, facing toward a big-screen TV playing cartoons. Some were there for a hearing on criminal charges. Others were foster youth waiting for news about their parents or guardians. Every few minutes the loudspeaker crackled and a hollow voice called another young person out to meet their attorney. Peace Over Violence maintained a standing monthly presentation on healthy relationships at the court, deep within the physical and institutional architecture of the slow state.

A woman introduced Anne and me: "These folks are here to talk about a very important issue, violence, so please listen." As Anne and I walked to the front, six or seven youth leaned forward in their creaking chairs. Others cradled their heads in their hands facedown on the mats in the front row, white earbud chords trailing down their necks. They did not register our presence. Anne began with what facilitators called "the check-in." She asked each youth to say their name and how they were feeling. She forced some enthusiasm into her voice, a skill she learned in training to build connection and momentum in fleeting interactions. Moving along the rows, she pointed to individuals so they knew when it was their turn.

I caught sight of a young man toward the back, who smiled and leaned toward the young woman next to him. They shared a conspiratorial laugh and I wondered if relationships ever start here. A few seconds later, her expression flattened and she yelled out, "He's being disrespectful!" She smacked her right fist against her open left hand and sternly said to no one in particular, "I'm going to have to take care of him." The boy put out his hands palms up and shrugged. Despite the setting, this felt like the schools I had spent the last year observing. Young people navigated their personal relationships within these massive institutions, with adults all around, but at a distance. Anne waited a beat, and when it seemed neither the young man and woman, nor the other adults, had anything else to say, she continued the check-in.

As she snaked around the room, most of the young people said they were "good," but some said "bored" or "tired." One young woman said, "I have no feelings." A boy said that he was "frustrated" and pulled his gray hood close around his face until only his eyes showed. Facilitators told me that they used the check-in to gauge the "emotional temperature of the room." It let them know if the energy was low, if there was some trauma bubbling, or if a short fuse was lit and burning. After months listening to young people describe how they were feeling, I had learned how this would go. There was a hidden grammar of emotion in the slow state, which was to be vague and unremarkable. The majority of youth described their emotional state as simply good, fine, or tired. On this day, waiting for their names to be called out in children's court, it was difficult to imagine what it meant to be good.

As sometimes happened, a young person, in this case a young woman with wire-rimmed glasses, said that she was "not good, not at all." This seemed to set off a small alarm in Anne. I could feel it too, an embodied sense that I picked up in training and from watching implementers at work. When a young person says that they are not good in front of a classroom full of peers and strangers, it means they are likely on the verge of crisis. Anne nudged in a smooth drawl, "What's going on that is making you feel bad?" The girl started to answer, "My mom, she—" but then, like something caught her, she stopped and shook her head. "Never mind." "You sure?" Anne nudged again, gently. "Yeah," the young woman said as she looked to the wall. Anne paused for several seconds, then moved on. If this was my only peek inside a room like this, I might have thought that her change of heart had something specific to do with the court and its representatives, or with Anne, or with her peers' eyes on her. But this happened nearly everywhere facilitators went. This is one of the things facilitators learn: young people want to talk, often badly, but then don't.

Anne continued, settling into a discussion of the roots of violence. She ran through exercises on how to identify an unhealthy relationship and how to help a friend. She finished by asking what the youth did to deal with violent feelings. One girl would scream into her pillow, several would listen to heavy metal alone in their room, another would go for long walks. This conversation seemed to be a release, and I could see people's body postures ease and some even cracked a smile.

In her study of school discipline, Ann Arnett Ferguson explores how institutional processes funneled Black boys in public schools into the "punishing room," where students were sent by adults when they were marked as trouble.[12] That room, and others like it, are symbolic and physical distillations of the larger system in many urban schools used to punish and mark youth, particularly Black boys. And yet, as Ferguson shows, punishing rooms are also sites of identity, power, and play: marginalized youth do not simply bend to labels, punishment, and school discipline; they have agency and make sense of themselves anew in the face of these forces. Young people's agency was evident one day, early in my research. I was new to a high school and the campus was vast and uneven and full of spaces hidden away from adult eyes, like the strange geometry of an M. C. Escher painting. I got lost. I weaved in and out of buildings, catching vignettes of kissing couples, girls snacking on contraband candy, and boys wrestling and laughing on patches of dead grass. It was the first time since I began observing violence prevention programs that I saw the hidden spaces that characterize so much of the underlife of young people in schools. Barrie Thorne described these relative free spaces youth develop within the disciplined structure of schools "like grass and dandelions sprouting through the cracks" in cement sidewalk blocks.[13]

The stories we hear about marginalized young people are pulled between poles of unstructured freedom and oppressive institutions. Yet, for even the most marginalized young people in the United States, daily life is shot through with pockets of something like state-sanctioned agency, as programs or campaigns come through promising a better life.[14] The programs I studied are just a few among a number of fleeting lessons throughout the daily lives of youth; posters in the halls, videos shown in classes, curriculums, after-school programs, social media campaigns, and more.[15] I came to recognize that there are places set aside for this kind of thing: A beige metal trailer on the outskirts of campus called the "Impact Office"; a YWCA in an office park; a windowless classroom wallpapered with students' art projects and crammed with cardboard boxes. They are, to build on Thorne's metaphor, curated gaps in the concrete, where only one type of flower is allowed to grow. These patches of programmatic empowerment often take place at the outer edges of labyrinth-like state institutions, but they are undeniable and scholars have not done enough to reckon with them. Urban public schools are not monolithic places where youth of color are relentlessly disciplined. Marginalized young people are also told that they are free, that they are responsible, that they can do anything they set their minds to. We must take these moments seriously, lest we ignore the shape of the contemporary state.

THE SHADOW STATE AND BEYOND

As we walked to his car after a session, a facilitator named Robert described a book he had read on the "nonprofit industrial complex." I knew the book Robert cited, *The Revolution Will Not Be Funded* by the INCITE! collective. In it, a range of academics and activists lay out the consequences of a sprawling system of nonprofits and funders, which secures inequality as it pacifies grassroots activism with band-aid measures. The authors argue that would-be activists are funneled into low-paying nonprofit work, which reinforces the status quo. Robert, who fit that description, agreed with the assessment of the book and hoped that funding might "dry up" for prevention programming—"then we could have a real movement," he said. Robert, like many facilitators, saw his work in the tradition of consciousness-raising and activism, yet believed it was tainted by the incentives of funding. And though this was true at one point, facilitation had become something different, a new kind of work for a new kind of state project.

Alongside the notion that nonprofits constrain movements, there is a second argument woven through *The Revolution Will Not Be Funded*, one I did not hear from facilitators: that together, nonprofits represent what Jennifer Wolch in 1990 called the "shadow state," which has grown up parallel to the prison-industrial complex and the military-industrial complex and partially fills in the gaps left by the dismantling of the welfare state.[16] Over the last several decades, the social organization of social support has changed dramatically, as the supportive arm of the state has been devolved and replaced by a swarm of nonprofits, charities, and foundations.[17] These organizations fulfill many of the roles of the state, but they do so in ways that are obscured and distant.[18] The slow state is coming apart and something different is coming together in its wake.

From this angle, the organizations that often play the role of independent actor in our everyday stories—nonprofits—are called into question. Today, nonprofits, funded in large part by state and federal grants, are the primary deliverers of services in the United States.[19] A study from the Urban Institute estimates that government agencies have as many as 200,000 contracts and grants with some 33,000 human services nonprofits: an average of six per group."[20] In this way, the growth of the nonprofit sector represents a dramatic shift in the way that the state approaches social problems: away from government bureaucracies and toward a system of grant-funded nonprofits. In Los Angeles, nonprofit organizations dot the landscape to an extent that dwarfs the number from a generation ago, with nearly 35,000 registered nonprofits in 2008, "representing seven percent of the gross metropolitan product and six percent of the labor force" in 2010.[21] There are dozens of organizations in Los Angeles working against violence alone. The Violence Prevention Coalition, established in 1991 by the Los Angeles County Department of Health Services, which promotes the public health approach to violence, listed 117 members in 2017, the vast majority of which were nonprofits.

The shadow state distributes services and social support through a market logic, as nonprofits and private entities compete for a narrow pool of temporary funding.[22] This is what Smith and Lipsky have called a "contracting regime." At the top, there are funders, who contract with organizations like the agency at the core of this book, Peace Over Violence, to implement a program within their desired parameters.[23] Grants rarely last more than three years, and organizations often have multiple grants at some point in "the cycle": drafting, submission, waiting, allocating funding, reporting on deliverables, repeat.[24] Funders might also hire grant-fidelity inspectors and technical assistance organizations to oversee the grant. At the local level, contracted organizations send programs, in the hands of trained facilitators, into schools and community centers.[25] Grants and curricula collapse the time horizons through which policy operates as they transform the kinds of work done by the state. This arrangement has led to new markets and commodities for temporally bounded policy—in short, to the ephemeral state.

Within the ephemeral state, this collapsing timeline is reorganizing the ground floor of social policy at those places where the state bumps up against the public. Facilitators set out not only to change citizens but to do so hastily before disappearing from their lives. No reliable numbers are available as to how many facilitators are in the United States today, but given the breadth of topics met with curricula, and the quick turnover of both employed and volunteer implementers, tens of thousands of people are likely to have been trained as program facilitators and likely millions have participated in at least one program. The facilitators of prevention programs are not the people at a heavy desk with a vast bureaucracy above them whom we usually think of as comprising the front lines of social support. Michael Lipsky, in a book which has had a lasting echo in sociology, coined the term street-level bureaucrats to describe how individuals manage the work of state bureaucracies—the slow state institutions of schools, police departments, welfare offices—that administer public benefits and sanctions. Unlike other street-level representatives of policy, facilitators' messages did not hinge on the promise of economic support or the threat of a fine or the restriction of liberty. They were not employed to provide any kind of support—financial, emotional, or otherwise—to youth participants. Their daily grind was built around providing messages and documenting the impact of those messages. They were, for the most part, undertrained and underpaid. While their bosses and managers felt the market pressures of competition and economic rationality, for facilitators, the most salient quality of their work was that it was fleeting, played out in a never-ending cascade of metrics, campaigns, and programs designed to be impermanent.

CHANGE PROGRAMS

I describe curricula designed to transform some social or cultural metric and their implementation as *change programs*. Hailed as a means to transform embedded cultural norms and prevent future harm, change programs are a slow-rolling policy revolution. Although change programs take a range of forms and names—including "norms change," "culture change," "positive youth development," or "health promotion"—they have several defining characteristics. They are temporary and bounded to a predetermined time and space. They are produced and evaluated in a market and operate through a tightly structured curriculum. Their goal is to change people in measurable ways. The CDC Training Prevention Guidelines state that program statements should define five elements, which are known as the ABCDE Method:

A—Audience: Who will change—the people you are training.

B—Behavior: What will change—the knowledge, attitudes, and skills you expect to change.

C—Condition: By when—the timeframe within which you hope to see change.

D—Degree: By how much—how much change you think you can realistically achieve.

E—Evidence: How the change will be measured—the surveys, tests, interviews, or other methods you will use to measure the different changes specified.

If you grew up in the United States in the 1990s or 2000s, a program has likely tried to change you. Your attitudes and behaviors, even your culture, were fodder. If you lived in a low-income, urban place, it is likely that multiple programs tried to change you. They may have been trying to change some of your most everyday and, perhaps, fundamental qualities:

how you talk with your peers or the people you love, your thoughts about violence to yourself or others, your sexual habits, your eating and exercise habits, and how you watch TV or listen to music.

This approach arose out of what public health has called "primary prevention" and it was honed through campaigns to increase seat belt use, curb smoking, and encourage people to wear condoms in response to the HIV epidemic.[26] As a category, change programs encompass the moral messages of marriage promotion and responsible fatherhood that were attached to welfare reform in the 1990s, except those messages were bound up with the conditioning mechanisms of incentives and punishments, neither of which are necessary aspects of change programs.[27]

In some ways, change programs mirror public education in that they provide knowledge. But the intended use of that knowledge is neither credentialing nor the production of a citizenry. Instead, it is to be used in personal lives.[28] The most apt analogy is to marketing: change programs transmit stories in order to direct behavior, attitudes, and norms. The weight of success is placed on the producer of the content, not the audience. Just as Coca-Cola doesn't (and cannot) require you to buy a soda, change programs do not exert force; rather, they pull the cultural levers available to position you to make a specific behavioral choice. This is a distinct kind of power, one which feels like a slight breeze on the ground, but looks like a storm system from afar.[29]

There is no comprehensive data on how many programs there are, but we can begin to put together a picture. For example, *Blueprints for Healthy Youth Development*, based at the University of Colorado Boulder, which assesses the evidence base on a range of positive youth development programs, had reviewed over 1,500 programs by 2018.[30] Change programs are now a common part of young people's lives and, taken together, they amount to a dramatic transformation in how young people experience social policy. In the United States, this type of programming has quietly become ubiquitous. Sixty-five percent of youth in the United States have gone through violence prevention programming.[31] For millions of young people every year, programs streak brightly across their lives, then disappear.

One reason for their multiplication is that the grants and curricula that undergird change programs make an incredible claim backed up by reams of evidence: that they simply and directly change individuals and culture writ large. This is the enticement of curricula: at-risk youth go in and healthy, empowered, nonviolent youth come out, and during that process, norms on the larger scale are changed. For example, programs designed explicitly to reshape and shift the masculinity of potentially violent and at-risk boys and men have multiplied at an astounding rate over the last decade. In a review of 58 programs aimed at encouraging healthy masculinities around the world, Barker et al. found that the programs could lead to a stunning list of positive transformations in men's attitudes and behaviors "related to sexual and reproductive health; maternal, newborn and child health; their interaction with their children; their use of violence against women; their questioning of violence with other men; and their health-seeking behaviour."[32] Drawing on ethnographic research conducted in the rooms where programs take place and out into the social worlds of those intended to be changed, this book casts doubt on the conclusions we may draw from these studies.

AT-RISK YOUTH AND THE UNEQUAL PAST

The fleeting interventions of the ephemeral state stand in contrast to the abiding harm and inequality in the lives of young people marked as at risk. The young people I encountered were haunted by the past. Zephire, a young man I met in a prevention program, put it this way: "Everybody comes from some past that they didn't do so well, were feeling bad. And that may lead them to act as some adults do now towards each other . . . they mistreat each other really horribly." The past, however, isn't a fair place. Difficult pasts aren't equally distributed: they are sorted along lines of inequality. Although violence occurs across society, it is multiplied by structural racism, heteronormativity, environmental hazard, deprivation, and so on.[33] To be an at-risk youth, in a way, is to have more than one's share of bad pasts.[34]

Los Angeles, like most cities, has seen a dramatic decline in violence over the last several decades. Yet even as rates of violence experienced by youth have decreased across the nation, the numbers remain stunning. Nearly two-thirds of all children in the United States will be exposed to violence in their homes, schools, or communities this year alone.[35]

Violence disproportionately affects those living in poverty and people of color, and can lead to post-traumatic stress disorder, economic hardship, and educational disparities.[36] The aftershocks of violence are acutely felt in health institutions. In 2011, more than 707,000 young people ages 10–24 were treated in emergency departments for injuries sustained from violence.[37] The criminal-legal system also deals with a share of the damage. According to the FBI, in 2009 approximately 86,000 adolescents were arrested for violent crimes.[38] These rates are even higher in poor and working-class urban "hot spots." In Los Angeles, at least 90 percent of the 120,000 young people living in the most violent neighborhoods will be directly impacted by violence. For tens of thousands of young people in Los Angeles, whether or not they have been perpetrator or victim, violence in a myriad of forms is common: part of the social fabric of their lives.[39]

While it may be spectacular and public violence that makes the news, close-up, intimate violence between people who know each other is far more common, even among youth. One study of middle-school students in "high risk urban communities" found that, of those students who had dated, more than three-quarters had perpetrated verbal or emotional abuse and nearly one-third had perpetrated physical abuse.[40] Another study of young adults ages 14 to 21 found that eight percent reported that they had kissed, touched, or "made someone else do something sexual" when they "knew the person did not want to." In 66 percent of the incidents, "no one found out" and the perpetrator did not face any consequences.[41] Other scholars have found that violence makes it more difficult to make friends, deters the completion of high school, and has long-term negative health consequences.[42] Interpersonal violence is pervasive and yet, for all the violence present in the lives of youth and the lasting consequences, the incidents themselves are often fleeting, or if they are persistent, they are obscured from public view, or hidden away in the past.

THE STORIES YOUTH TELL AND THE ONES THEY DON'T

It was the third day of class at a charter school for system-involved youth, when Anthony, an 18-year-old Latino young man to whom I had never spoken directly, told me his story. There had been a pause between two units of a prevention curriculum and I had gone to the bathroom. I was digging around for the paper towel dispenser when he came in. He looked right at me, eyes glistening, and I knew something was wrong. He spoke in a staccato: "I did something I'm not happy about, but that I don't like telling people." He loved his girlfriend, he explained, but they were always yelling at each other and he worried what he might do if she "kept pushing him." His girlfriend made him cut himself and he got really mad at her and he didn't know if he could take it. He wanted to get counseling. He wanted my help and I was unprepared. He did not want to call the anonymous hotline that the organization ran because he did not trust them. He did not want to tell anyone at his school. He had approached me at his own peril. He was nervous that I might "get him in trouble or something," but he desperately wanted to know what to do. I encouraged him to consider the hotline. I emphasized that it was truly anonymous. I tried to work out someone at the school he could trust with his story. None of it seemed to convince him. I'm not sure what I could have said to get him to confide in someone who could provide the support and counseling that I believed he would benefit from and that I was unable to provide. According to facilitators, what happened with Anthony was common. Young people would approach them out of the blue to tell their stories. But other times, young people would shut down when asked about their lives. Some would get frustrated, or cry without saying why.[43]

Many young people were trapped in the stories of their past, but change programs did not have a way to hear those stories. The past, it turns out, is a problem for an ephemeral policy. Sociologists and policy makers alike have few ways to make sense of the lasting consequences of trauma and violence beyond the personal and psychological. The response to the past was to change young people's futures, not reconcile their trauma or change the situations that enabled it.[44]

Stories are social objects. Making order from chaos, they unfold action over time as a series of events or scenes, which individuals use to make sense of the past, present, and future, and the links between them. Certain details are privileged and others omitted. Stories have characters, plots, scenes, props, and make us all into actors. That is, stories have power: they *do* things.[45] Stories can be used to do all kinds of things: to build social movements or to navigate the law in court proceedings or to trigger punishment. This is, of course, what Anthony was scared of: that his story would cause an institutional response. Telling a story, depending on how you tell it, can get you support or mark you.[46] Stories can also organize the disjointed raw material of experience into an identity and in turn drive personal action and meaning.[47] Social location—gender, race, and class—become a part of stories about who we are and who we want to be.[48]

Young people are not the only ones who tell stories about their lives: the state tells stories, too.[49] The stories of the state are often narratives of social location, as social policy works to actively transform meanings around race, socioeconomic status, age, gender and sexuality, and with them, identities.[50] The stories told by the state create the world they tell of, or at least a version of it. At the same time as they provide services and sanctions, social policies divide people into new categories—such as "at-risk youth" and "nonprofit organization"—and give meaning to categories.[51] The stories that social policy tells constrain and enable how people make their lives legible.[52] Although all social policy tells a story, the ephemeral state is, above all, a storytelling apparatus. Within it, narratives are the core mechanism of policy action, from the statistical stories of risk data, to the transformation stories of evaluations, to the blunted stories told to mandated reporters in schools.[53] This book is an ethnography of those stories.

VIOLENCE AND THE STATE

The state and violence are historically and theoretically linked. Max Weber, in a 1919 lecture, defined the state as "a human community that (successfully) claims the monopoly of the legitimate use of physical force within a given territory."[54] Since then, scholars have sought to tease apart the relationship between the state and violence. This makes violence prevention a vital and intriguing site for understanding how the state functions and how the meaning of violence is legitimated, contested, and transformed. In the world of violence prevention, it is taken for granted that a well-designed curriculum could change norms around violence, but, if we take a step back, we can see how audacious and strange this is. Throughout history, violence has been viewed, in turn, as innate to mankind, as held in check by the state, as a failure of state power, and as a widespread cultural norm. In violence prevention there is a novel way of thinking of violence—as the byproduct of behaviors and risk factors— and with it, new ways to think about the state.[55]

In all my time in the field, I saw a dozen or so instances of play fighting, most of which were among boys and rarely between a boy and a girl. I saw a few exchanges that could have been considered verbal or emotional violence. Still, the language of violence was ever-present. It was on every branded poster, pin, and T-shirt that read Peace Over Violence, of course. But it was also on our grants and in the mouths of teachers and administrators. In the world of social policy, where lived stories rarely appeared, there was a swell of discourse on violence, but rarely did I witness its physical manifestation. Foucault argued that sexuality was created and defined by the multiplication of discourses around sex that arose in the nineteenth century: that an obsession with sorting and categorizing varieties of sex and deviance gave power and meaning to the concept. Something similar may be happening with violence.

Violence is no one thing. When we name something violence, and then, further, sort it into a specific subspecies, we place it as a point in a kind of story of morality and policy. These categorizations are fiercely contested and call up moral questions of intention, harm, physicality, power, and choice. Policy stories about violence have high stakes for the allocation of funding, the framing of problems, the assignment of victim and perpetrator labels and legal repercussions. Control over the story of violence comes with a kind of power, and various institutions jockey for that power. This seems obvious when it comes to the military or the police, but it is also true of social movements, support agencies, and healthcare policy. For this reason, the ways that groups and institutions frame violence have consequences. The courts may determine if an incident rose to the legal definition of violence, while a guidance counselor may gauge if an incident was emotional violence in order to determine the best course of treatment. A referee may decide if a foul was flagrant and in war, policing, and sport violent actors may gauge the effectiveness of the violence in order to award medals and acclaim.

Anti-violence organizations do not agree on what violence is. Instead, there are competing organizational stories of violence and various kinds of data that they draw on to make their case. To use criminal-legal data, which is affirmed by the weight of the bureaucratic state, results in a narrower categorization. Alternatively, drawing on hospital records of injuries, many of which never go to the criminal-legal system, provides a broader definition that still requires some formal authority. In contrast, surveys or interviews from self-defined survivors and victims offer a different accounting, which often varies considerably from formal reports from police and hospitals. This is particularly important for underreported crimes such as sexual assault, as well as threats and emotional violence for which the act may be contested or subjective. In addition, organizations and institutions must decide whether or not they believe that a person can consent to violence: If a person approves of their own harm, is it violence? In practice, this meant that some organizational definitions include self-directed harm, such as suicide or cutting, others discount consensual harm, such as in football or BDSM, and others only count nonconsensual harm directed at others.

These questions, while moral and theoretical, are also practical in the daily work of violence prevention. When I first entered the field, the Violence Prevention Coalition of Greater Los Angeles had, after decades and a contentious debate, only recently come to a formal definition of violence. They decided on a definition that "excluded suicide but included football." Weiss, who founded VPC, in a 1996 article made the case that the public health definition of violence requires intention, so as to distinguish it from the public health data on injuries from accidents. As Weiss put it: "public health records focus on the victim, criminal justice records focus on the perpetrator."[56] VPC's definition was less expansive than that of the World Health Organization, which defined violence as "the intentional use of physical force or power, threatened or actual, against another person or against a group or community that results in or has a high likelihood of resulting in injury, death, psychological harm, maldevelopment, or deprivation."[57] This is, if you pause to look at it, a stunningly broad definition, full of flexible terminology and concepts, such as power, threats, community, likelihood, and psychological harm. It is also a definition that lacks a notion of consent. In 2012, the Department of Justice changed their definition of sexual violence to "a sexual act committed against someone without that person's freely given consent." The changes to the definition of sexual violence, for the first time, included nonheterosexual violence. When the definition of sexual assault changed, it meant that whole new actions, things that real people did, meant something different to the state.

The formal definition of violence at POV, which I heard dozens of times in trainings and presentations, was this: Any act, action, or force that causes harm. Many facilitators emphasized, as a manager named Joan did: "Our definition of violence doesn't include intent. If you hurt somebody, physically or emotionally, it doesn't matter what you intended to do—violence is violence." There was also an informal and contradictory mantra around POV, "violence is always a choice," which aligned with the use of violence in self-defense classes and with the logic of prevention more broadly. These two definitions signal the contentious debates over the meaning of violence that have taken place during the more than forty-year history of Peace Over Violence and the state more broadly.

A NEW POV

Peace Over Violence is located in a two-story modern box in the shadow of skyscrapers just north of Wilshire Boulevard. Since they moved in, development has steadily marched through the neighborhood, with a new towering hotel and apartment building on one side, and a rundown lot destined for redevelopment across the street. The building is quietly fortified with a metal screen that rolls down in front of the door and a mechanical gate with a passcode for the parking lot on the roof. Multiple times each day, whenever someone pulls in, the building rattles. During the day, with the metal screen up, the front is glass, and you have to press a call button to page Sandra at the front desk to let you in. Through the glass doors, it looks like a corporate office. Sandra, who is Latina and grew up in Los Angeles, is often behind the desk and partition wall, a phone curled between her ear and shoulder while clicking on the computer. This is the "seventh or eighth" nonprofit job Sandra has had. After her family member died of a drug overdose, she started working in a recovery center for women and then after that "kept staying in the nonprofit organizations." When I asked how she felt about POV, she said that "what they do here is something that everybody goes through almost. If you think about it, everybody has experienced some sort of domestic violence or sexual assault, something even if it's not a major thing. That's what I liked about it is that it's universal. Everybody goes through the same thing."

Peace Over Violence was where I began my research, and it remained my touchstone throughout. However, to study how stories circulated through the ephemeral state, I conducted over three years of ethnographic research in the world of interpersonal violence prevention in Los Angeles. With the door cracked open by Peace Over Violence, between November 2009 and May 2013, I shadowed stories back and forth across contexts: the booming market for programming, an organization striving to keep pace, the classrooms where programs were implemented, and the lives of so-called at-risk youth.[58]

During the course of my fieldwork, I spent time in 20 program contexts across Los Angeles, including large public high schools, a continuation school for "troubled" students, a wealthy suburban school, the children's court, afterschool programs, and more, sitting in on programs and at times implementing them myself.[59] Most of the schools where youth programs were implemented were also schools marked by disadvantage and crime control approaches, as grants focused on specific geographic communities or demographic populations seen as at risk.[60] The audience for programming, in line with the population of the Los Angeles Unified School District, was almost entirely youth of color. Only two of the 20 sites were populated by a majority of white students. In total, I observed over two thousand students enrolled in violence prevention programs. During the course of my ethnographic research, I also conducted dozens of informal interviews with youth and with various participants in and around programming, including campus police, teachers, and guidance counselors. I conducted in-depth, semi-structured interviews with 32 youth.

The world of violence prevention is made up of moving pieces. In addition to my time in schools, I participated in trainings and regular meetings of facilitators and other organizational staff, during which time they discussed challenges and strategies of facilitation. During the third year of participant observation I conducted in-depth, semi-structured interviews with 11 program facilitators. In addition, I interviewed 10 employees working in various other departments in the organization. I also attended conferences, meetings, and webinars in the broader world of Los Angeles violence prevention. I talked with professionals in the field of public health who ran technical assistance and taught workshops on effective prevention. I read as many violence prevention curricula as I could find and the public health research on violence that undergirded program content.

How did violence become preventable? Chapter 2 draws on in-depth interviews, primary organizational documents, and secondary sources— including a study of Peace Over Violence (then the Los Angeles Commission on Assaults Against Women) between 1972 and 1990—to trace the trajectory from feminist consciousness-raising, which centered on personal narratives of interpersonal violence, to contemporary interpersonal violence prevention, with its focus on data and evidence. With the expansion of the nonprofit sector, change programs arose in the 1990s to fill a gap created by the expanding punitive state and the devolving welfare state. In tracing this history, I develop a theory of *curricularization*, a process whereby human conditions and social problems become formalized into problems met with narrative curricular interventions.

What is lost when a life becomes data? Chapter 3 examines the cultural consequences of risk data, as statistical methods change the way we think about and act upon the problems of personal lives. In contexts marked by ubiquitous crime control, fraught intimate relationships, and persistent trauma, the process of stripping out social context that gives population data its power is multiplied. Ultimately, this widens the gap between personal stories and statistical lives, making experience less recognizable and limiting the usefulness of risk analysis on the ground as it distances youth from the state. In contrast to the statistical lives of youth marked as at risk, the chapter sketches textured portraits of young men and women coming of age and forming relationships within a world of temporary programs.

What is the work of the ephemeral state? Chapter 4 explores the social organization of the interactions between facilitators, who act as street-level representatives of social policy, and the subjects of the ephemeral state, in this case young people marked as at risk. The ephemeral state, and its multiple overlapping interventions, give rise to new processes of marking risk and enrolling young people in programming. At street level, the ephemeral state produces a constant churn of temporary encounters with social policy. Inundated by an avalanche of metrics, facilitators distrust the ephemeral state, but ultimately participate in its validation.

Can a story change a life? In chapter 5, I take up the seemingly simple question of whether or not these programs succeed in changing narratives. Drawing on excerpts from widely used curricula and classroom vignettes of role-plays gone wrong, games with contradictory messages, and narratives of violence stripped of emotion, I provide a rare look inside the rooms where violence prevention curricula, intended to reshape intimate thoughts and feelings, are brought to life. The new narratives of prevention, untethered from personal connection and failing to engage with the jumble of narrative projects that make sense of lived experience, collide and fracture in a form of *narrative entropy*. Youth pick up the pieces, drawing on their own experiences to resist and transform the messages of programming, often in gendered ways.

How do young people come to understand the state? The final empirical chapter examines how young men and women marked as at risk engage with adult representatives of the state in their lives. Young men and women marked as at risk, unlike their hypercriminalized peers, experience a cascade of cultural frames from state-aligned adults, teachers, administrators, school resources officers, and guidance counselors. In practice, I argue, young people come to understand the state through the lens of interpersonal interactions, or what I call *policy in person*. This has consequences for the ways that young people make sense not only of the state, but those closest to them. Young men seek out meaningful connection outside of institutions, and many young women cultivate individual success within them.

2 How Violence Became Preventable

THE VIOLENCE PREVENTION COALITION'S STATEMENT OF COMMITMENT TO
A PUBLIC HEALTH APPROACH TO PREVENTING VIOLENCE

As members of the Violence Prevention Coalition, we desire a society committed to preventing violence before it starts and that allows everyone to thrive, even those struggling to overcome economic, social and political challenges.

We believe violence is a public health issue and that eliminating violence enhances the growth of a healthy society.

We believe in applying to the prevention of violence the tools that have been successfully used in addressing public health issues. Having pledged to support the public health approach, we share the common purpose of reducing, and, where possible, eradicating through prevention and intervention efforts all forms of violence.

We believe in preventing violence, though we also recognize that violence must often be addressed when and where it happens, as well as in its aftermath.

We believe the public health approach will assure that policies and direct actions meant to prevent violence both protect and promote community health, while also supporting the positive growth of individuals living in communities.

We believe that violence is a learned behavior. We also believe that if violence is learned, then people can also learn alternatives to violence.

We believe that the success of any violence prevention approach hinges on the comprehensive involvement of public and private institutions and the people who lead them, including schools, businesses, law enforcement, spiritual centers, families and all other parts of a community.

We believe that reliance on law enforcement as the primary means of addressing violence runs counter to the society we want. We believe that the practice and policy of law enforcement must meet rigorous tests of fairness and humanity, and, in all cases, incorporate a broader plan for addressing violence rooted in the public health approach we value.

We believe that a public health approach strengthens any plan for addressing violence by:

1. Relying on factual, verifiable data for describing and monitoring the magnitude, scope, characteristics and consequences of violence at the local, state and national level.

2. Identifying the many, complex economic, social and political conditions that are likely to increase or decrease the risk of violence.

3. Valuing and incorporating the views, ideas and experiences of individuals and communities, particularly but not limited to those most affected by violence.

4. Designing and implementing strategies and programs for preventing violence based on the facts, findings and conditions described by the data.

5. Using proven methods to evaluate the results of strategies and programs.

6. Disseminating what has been learned about promising and evidence-based practices with the aim of assuring adoption of new knowledge and insight by the greatest possible number of individuals, community leaders, organizations and institutions.

[Note: This is an agreement signed by organizations and individuals that join the Violence Prevention Coalition of Greater Los Angeles.]

.   .   .   .   .

"It's a paradise—small—but we still have violence. We still have people," the pastor from a California coastal town began in a practiced rhythm. He glanced out the tall windows of the Peace Over Violence office at the traffic light. The words "paradise" and "small" sounded like code words for wealthy and white. One of his congregants had brought a local domestic violence shelter to his attention and since then he had partnered with athletic coaches, some of whom he golfed with, to "do something about violence." They put on a Walk a Mile in Her Shoes march: he chuckled and shook his head as he recounted the male coaches and football players stumbling in red pumps.[1] Inspired by the success of the event, the pastor wanted to launch a program for young men in the community. I was intrigued. In the face of violence, this man of faith did not look to scripture or morality; he sought out answers in programs and campaigns.

Ella, a POV manager, darted out of the room and returned with a glossy trifold brochure that described the organization's in-house curricula, In Touch With Teens (ITWT), which staff casually referred to as "it-wit."[2] "It sells for $230," Ella said matter-of-factly. "You can buy it online, it's very easy." Joan, a higher-up, chimed in. Joan suggested a two-day training, adding, "we have done it all over the country." That was when I caught on to the scene unfolding in front of me: this was a sales pitch. I thought back to a flyer for a training from a prominent anti-violence organization that I had seen at a conference: "Tuition is $500 per person. This fee includes a full copy of the curriculum, certificate of completion, and continental breakfast each day." And at the bottom of the flyer: "Space is limited, so please act now!" That was the competition.[3]

Originally written in the 1990s, and revised in 2009, ITWT was the program that the organization defaulted to for one-time presentations, fundraisers, and for their Rape Prevention Education (RPE) grant, which was the longest-running prevention grant at the organization. In a given year, the RPE grant would fund staff to reach as many as 1,500 students across more than 400 sessions. It would also support professional training for over 100 people, which enabled them to implement the program on their own. RPE was just one of POV's prevention grants. In 2012 alone, POV received over one million dollars from government agencies and private foundations for prevention programming. With that funding, a team of implementers and volunteers reached over 20,000 Los Angeles youth that year, a massive grant-funded endeavor to transform cultural norms and, possibly, stop violence before it occurs.

The pastor was losing interest; Joan pushed harder. She recounted a story about a time that POV applied for a grant only to discover that other organizations competing against them were also using ITWT. The pastor cocked his head skeptically. He asked if the curriculum included a mentorship component. Ella and Joan did not answer that question and Joan told him that they have "had a lot of luck with in-school, curriculum-based programs," which is what ITWT is. It is not a mentorship program. The pastor asked about a mentorship program from another organization, and Joan responded that "a lot of that came out of our curriculum" and then, after a pause, said, "we can train your team on it though." Ella, hesitant, corrected her: "No, we can't." "We can't? Who can train on it?" Joan asked, rhetorically. Joan looked at the pastor and explained: POV was one of the first to *implement* the program, but they were not certified to *train* on it. They can, however, train on ITWT, she added, because they created it. Ella gave the pastor a copy of ITWT and he thumbed through the glossy pages of the thick white binder slowly, his expression flat as smiling teens and bright text flipped by promising a world free of violence.

The office was decked out with Peace Over Violence branding, which had won a design award. The logo echoed across pamphlets and curricula, on mugs and posters and pins. The office aesthetic was crisp and hopeful: blue-sky walls, open floor plan, glass and pale wood, branded black and white pictures of smiling people ringing the walls. Rob, the second facilitator I had ever met, was in one of the posters, holding a determined stare. Another captured a young man I recognized from a youth group, eyes wide with a surprised smile. It had been a few years since that snapshot and today he was unlikely to let such a moment of unrestrained happiness slip through. On each poster, below their faces was the logo, with personal mantras pasted in where Peace would be. Love. Confidence. Youth. Feminism. "Our name is an engine," the director often said. On the wall by the front desk was a towering plaque, with etchings commending major donors. Across from that was a display of brightly colored trifold sheets outlining POV's numerous services: counseling, education, prevention, hotline. One of the graphic designers had told me, "The only thing that changes is the topics . . . it's just pretty much the same as any other company, like Coca-Cola or whatever, that [has] branding . . . I think there's not much different."

The conversation with the pastor turned to prevention strategies. "What about youth clubs?" he asked. Joan shrugged, "They stole clubs from us." It was unclear who "they" were, but clubs were components of several new violence prevention programs. The pastor, literally, was not buying it. Joan recommended a pledge, a scripted public statement to be spoken by young men promising not to be violent. The pastor perked up and asked if the pledge came out of the ITWT curriculum. Ella answered yes, but as the pastor flipped through in search of it, Ella hedged, "no, it isn't in there." The pastor closed the binder definitively and thanked them for their time. He would think about it. Halfway through the doorway, he turned back and asked Joan to put him in touch with another organization about their curriculum. She agreed, albeit reluctantly. In the market for anti-violence it seems better that someone else get the sale than no sale at all.[4]

Programs are commodities, bought and sold in an expanding market-place.[5] In order to get by, organizations sell curricula, and the wider the audience the better. In this regard ITWT was treading water. Teachers in

Los Angeles wanted it in their classrooms and so did students. The paid staff was unable to keep up with demand, so volunteers covered some implementations. What eluded the curriculum and dogged the managerial staff, however, was reaching the next tier of national recognition. This would require spending time and resources to evaluate the curriculum—ideally through a randomized control trial—and acquire an "evidence-based" certification.[6] The market was booming and competition was intense.

I often thought back to the pastor, thumbing through the pages of ITWT, and wondered about all that had to happen to put that binder into his hand with the promise of preventing violence. When you look through a violence prevention curriculum, or any of countless other change programs, it is easy to miss the messy history that made that carefully assembled and brightly designed object possible. This chapter resurfaces that buried history as it recounts the genealogy of interpersonal violence prevention curricula, making them visible as artifacts of three processes.[7] The first was the reorganization and devolution of institutions of social support into a shadow state composed of nonprofit organizations, which opened up new markets for temporally bounded policy.[8] Those new markets were not just a stripped-down bureaucratic state, but were constructed from the remains of social movements. Second, personal stories, in this case the raw stories that bubbled up through consciousness-raising groups, became hardened into impersonal and largely de-political policy objects. Stories of gendered violence, oppression, and pervasive harm became the glossy narratives sold in curricula.[9] Lastly, technological and analytical advancements enabled an explosion of longitudinal data on social phenomena on one hand and evaluations metrics on the other, reshaping the terrain on which social change was imagined and managed.[10] Taken together, these three process explain one way that social issues become problems met with curricular programs.

I focus on a historical case study of interpersonal violence prevention curricula at the Los Angeles Commission on Assaults Against Women (LACAAW)—the organization that would eventually become Peace Over Violence—and the wider political contests around interpersonal violence in Los Angeles between the early 1970s and the early 2010s. In order to situate processes in time and place, I delimit three historical periods in which macro social and political shifts acted as "switches" in the tracks, enabling transformations in how the state thinks about and acts on violence and, in turn, giving rise to violence prevention curricula.[11] The history picks up at the end of the feminist movement, which had made violence knowable as a systemic source of oppression and inequality, and examines what happened next. First, the period of backlash to and institutionalization of anti-violence activism that followed the feminist movement. Second, the surge in crime control logics in response to rising rates of violence. And, finally, the solidification of public health as a cornerstone of modern government. This is how violence became preventable.

A MOVEMENT IN PLACE (1972–1989)

In 1972, a group of women, most of them "counterculture white feminists" according to Nancy Matthews in her book about Los Angeles feminist activists, began the first rape crisis hotline in the city with a phone at the Westside Women's Center.[12] The "Anti-Rape Squad," as they called themselves, had bubbled up out of their ongoing activism, which included both organizing consciousness-raising groups and "guerrilla tactics" such as "going after rapists and confronting them" on the streets of Venice and publicly calling out local police officers for failing to respond to rapes.[13] In today's era of "fluoride feminism"—in the water, everywhere and nowhere—it is easy to forget that even though it was a national movement, feminist activism, without the internet or the smartphone camera, was composed of stories circulated in voice and on paper—it was physically manifest.

Over telephone lines and in consciousness-raising groups, women told of the grim and hopeful turns that their lives had taken. Activists worked out ways to support the person on the other end of the line or in the circle of the group, providing what we now call counseling, and at the same time took up a kind of informal data collection of the narratives of women across Los Angeles. The voices on the line and in groups told stories, and those stories revealed patterns of gendered violence, systemic failures, cycles of abuse, and strategies for navigating pervasive threats.[14] The hotline and consciousness-raising groups, alongside community education, provided a foundation for seeing women's experiences and traumas as more than the consequence of incomprehensible individual actions, but as byproducts of a system of inequality and patriarchy. The personal was political, not in the sense of the personal as individual, which is how it is used today, but personal in that it was everyday. With little access to traditional levers of power, women mobilized their stories to make new kinds of claims on the state, calling for protection from harm and institutionalized support. In the 1970s, feminists made intimate life visible and argued that, perhaps, it could be made just.

Movements do not last forever—they are defined by their ephemerality. They either win outright (rarely), fade away (sometimes), or dig in (often). Scholars of organizations and movements call what happened next for feminist anti-violence institutionalization, the process whereby movements become permanent and, in many ways, part of the mainstream.[15] As the brush fire of feminist grassroots activism receded, the remnants of the movement took root in places where there was enough energy to sustain them. In these nascent hubs, largely in urban centers, groups began to puzzle out how to make their politics a reality in the long run. In Los Angeles, several groups, including the anti-rape squad, were doing just that. Matthews notes that the racial and class geography of the city influenced the political possibilities of crisis centers.[16] The anti-rape squad, more white and middle class than the other activist groups, was more easily folded into the city government. In 1973, as part of the work of a new city councilwoman, Pat Russell, to turn the loose collective into a task force for the city, the group took on an official title, the Los Angeles Commission on Assaults Against Women (LACAAW) and received $600 from the City of Los Angeles to fund their work for a year—about $3,000 in 2017 dollars. The agreement with the city fell through not long after, but the name remained for another 33 years, an artifact of the institutionalization of a movement and its incorporation into the city's infrastructure. At LACAAW and similar organizations around the country, the ensuing years were marked by the quiet ceding of ground to organizational practicality in the face of budget concerns. LACAAW began to pay their co-directors and "got structured." The activists reframed their radical movement work as expertise that could improve how the city government managed violence.

Pushed by the "state's grant economy," anti-violence organizations across Los Angeles either fell apart or survived by adapting to their new reality as service delivery organizations.[17] By the close of the 1970s, the remaining members of LACAAW, without the momentum of a grassroots movement to sustain their work and in the face of a contraction of government funding, nearly disbanded. A $150,000 grant from the National Institute for Mental Health for community-based rape prevention had run out and there was no sign of additional funding on the horizon, at least without sacrificing the ideals of the organization. At the time, much of the financial support for rape crisis organizations required organizations to collect data on the people, predominantly women, who called. LACAAW, distrustful of law enforcement from the outset, had long objected to this requirement because they feared that authorities would use the hotline data against callers at trial. Unwilling to cede this principle and with seemingly no options left, interim director Judy Ravitz set out on a last-ditch effort to attract funding by further formalizing the organization: establishing an executive board, repairing relations with law enforcement, and emphasizing prevention. Not long after these changes took hold, the organization received $50,000 from a newly established program out of the California Office of Criminal Justice Planning (OCJP) to provide direct services to survivors and train district attorneys and law enforcement. The funding from OCJP marked a new era for LACAAW, one that was echoed across the United States, with short-term funding for local services overtaking grassroots organizing as the driving force behind feminist anti-violence organizations. Alongside the bolstered funding, this formalization came with new strings. The organization was more exposed than ever to the oversight and uncertainties of the grant funding market and, freshly designated as a 501c(3) (and thus exempt from federal income tax), it was restricted in its actions in local, state, and federal politics. If LACAAW was going to change society, they would have to do it outside of party politics.

Meanwhile, far afield from the daily work of responding to violence, government agencies set in motion a transformation in how the state conceptualized and approached violence. In 1979, the landmark *Healthy People* report, which proclaimed that "prevention is an idea whose time has come," stated that violence, defined crisply as intentional injury, was not only a criminal justice issue, but a public health problem on a national scale.[18] The report listed "control of stress and violent behavior" as one of fifteen priorities in health, and in 1980, the report's findings were translated into measurable objectives in *Promoting Health / Preventing Disease: Objectives for the Nation* (a companion piece to *Healthy People*). By 1983, the Centers for Disease Control (CDC) established the Violence Epidemiology Branch, which applied the tools of disease monitoring to violence. Two years later, the Report of the Secretary's Task Force on Black and Minority Health identified interpersonal violence, and homicide in particular, as major contributors to health disparities among African Americans. The assistant director of LACAAW, Cathy Friedman, who began writing grant proposals for LACAAW while finishing her master's in public health during this time, explained to me that the medical literature she was reading at that time contained "nothing on violence, nothing on women's health. And then there was an AMA journal on domestic violence. All of a sudden I was like, 'Hey, this is interesting. There's some domestic violence showing up. Violence against women is showing up . . . Finally, this issue I've been immersed in for years is starting to come up in Public Health.'" A new kind of story about violence was coming into view.

These extensions of public health research into feminist anti-violence, largely in the form of new kinds of data, were barely felt by the women working on the ground at LACAAW. They were busy reconfiguring their approach in the wake of an anti-feminist backlash against the advances eked out over the previous decades and the "Reagan Revolution" of the 1980s, which had privatized and devolved many federal programs across the board in favor of local service provision.[19] In 1985, amidst these macro-level shifts, Patti Giggans, who had been a volunteer at the organization, became executive director—a position she still held in 2018. Over the ensuing years, LACAAW and organizations like it learned to scrape by on small donations, volunteer labor, and peripheral grants from state and city agencies. At the close of the 1980s, LACAAW had become firmly embedded in the operating infrastructure of Los Angeles.[20] They competed for and won temporary funding across a patchwork of areas—child abuse prevention, crisis counseling, and teen dating violence prevention—under the umbrella of a cohesive response to violence. Across the country, feminist crisis hotlines became part of what some have called the new urban governance: a shifting cluster of philanthropies, government agencies, and for-profit firms that distribute resources and services and create forms of solidarity, collectivity, action, and cultural practice in cities.[21]

When George H.W. Bush accepted the presidential nomination in 1988, he described a new approach to social support: a vast sea of charitable, volunteer, and nonprofit organizations—"a thousand points of light in a broad and peaceful sky"—as an alternative to governmental intervention. "All the community organizations that are spread like stars throughout the nation, doing good." These organizations would require grant funding, and by the end of the 1980s, the annual budget at LACAAW had grown to $800,000, largely thanks to increases in funding for community organizations. As these grants sustained or expanded ongoing programs, they also furthered the reorganization of LACAAW into a machine built to harness the whims of the grant system: a flexible organization built on top of the shifting fault lines of short-term funding.

It was one such grant that allowed LACAAW to create and implement one of the first in-school interpersonal violence prevention programs in the country, although it was short-lived. Leah Aldridge, who had recently started as a hotline volunteer at the time, explained to me: "We did a child abuse prevention program through OCAP, in Office of Child Abuse Prevention, in third grade, sixth grade, in a number of schools, and then [Governor George] Deukmejian cut that out of the budget in the late '80s so we lost that." While LACAAW had received significant funding for dealing with crisis and counseling, the organization struggled to sustain funding for prevention. At the time, California only funded one grant, $50,000, to prevent domestic violence across the state. During these years, prevention held promise, but it was largely focused on teaching safety strategies and it was unclear if or how anyone would know if it worked.

At the close of the 1980s, a lot had changed for LACAAW. Women's stories, and the feminist activists who propelled them into the national consciousness, had shown that interpersonal violence against women was dramatically underreported and held long-term consequences for survivors and communities. They had convinced a growing number that violence against women was part of a pervasive cultural pattern that could be transformed. This narrative had circulated through institutions and politics and come out the other side diluted. As violence against women gained legitimacy as a focus of public health research, the feminist movement, along with its focus on inequality, power, identity, and care work, lost standing in the cultural imagination and in institutions. At the same time, the notion that violence was a cultural trait, not the action of a few bad actors, worked its way into the public consciousness and state policy. With a public health literature supporting them, anti-violence agencies were increasingly able to make their case to funders, but they often did so without their feminist politics. The public health approach validated women's stories of violence even as it depoliticized them. Loosed from the movement and subject to the shifting tides of governmental management and funding demands, anti-violence agencies were about to experience a dramatic course change.

CRIME CONTROL (1990–2000)

At the start of the 1990s, rising violence in cities across the country, dubbed an "urban crime wave" by media and politicians, sparked a panic around young Black and Latino men.[22] It was concern over interpersonal violence, specifically the pervasive trope of young Black and Latino men sexually assaulting women, particularly white women, that was used to justify increased policing and the incursion of crime control tactics into everyday lives in marginalized communities.[23] The panic that propelled the multiplication of "tough on crime" policies also paved the way for the collapse of support for rehabilitation and welfare.[24] Violence, it seemed, was a problem of young men of color, and one to be met with "control."

Los Angeles was ground zero for many of the new policing tactics honed during this era. In 1992, after two LAPD officers avoided prosecution for the videotaped beating of Rodney King, the L. A. uprising set off bubbling tensions and saw one of the first uses of paramilitary policing tactics in U.S. cities. Police Chief Daryl Gates pushed other new forms of policing, such as broken windows policing, which promised to deter crime by curtailing small violations in urban neighborhoods, as well as gang task forces, and new statistical surveillance technologies, such as Compstat, which allowed police to track and map the locations of reported crimes.[25] Taken together, these new policing approaches functioned to "govern through crime" and fed a massive boom in the prison population, as well as those under carceral supervision more broadly, largely by incarcerating Black and Latino men.[26] Young men of color and their physical movements—specifically their friendships, affiliations, and public actions—were increasingly seen as criminal and pulled into the orbit of criminal-oversight institutions in a process that sociologists have called *criminalization*.[27] A 1994 commission on juvenile crime in Los Angeles began with this startling paragraph:

> When police arrest 14- and 15-year-olds who shrug off cold-blooded, unprovoked murder as a rite of passage, the rational public response is fear and anger: How can we protect ourselves? How can we make them pay for what they have done? And then at the policy-making level, the secondary but more productive response of perplexity sets in: How did these children become settled in lives of unthinkingly vicious, violent crime? What can we do to prevent coming generations from repeating the pattern?[28]

The statistics and media attention placed urban youth violence, and the young Black and Latino men who were seen as the primary culprits, at center stage and shaped the "tough on crime" politics of the decade. But, as the final sentence of that quote suggests, the door to prevention had been opened, just a sliver. In Los Angeles and cities around the country, a new crop of nonprofit organizations began to approach "urban violence," including, in 1992, Homeboy Industries in Los Angeles, which was established as a religious gang recovery organization with the motto "Nothing stops a bullet like a job" and would eventually partner with Peace Over Violence.[29] In 1983, Gates himself had co-created the Drug Abuse Resistance Education, or D.A.R.E. program, one of the first prevention programs to achieve widespread adoption. The mix of pervasive policing and prevention programs that marked Gates's approach would set the model for the United States for decades to come: a well-funded and institutionalized police force and a raft of grant-funded prevention organizations.[30]

In the midst of the crime wave, public health practitioners escalated their efforts to use data to connect early risks with later violence.[31] Billie Weiss explained to me how, while she was an epidemiologist at the Department of Health Services in Los Angeles in the late 1980s, youth violence came to the attention of the public health world: "young people in Los Angeles County were not dying of infectious diseases, but they were dying of injuries . . . violence was the primary one and it was killing more young people between the ages of 15 and 24 than anything else." According to a pamphlet put out by the Centers for Disease Control and Prevention (CDC) titled *The History of Violence as a Public Health Issue:* "from 1985 to 1991 homicide rates among 15- to 19-year-old males increased 154 percent, a dramatic departure from rates of the previous 20 years for this age group. This increase was particularly acute among young African American males. These trends raised concerns and provoked calls for new solutions." In 1990, in order to better understand these trends, the CDC established the Youth Risk Behavior Surveillance System—a massive data-collection endeavor—to monitor "priority health risk behaviors" among adolescents, including violence-related behaviors. On the back of new quantitative data, Weiss, along with Deborah Prothrow-Stith and Larry Cohen, formulated the argument that would open the door for public health into the world of programs, she explained: "[Violence] was impacting the health of young people more than anything else."[32] It was way over what could be expected, which is the definition of an epidemic. So it was a huge epidemic."[33] With the support of Shirley Cannon, who was a pediatrician and the head of Infectious Disease / Communicable Disease Control for LA County, and after a lot of "shopping around looking for grants," Weiss and the others received a CDC grant to study injuries from violence in Los Angeles.

In 1992, the CDC received its first appropriation aimed at curbing the high rates of homicide among youth. The following year, the CDC published *The Prevention of Youth Violence: A Framework for Community Action,* which stated: "We can reduce the violence. We can change our lives," and outlined the steps necessary to implement a public health approach to youth violence prevention.[34] Violence became part of the surging study of "health-related behaviors," which linked up everyday activities, such as eating, drinking, moving, driving, and sleeping, to major health problems. In the process, the meaning of health was redefined. Health no longer meant the absence of noticeable disease; current actions were read for signals of future danger.[35] By 1993, several violence-prevention programs were being developed, undertaken, and evaluated in schools and communities across the United States, some under the CDC's newly established Division of

Violence Prevention.[36] These evaluation studies were among the first to use randomized control trials, much like the ones developed to test medical and pharmaceutical interventions, to specifically assess the impact of programs on violence-related behaviors. These programs demonstrated to funders and organizations that significant reductions in aggressive and violent behavior were possible with specific interventions. It seemed that changing attitudes and behaviors, much as feminists had contended, could prevent violence.

Support for a public health approach to violence grew and Weiss's team decided to "find anybody in the county who was doing anything that looked like violence prevention or working with young folks to try and keep them safe." This brought them into contact with LACAAW and other domestic violence and sexual assault organizations, as well as the district attorney's office, child abuse prevention advocates, the LAPD, and the sheriff's department. Weiss told me, "We all got in a room and started talking and I talked about what the public health model was about, that it was really . . . [that] you could measure [violence] and monitor it and you could see where it was going, see who was at risk, where the risks were, and so forth." Gathered around the promise of quantifying violence, this collection of criminal justice, public health, and feminist organizations would eventually become the Violence Prevention Coalition of Greater Los Angeles (VPC), a political force for promoting the public health approach to violence prevention in Los Angeles that would later count dozens of local organizations among its members, producing a model that would be echoed in cities across the country.

Meanwhile, tensions between public health quantification and con-sciousness-raising narratives were evident on the ground. In 1990, Leah Aldridge joined the staff full-time at LACAAW as a community education coordinator, a position that was funded out of a small grant from the Office of Criminal Justice Planning (OCJP) for the State of California. She saw her position as an echo of the community education of grassroots feminism, dedicated to "moving sexual and domestic violence out of the shadows into the public sphere, if you will . . . just saying, 'This is what life is. This is who it happens to. These are some of the myths and realities of life.'" LACAAW ran up against pressure from OCJP to deliver programs to large volumes of youth with broadly accessible "universal" programming. Aldridge told me:

"They wanted just counting heads mostly . . . there was a formula, and the numbers changed according to population. In Los Angeles, we had some very high numbers." LACAAW adapted their educational tactics to reach a wider audience and drew on their connections with organizations and institutions—largely schools—serving young people across Los Angeles. Aldridge explained: "in addition to wanting to change the world, there was a practicality in our approach." Students were a captive audience, and the schools, strapped for resources, were eager for the additional support. Youth became the central focus of programming for LACAAW, in large part because of funding pressures to maximize the size of their impact.

It was out of this strange mix of forces—fear of violent crime, the dawn of the "evidence-based" movement, and a long-standing feminist organization—that one of the earliest interpersonal violence prevention curricula was born. Feeling constricted by the victim and perpetrator focus of the criminal justice approach that dominated funding at the time, Cathy Friedman suggested that LACAAW harness the momentum around violence prevention to apply for funding to write a teen abuse prevention curriculum that focused on abuse in relationships, not violent crime. They were awarded the funding, and with $42,000, they went to work designing a curriculum. Aldridge described the process as "very unscientific" as they stitched together content from existing educational materials with their own informal research in classrooms.[37] Without an institutional network to turn to, Aldridge ran a rudimentary search on the internet and drew from what was then called the Marin Abused Women's Center, "a little thin curriculum and it was called TAP, Teen Abuse Prevention." They also pulled in testimonials collected for *Dating Violence: Young Women in Danger,* a 1991 book by Barrie Levy, a former co-director of LACAAW. Aldridge explained: "It was skills for building a violence-free relationship. It didn't have a real public health prevention swath across it, but it was about never getting into an abusive relationship to begin with, which nobody had really developed a game plan for how to do." With funding from "Teen 1 Media, which was a division of Toyota of Lexus or something," they turned the testimonials into a poster campaign, which they brought into classrooms across the city.

Similar struggles likely played out at other feminist organizations across the country, given the opportunities that public health funding promised and the alignment of prevention and feminist thinking around cultural change. As they saw funding opportunities opening up, Aldridge, alongside Friedman with her public health background, worked to refine the language of feminist consciousness-raising into public health prevention messages. She told me:

> Nobody, to my mind, had ever figured out how to talk about the cycle of violence as a prevention strategy, or had pointed to the cycle of violence rather as being an indicator how the cycle of violence can be used as a warning sign in the effort to prevent dating violence. Nobody had talked about that, looking at [that] from the notion of patterns . . . and therefore, when you begin to recognize these, you need to make different choices or bust a move or whatever . . . I was trying to figure out dating violence—nobody knows it when [they're] in it. How do I teach someone what it is that they need to know: what's symptomatic, what's a predictor of the abusive relationship . . . We had previously used the cycle of violence as a way of proving that you were in an abusive relationship. Now how do I take that and move it from being an indicator or evidence to being a predictor?

In her description, one can see how Aldridge and Friedman reformulated consciousness-raising narratives into prevention. This meant making violence and the precursors of violence visible not just in male perpetrators, but in everyone. Aldridge told me, "I had to locate or situate the behavior within each of us as opposed to a perpetrator, someone over there. As a prevention strategy, I had to make this about *your* behavior."

Although it would take years for curricula to enter the mainstream, at the national level, the precursors of this shift were exemplified in 1994, when President Clinton signed into law the Violent Crime Control and Law Enforcement Act, Title IV of which is often referred to as the Violence Against Women Act (VAWA).[38] Much of the funding provided by the act went into crime control and policing in working-class and poor urban communities. On the ground, this often negatively impacted women in communities of color and poor communities, perhaps more than it helped, and many of the mechanisms for providing meaningful law enforcement responses to violence against women failed to materialize.[39] The lasting legacy of the bill has been the entrenchment of crime control and hyperpolicing more deeply into poor Black and Latino urban neighborhoods. However, the crime legislation also invested in the public health approach to violence, albeit to a far lesser extent, as it launched the first national violence-against-women survey, established rape prevention and education programs (called RPEs), and called for local demonstration projects—community laboratories for new programs—to coordinate the intervention and prevention of sexual assault and domestic violence. Marking a significant shift, the CDC, not the DOJ, was given the federal responsibility to administer the efforts, drawing a clear line: the criminal justice system was responsible for perpetrators and suspected perpetrators of violence—largely dramatic public violence—and the prevention of violence in interpersonal relationships was a public health issue. Up until that point, LACAAW had only received state-level funding for prevention, but VAWA began to deliver what would remain a steady stream of funds for wide-ranging projects from legal services to disability services to transitional housing to a program to engage men in anti-violence.

The raced and classed logic that dominated the era continued to shape policy debates after the crime bill. President Clinton, pushed by a powerful discourse that painted poor and working-class people of color in general—and Black women in particular—as welfare cheats, orchestrated a withdrawal of the state from social support. In 1996, Clinton signed the Personal Responsibility and Work Opportunity Act, which transformed welfare into a temporary program and attached work requirements to welfare benefits. Much of the burden of welfare reform fell on single mothers, a disproportionate number of whom experienced domestic and sexual violence.[40] For victims and survivors of violence against women, these reforms limited social support, cutting off cash assistance, addiction treatment, and rehabilitation, and instead required curricular training in parenting, marriage, and work.[41] This dissolution of social support, which had begun under Reagan and been accelerated by Clinton, left few state-implemented responses for interpersonal violence outside of the criminal system. Aside from limited funding for crisis hotlines and court-mandated anger management classes, social policy largely gave up on sustained support for those in the throes of violence and embarked on a decades-long experiment in mass incarceration. For those interested in alternatives to policing, public health prevention presented one of the few viable options. Rather than support "dependency" or drain the state, public health shifted the frame to focus on transforming those marked by data as at risk. The message was clear: you are at risk or you are too far gone.[42]

At the close of the 1990s, a new wave of youth violence captured national attention, this time perpetrated by young white men against their peers in suburban schools, most prominently in 1999 at Columbine High School. In the years that followed, concern over bullying—a form of interpersonal violence, although it is rarely seen that way—would bring violence prevention into even more schools, but in ways that reflected gendered, raced, and classed notions of difference.

PRIMARY PREVENTION (2001–PRESENT)

As the tide of violence began to recede from urban communities in the late 1990s, the data collection mechanisms and programming approach honed by public health remained.[43] Bolstered by success in discouraging smoking, encouraging seat belt use, and stemming the spread of AIDS, public health advocates turned their attention to interpersonal violence in force.[44] In 2001, a second meeting of the State of California's "Little Hoover Commission"—the same one that had stoked fear of teenagers shrugging off cold-blooded murder—which included the governor, superintendent, attorney general, and representatives of the police department and social services, cast youth violence in a starkly different light than the racialized and gendered moral panic at the height of the crime years. The report began, "Violence stalks California's young people like the plague," and then continued:

> A growing body of evidence reveals that most violence is learned behavior. Before they were perpetrators, many offenders were victims. The abusers were abused. The heartless were not loved. The evidence also is increasing that many strategies can cost-effectively intervene in young and troubled lives to prevent harmful and costly behaviors. Emotional wounds can be healed. Stress can be managed. Respect can be learned and earned. Tutoring, mentoring and counseling can restore trust and hope.

At one point, the report states that the evidence was sufficient to make prevention a priority above crime control: "Until now, the State's policies have reflected a skepticism about prevention programs. The State funds them as experiments or purchases them as luxuries. The evidence now compels a contrary conclusion: Prevention can consistently and reliably save lives at far lower costs than what crime and violence inflict on public budgets and private lives."[45] A new moral consensus was coming into view around prevention, and with it, a distinct view of how young people should be understood within social policy.

There was no institutional center for this new approach, and programs sprung up out of nonprofits, foundations, and academic departments around the country. The laboratory of prevention efforts during the crime control years spawned dozens of programs, many claiming some level of success at youth violence prevention and clamoring for funding. Organizations like LACAAW, nimble from decades applying for grants, jumped at the opportunity. Weiss, who in the 1980s formulated the argument that youth violence had become a public health epidemic, explained to me that there was a move away from counting participants and a "big push for evaluation" in the early 2000s that shaped how funding was distributed: "It's a sea change in the way money is allocated to all sorts of issues but that is definitely a public health mantra. If you can't show that it works then really how do we know you're doing anything but feel-good stuff?" One touchstone for the shift to linking programs and evaluation was the Drug Abuse Resistance Education, or D. A. R. E. program, which sent police officers into middle schools to encourage young people to "just say no" to drugs. D. A. R. E. received $20 million a year at its height in the mid-1990s. However, evaluations showed that the program did more harm than good, in large part because police officers were not seen as trustworthy messengers for young people skeptical of authority.[46] Nonprofit organizations leveraged their position at the outskirts of the state to make their case.

In 2001, the U. S. surgeon general released *Youth Violence: A Report of the Surgeon General*, which aggregated the achievements made in the prevention of youth violence throughout the 1980s and 1990s, and quantified patterns of offending, risk, and protective factors. In 2002, the first state-based surveillance system to link data from multiple sources to enhance violence prevention efforts, the National Violent Death Reporting System (NVDRS), launched in six states. In the years that followed, the NVDRS expanded to include 17 states. These new forms of evaluation and measurement enabled a workable system for counting and correlating risk factors and outcomes. Risk data and program evaluation made violence legible in numbers to an unprecedented degree and defined the variables that would be used to determine effectiveness going forward.

As funders emphasized measurable effectiveness, organizations felt new market pressures. At LACAAW, Aldridge told me, the evidence-based push was "impactful":

> We realized we had to sharpen and crystallize our approach. We know we were doing it, but we didn't have all the pieces in place, and maybe we didn't even have them in the right sequence or whatever. We had to get clear about language: a predictor in sexual assault is something different than it is in public health. We knew we had to get some research and evaluators associated with us; wasn't easy . . . We did it once with the Violence Prevention Coalition and the LA County Department of Health when Billie Weiss was there. They evaluated the tool—[to see] if it was an effective tool—and evidence came back that it was an effective tool.

This process pushed LACAAW, according to Aldridge, "to backpedal and spin and raise the muscles and evolve and adapt and overcome. We were up for the fight." This fight would look very different from the social movement battles that gave shape to LACAAW. It was not a war with a powerful institution, but competition in an open market.

In order to make products that could succeed in the growing marketplace for prevention, LACAAW began to develop programs that expanded their focus outside of interpersonal violence and gender-based violence. This took their youth programming in two distinct directions. The first was toward gender-based youth empowerment. For example, out of a program for incarcerated juvenile women, LACAAW developed BeStrong, which emphasized women's empowerment through healthy relationship education and financial literacy. The second direction was into "youth violence" more broadly, a nexus of interpersonal violence, bullying, gang violence, abuse, and trauma.

By 2004, Aldridge recognized that the in-flux of money and status had brought an increasingly polished character to the work, as fresh university graduates in public health and social work showed up who were interested in prevention with youth. On the back of growing funding for curricula, the organization grew from one prevention staff member on one project when Aldridge began, to 18 projects and 12 staff by the early 2000s. The organization continued to take on new prevention and education initiatives, including a growing national sexual assault awareness campaign called Denim Day, which used media and print campaigns to raise awareness about sexual assault. During this time, one of the vestiges of LACAAW's social movement origins disappeared. In the early 2000s, for their annual youth sexual assault awareness day, LACAAW would hold a massive rally, though they often struggled to get students to the event during school hours. By the late 2000s, as one organizer explained, they were able to hold events *in* dozens of schools. The legitimacy that came with the public health approach was a boon for LACAAW, not only allowing them to reach significantly more young people, but to do so within the institutions that shape their worlds.

In 2006, the organization enacted a change they had been contemplating for years: leaving behind the LACAAW name and taking on a new one.[47] The word "commission" and its association with a city agency made little sense in the context of a national market for programs, and they needed a name that could be a "brand." Friedman explained, "As we had more youth involved in the organization and more men involved in the organization, we found that concept of 'assault against women' very limiting for our constituency." LACAAW, like other violence against women organizations across the country, was looking to change its image, and in the process, broaden the array of funding they had access to by taking on a clear and marketable brand identity. For over a year, they worked with a design team to craft a new name, with "brand guidelines"—visual rules for their logo and associated materials—which are, as one staff member put it, "very, very serious." In 2006, the Los Angeles Commission on Assaults Against Women officially became Peace Over Violence. With the new name came a new motto, one which built on the promise of public health prevention: "Violence is an equation and it can be solved one on one, one by one."

By the mid-2000s, state and federal agencies, as well as national organizations and foundations, had built up a dense web of funding for youth violence prevention programs in cities across the country. POV benefitted from these new flows of funding. In 2005, the California Coalition Against Sexual Assault received $1 million from the CDC to develop a program from the Washington, DC–based organization Men Can Stop Rape, which focused on encouraging bystander intervention by men. POV was one of six pilot sites where the program MyStrength was implemented.[48] In 2010, POV was awarded a spot in a massive four-year undertaking by the foundation arm of pharmaceutical company Robert Wood Johnson and the health plan provider Blue Shield of California, which together spent $18 million at 11 sites across the country for a middle-school healthy relationship program called Start Strong.[49] Futures Without Violence, one of the biggest names in violence prevention in the United States at the time, formerly the Family Violence Prevention Fund, provided technical assistance for a curriculum created by Hazelden, a drug abuse recovery nonprofit. Since the close of that project in 2014, the curriculum component, Safe Dates, has been adapted for use in public health departments across the nation.[50] In my time at POV, the organization was funded for at least eight prevention grants. All of these were complex, multiyear undertakings, often mixing public and private authority and multiple agencies.

By this point, violence prevention was incorporated into a large and varied field of youth programming, which had distinct theoretical and organizational frameworks. A backlash to the "deficit model" that had long dominated youth programming sparked a shift to a more empowering and positive frame in the field of youth programs.[51] This pushed public health further out of view in curriculum content, even while it served to organize much of the data, evidence, and funding that undergirded it. Instead of health, these programs shared a new focus on a discourse of personal choice.[52] In 2006, the CDC, with a nonprofit called Break the Cycle, launched Choose Respect, which they dubbed "the first national communication initiative designed to prevent unhealthy relationship behaviors and dating abuse." POV would later follow suit, launching a Choose Peace campaign in 2010 and a Make a Choice campaign in 2015. This was the mission statement of their 2010 Choose Peace campaign:

> At Peace Over Violence, we realized that we cannot work to eliminate sexual assault and domestic violence in isolation, without regard for the connection that these particular manifestations of violence have to other forms of violence in our society. If we want to empty our prisons, to be safe in our homes and our communities, and to build healthy relationships, families and communities free from sexual, domestic and interpersonal violence, we have to protect children from experiencing or witnessing violence, or get to

them as soon as possible after that experience and teach them that there is another way to relate to others. We have to teach them that violence is learned and can be unlearned, that violence is a choice, and you can choose peace over violence.

Prevention programs aimed at shaping the choices made by youth had become a significant tool of social policy, meant to shift statistical factors that were out of view of the participants.[53]

A WORLD OF PROGRAMS

Light poured through the windows and across the conference table in the second-floor offices of the Violence Prevention Coalition of Greater Los Angeles (VPC). The VPC is housed within the California Endowment, the largest private health foundation in the state with over $3 billion in assets. Five of us were there for a VPC training, including a representative from one of the Department of Justice "weed & seed" sites across the Central District of California, the head of an addiction and recovery center, and a staff member from the University of Southern California Violence Prevention Institute.[54] I thumbed through a thick printout of PowerPoint slides while an aide from tech support fiddled with the projector. VPC was going through seismic changes, including a new director, Kailee Shilling, who had formerly been the director down the street at Homeboy Industries, a gang recovery agency. The folders on the desk, we were told, were leftovers bearing the organization's old logo—hands holding flowers. A scene of a rally in the introduction video flashed across the projection screen and Billie Weiss, who founded the organization, said to us, "We don't do those anymore."

The goal of the VPC on paper, as described in their purpose statement, is to promote the public health approach to violence through their member organizations. In 2011, 40 years after it was first founded, Peace Over Violence signed on to a pledge—alongside over a hundred other members of the VPC—which frames violence in these terms. The public health model and the medical model are different, Weiss explained. "We don't have cures," she told us, "you have to change the norm." Weiss, and the slides, defined the public health model as a "vaccination to prevent disease." In this case, however, the disease is cultural. Another slide stated that "the causes of injuries and violence are understandable and predictable and resulting injuries are preventable!" She laid out the public health approach: (1) define problem; (2) identify risk/protective factors; (3) develop strategies; (4) promote widespread adoption. I realized that I was sitting through step four. Weiss, it seemed, had given versions of this talk dozens, maybe hundreds of times. She explained that she believes in data. She talked repeatedly about the things that there is "good data" on, about "data surveillance": watching the data for trends. "We push evaluation, evaluation, evaluation."

In all this, Weiss echoed a special comment in the *Journal of the American Medical Association* from Harvey Fineberg, former head of the National Institutes of Medicine, who explained how prevention flips the medical approach to health problems on its head:

> Prevention reverses the usual order of clinical thinking: it often starts at the population level and then translates information back to the individual. Rather than dwell on the pathology of disease, preventive medicine focuses on risk. In curative care, the goal is usually to restore patients to their earlier, normal state of health. In prevention, as in dealing with hypertension or elevated cholesterol levels in a community, the goal is to shift the entire population-wide distribution to a healthier level, thus changing the norm. In curative care, the principal professional responsibility is to the individual patient, whereas in preventive care, focus is often at the population level and entails a responsibility to the entire community. In curative care, solutions involve prescribing medication, performing operations, or delivering other clinical therapies; in prevention, there is a much wider array of possibilities, from changing behavior choices to altering social conditions.[55]

There is a cliché that when you have a hammer, everything looks like a nail. Well, in public health, and increasingly social services more broadly, nearly everything looks like "behavior choices." Not long into my research, on the other side of the country from Los Angeles, during the opening of a conference on the bystander approach to violence prevention, the president of the host university explained how he saw the goals of the conference as aligned with the work of the university, explaining, "we're an institution that can change culture." As a mission statement and job description, culture change is a strange demand. We might ask: which culture should change? Who decides which culture it should become? How does one go about changing something as omnipresent and simultaneously personal as culture? What does the evidence of cultural change look like? At the conference, during a pause between breakout sessions, I went into a room labeled "materials" and walked up and down rows of tables, nearly two dozen in total, and on each one was a different program for sale, with campaigns and curricula sprawled across them: dozens of ways to change behavior choices and prevent violence.[56]

Although the pathway I have laid out, from movement to program, may be specific to a subset of programs—D. A. R. E., for example, took a different route—the underlying social process is of a distinct type. The curricula laid out at that conference, like the programs developed by POV, as well as countless others, are the result of a process that I refer to as *curricularization*, whereby social problems and issues come to be defined and treated as short-term educational and pedagogical problems.[57] Violence, within this model, is not a problem for police detectives, emergency room doctors, trauma therapists, or urban planners, but for the organizations that fund, create, implement, and evaluate programs: the ephemeral state.

What kind of solution is a curriculum? Curricula signal a new kind of governmental product, one that can be bought and sold on a market, and implemented in order to govern citizens. The realm of the curricular is concerned with the transmission of a message, often related to personal and at times intimate life. In this way, curricula bring a raft of otherwise private issues into the purview of the fields of education, marketing, and public health communication. Through curricularization, issues become objects seen through the lenses of curricula design, campaign design, technical assistance, instructional training, exercises, technical assistance, and programmatic evaluation. Curricularization, with its defining notion that cultures can be changed through programmatic intervention, carries with it the implication that if a problem can be met with a curriculum, it does not need to be met with economic support, medical intervention, or legal remedy.[58] In doing so, it may undermine structural approaches and hasten retrenchments of the welfare state, even though it may benefit those enrolled.

Designing and producing curricula in response to social ills has occurred for decades, but advances in statistical analysis and the reorganization of the state into fleeting and outsourced funding models have

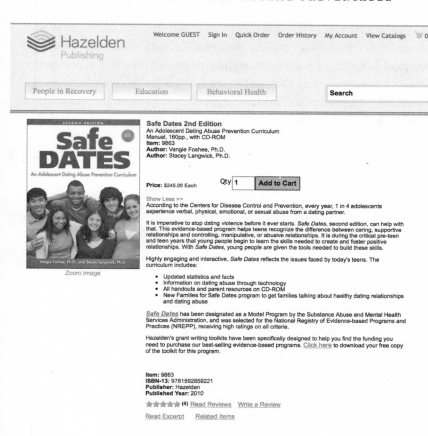

Figure 1. Safe Dates for sale. Screenshot by author.

transformed it, providing new legitimacy and reach. The history I have recounted here—of the transformation of stories of interpersonal violence into prevention curricula in Los Angeles—is just one example, but it speaks to the power of this process. In regards to interpersonal violence, curricularization incorporated a significant portion of feminist activism and marshalled an alternative to crime control approaches and social support. It made violence preventable.

Curricularization shifts the kinds of questions we should ask and the debates we should have. How are conceptions of agency and social control transformed if programs effectively transform culture and behavior? Who are the social actors on the ground, and how do they enable or redirect this process? What does it mean that the government funds the creation of culture change and puts that ability up for sale? Who should receive these lessons, which ones should they receive, and how might those lessons create or challenge inequality?

3 Statistical Lives

Individual-Level Risk Factors
Acceptance of violence in dating relationships
Adolescent antisocial behavior
Age (older than age 18)
Aggression-tolerant attitudes
Alcohol use
Anxiety
Child's sex
Chronic offenders of violence throughout adolescence
Depression
Drinking—frequency by volume
Drug and alcohol use
8th grade sexual initiation
Emotional distress
Fighting
General aggression
General antisocial behavior
Having sex before love-telling

Relationship-Level Risk Factors
Aversive family communication
Childhood physical abuse
Early involvement with antisocial peers
Engagement in peer violence
Exposure to father-to-mother violence
Exposure to interparental violence
Exposure to mother-to-father violence (Low)
Father-child hostility
Friends perpetrating adolescent dating violence
Friends victims of adolescent dating violence (Low)
Friendship quality

Harsh parenting practices
Higher number of sex partners
History of physical aggression
History of sexual aggression
History of verbal aggression
Hostile / conflict couple relationship
Hostile friendships
Increased involvement with antisocial peers
Late increasing pattern of violence in adolescence
Marijuana use
Negative parent–child interactions
Parental marital conflict
Parental monitoring (Low)
Parent–child boundary violations
Partner's use of physical aggression
Prior dating violence
Race / ethnicity
Sex desirability
Substance use
Suicide attempt
Total drinking
Trauma symptoms
Trauma-related anger
Unskilled parenting
Use of aggressive media

[Note: This is a list of variables that were reported more frequently among individuals who perpetrated dating violence than those who did not, drawn from Vagi et al. 2013.]

.   .   .   .   .

Risk treats life as an equation. A computer program takes race, gender, socioeconomic status, and whatever else the user feeds it, and runs it all through an algorithm. Out the other side comes an echo of lived experience. Pulled together, sequenced, and laid out, these factors compose what Harvey Fineberg, former head of the Institute of Medicine, has described as "statistical lives." Fineberg lamented that the statistical lives produced by public health data were far removed from the "personal stories" that animate experience.[1] But these two ways of describing a life are not as disconnected as they seem. Risk data does not just recount the edges of a life, it defines the stories we can tell about how lives should unfold.

Risk, that seemingly objective arbiter, is produced through a specific set of techniques.[2] Here is how: First, researchers and policymakers extract points of data from the raw material of lived experience. They use surveys that draw on representative samples of a given population and questions about demographics, such as age, race, and gender, as well as experience, such as having perpetrated or witnessed violence. Or, they take the bureaucratic data of institutions such as police departments, emergency rooms, and rape crisis centers.[3] Despite a wide array of human experience and attributes measured on surveys, this process constrains the field of vision. Lives, after all, are complicated and at least some of what people experience is noise that distracts from seeing the link between cause and effect. Risk data draws its power from stripping away the static and residue of social life.

Second, the data for hundreds or thousands of individuals are put together in a file. When they are analyzed, experiences and identities are treated as factors, that is, they are isolated. Analysis can then take those factors, and map patterns of relationships between them. Complex lives are abbreviated to a wide variety of individual factors that are treated separately or sometimes in relation to intersections with additional factors. In public health, statistical analysis allows us to see how some kinds of experiences—call them outcomes—tend to follow others—call them factors. If the outcome is good, the things that lead to it are protective factors. If it is a bad outcome, the things that precede it are risk factors. What happens to you, happens for a reason.

Then, there is the big leap: experiences become prophecies that can be applied to a different set of people.[4] In this way, strangers' experiences with violence and trauma can cause someone whom they have never met to be labeled as at risk. Crime data is used to mark noncriminals as at risk and injury data is used to mark healthy people as at risk. The meanings jump between arenas and individuals. Risk data are, in a sense, a map of the past that is used to predict the future. In fact, one survey of high school seniors is called "Monitoring the Future." This creates a kind of solidarity that borders on poetic: a stranger's pain predicts my own and my humanity is bound up in theirs. But it also serves to take away the particulars of experience and replace them with a generalized trajectory.

Risk, Ian Hacking tells us, is a recent invention. The first iteration of risk, which arose with simple probabilities, enabled the threats of the future to be met with insurance and a range of technologies of government; what Nikolas Rose described as "a family of ways of thinking and acting that involve calculations about probable futures in the present followed by interventions into the present in order to control that potential future."[5] Writing in 1991, French social theorist Robert Castel argued that this way of thinking of risk had political and even existential consequences in the mental health fields. Castel wrote that prevention strategies "dissolve the notion of a *subject* or a concrete individual, and put in its place a combination of *factors,* the factors of risk." Castel contended that by looking at individuals as risk factors, professionals might find it difficult, if not impossible, to see the person through the haze of statistical risk. On a large scale, Castel worried, risk might erase the individual entirely.[6]

In the last 30 years, advances in statistical technology and access to personal data have multiplied the scope of the statistical process and given rise to a staggering catalog of risks and protective factors. C. Wright Mills, in a classic tome of modern sociology, once argued that to understand any one person, we must situate their biography within the tides of history.[7] Risk data was not what he had in mind, but it has put his call into action to an unprecedented degree and into a novel form. We are each a small cluster of data points in a stream of billions, tying the past to the future.

However, statistical data does not simply reflect reality, but, as scholars have argued, actively creates it. Statistical representations "invent and transform collectivities and social reality . . . These have effects on how people conceive of themselves and others."[8] We can see this in action as risk data takes on a life of its own and reverberates across grants, curricula, fact sheets, PowerPoint presentations, and the formalized discourses of social policy, far beyond the people it echoes. Technological inventions such as risk analysis are also cultural processes, producing value differences, redrawing symbolic boundaries, and constructing new kinds of subjects.[9] Risk data has produced at least two new subject positions, that is, two kinds of people who did not exist before: the preventionist and the at-risk youth.

The preventionist has learned to see risk in all parts of daily life. As one facilitator told me, "I wish I could turn it off when I'm listening to music or watching TV . . . I wish I could turn it off. Like in my house, like if I hear a woman scream . . . I wish I could turn it off when I'm talking to my friends because I'm sure they would appreciate that. This is just the way I look at things at this point." This is, above all, a way of seeing behaviors, one that I contend aligns with the structure of the ephemeral state. From the perspective of the preventionist, behaviors are linked up to potential futures and individuals are statistics.[10]

Risk data also makes possible the subject position of the at-risk person. Unlike the deviant, who lies outside the boundaries of social norms, or the criminal, who runs afoul of the legal system, the at-risk person has a past correlated with a harmful future: those who have never done violence but one day might because their statistical lives suggest as much. They are nearly always young because that moment in the lifecourse occupies a place between the accumulation of risk in childhood and irreparable action in adulthood. Statistical risk has been personified into individuals at risk, and in the process, cultural categories have been reshaped and inequalities obscured. In practice, risk creates distance between the ways that young people experience their lives and the ways that adults experience young people.

A range of critiques have been leveled against risk data.[11] Some have argued that it fails to capture enough detail of lives or that it overlooks too many associations between factors. These arguments boil down to the idea that risk data fails to work as well as it could. My argument differs. I contend that risk data has cultural consequences that have not been adequately explored, regardless of how accurately they capture reality.[12] These consequences are likely to escalate even as we hone statistical approaches. Statistical analysis of risk data changes the way we think about and act upon the problems of personal lives, but we do not yet grasp what is lost when personal lives become data.

WHAT RISK ERASES

In 1983, when statistics on domestic violence and sexual assault were just beginning to enter mainstream conversations, feminist activist Andrea Dworkin talked about what those numbers meant in personal terms:[13]

We use statistics not to try to quantify the injuries, but to convince the world that those injuries even exist. Those statistics are not abstractions. It is easy to say, "Ah, the statistics, somebody writes them up one way and somebody writes them up another way." That's true. But I hear about the rapes one by one by one by one by one, which is also how they happen. Those statistics are not abstract to me.

While I dug through the dense morass of statistical data on violence and risk, I thought about how much had changed since the early feminist strategies for counting, the kind Dworkin talked about. After all, feminism was founded on a kind of data too: the stories told between women which, taken together, built up a systemic critique. Those stories are different from what we have today. They were largely told within the confines of real connections—not anonymous or massive, but personal and shared.

Risk data, I contend, converts the byproducts of structural inequalities into legible interpersonal health patterns. Social inequalities, particularly racism, poverty, and heterosexism, are aggregated and resorted into new categories. As a result, they are thought of as different kinds of problems. Janet Shim, writing about the social origins of heart disease, describes the hidden "politics of causation" in medicine. We often think that race is associated with heart disease, but Shim argues that it is structural racism—the way that people of color are treated—that causes increased rates. To make an argument about causality means picking a variable to start at and inevitably erasing some aspect of causation.[14] Drawing on risk data, prevention locates risk in the small-scale world of behavior and personal experience, disconnected from institutions and identity. The causes are made to be interpersonal, emotional, and habitual, but not economic, medical, or political.

Statistical analysis trades specificity for generalizability, and thus buried within risk factors are whole lives. Statistics are the byproduct of aggregated and analyzed individuals who, once viewed in clusters and categories, reveal patterns of experience. However, experience is messy and violence is a fundamentally unstable category, filtered through prisms of power and identity.[15] If we take risk factors apart and unravel the experiences that accumulate into them, we can see what risk erases.

The attitudes and behaviors of the young people I talked to looked a lot like their peers' in middle-class and wealthy communities. Several used marijuana or drank recreationally. Most engaged in sexual activity. Nearly all had friends and loved ones involved in what would qualify as dating violence, although they rarely saw it that way. Those who had partners sometimes got into heated arguments. Several talked about situations in which they believed it would be okay to yell at or fight playfully with a partner.

The three most common risk factors—in the technical sense—that arose in my interviews with youth were: witnessing violence in the home, showing signs of trauma, and displaying aggression.[16] Every young person I talked to described one or more of these factors, yet I found that each risk factor encompassed incredibly diverse experiences and often obscured the mechanisms that might increase the chances of future violence. In other words, risk factors shift our gaze onto the markers of risk and away from the facts of young people's experiences with violence. The stories that follow, of fighting at home, traumatic experiences, and aggressive behavior, signal the limitations of risk factors for understanding daily life in marginalized places; at the same time, they provide a glimpse of the underlying tensions wrought by pervasive violence, trauma, and policing, and how structural forces are erased in the production of risk factors. To begin the story with risk factors—trauma, disengagement, isolation, or distrust—erases the forces that gave rise and shape to them. These things are not just factors that produce harm, they are harm themselves, beget by specific arrangements of history and structure.

"Witness or Experience Violence in the Home"

Tensions at home were pervasive and many young people witnessed tempers boil over into yelling, aggression, or physical violence. This seemed like a clear-cut risk factor. After all, young people who grow up in violent circumstances might also be the object of aggression or, because we all learn something about relationships from our families, they might be more likely to enact violence themselves. Yet, although many young people experienced fighting between adult family members, I found that it took a dizzying range of forms, making it difficult to interpret using a risk factor logic of cause and effect. Violence in the home, after all, is often violence among the people with whom young people feel closest. For this reason, its ramifications were shaped by—and echoed through—all of the complex emotional dynamics of those relationships: between a husband and wife, a niece and her aunt, a mother and a daughter. Beyond that, these relationships were not isolated. They were bound up with economic pressures and shifting notions of gender in family life, often agitated in the economic pressure cooker of long work hours for scant wages.

Sky, a 17-year-old with bleach-tinged hair who identified as "Mexican and Honduran," spoke in a level tone as she described her parents' constant fighting as inseparable from the love they felt for each other: "My mom's like, 'Oh my God, do this, do that!' My dad is just laid back like, 'You know, woman, leave me alone,' and that results in fighting . . . They've been arguing for the past 15 years. I know the love is there, or else one of them would have left already." While Sky disliked her parents' fighting, she decided it was okay in the context of what she saw as "goofy" love. It was easy to imagine that this perspective, if carried forward, could impact Sky's future experiences in relationships. In this way, it was not the experience of witnessing violence, but the way that Sky interpreted it as part of an acceptable pattern of gendered interaction, that felt like a risk.

Many young people had previously learned that violence and aggression were unhealthy and tried to intervene when they saw it in their family. Take for example Misty, a 17-year-old Bangladeshi woman, who recognized that her aunt was in a destructive cycle of emotional abuse and tried to intervene. She told me, her voice sliding between frustration and resignation: "It gets so bad there. It's actually both of them trying to put the other one down, and then at times my aunt, she just gets so down and then one time she tried to kill herself." Misty felt "helpless in that place," but mustered the courage to talk with her aunt and uncle, but they "got back into the honeymoon [phase] again." "They were like, 'Oh, you're so young you don't know anything. You shouldn't even be getting into the whole conversation.' And they were also like, 'Oh, it's not your life, it's my life and I can live it the way I want to.'" Unlike Sky, Misty did not believe that fighting could be part of love. However, when she intervened, she received the message that violence was a personal choice and that only those in the relationship were in a position to deal with it.

For other young people, aggression between parents was beside the point. Valeria was 18 when I interviewed her in the guidance counselor's office at her high school at the edge of downtown Los Angeles. Valeria spoke casually about the fighting and confrontation that were seemingly constant aspects of her life. Her father was not around and her mother was a bartender and "at night sometimes she just hangs out and drinks and she comes home drunk and stuff." This was a source of tension between the two of them while Valeria was growing up and they fought often: "We would always argue about random things in the house, or about school and the people I would hang out with . . . I would judge her of the certain things she did. And she would judge me of the certain things I would do." Valeria was most critical of her mother's hypocrisy and seemed less concerned with her mother's use of physical violence as a form of punishment: "She used to get the *chancla* [sandals] every time I would do something bad or like used to whoop me when I would do something bad." Growing up in "that environment" shaped how Valeria planned to raise her own kids: "It made me a better person, because I know now I won't do that to my kids, unless they're actually—like they really deserve it." Valeria, unlike Sky and Misty, described how she might use corporal punishment as an adult. However, Valeria's relationship to violence was different from the other young women's, couched as it was in the ongoing tensions in her relationship with her mother.

Valeria, Misty, and Sky experienced fighting, aggression, and violence at home in ways that would mark them as at risk. However, a risk factor fails to capture these young women's experiences and the diverse ways that violence was embedded in economic and cultural positions of families in Los Angeles. What they did share, however, was a position as young women of color from low-income families. We know from sociological scholarship that, because of this position, they are likely to face increased violence, marginalization, and economic subordination. However, those forces, as well as the pressures felt by their parents, were invisible in the risk factor. To put it another way, "witnessing or experiencing violence in the home" is perhaps more likely an effect rather than a cause.

"Are Depressed, Anxious, or Have Other Symptoms of Trauma"

Most of the young people I interviewed had experienced something that would be considered traumatic. Many had lost loved ones to illness or violence, had family members in jail, had witnessed shootings, or had been beaten up or harassed. While trauma is a fact of life for young people in every city and town, it was clear that young people in the marginalized neighborhoods of Los Angeles dealt with more than their share. Flora, a Latina student, told me that she felt the weight of violence as ever-present: "It's being everywhere. It's not only South Central, it's West LA, it's in the mountains. Yeah, it's everywhere. And like where I used to live, um, I grew up in another country and it's like next door, in front of my house, right in my door. Like yeah, everywhere."

I talked with Flora the day after a group of young people went to see *Fruitvale Station*, a film that chronicles the last day in the life of Oscar Grant, a Black man who was shot and killed by a white transportation officer in Oakland while lying on the ground with his hands above his head. When I asked Flora, who is Latina, about the movie, she explained that it reminded her of what happened to her father:

> I felt like I was living [it] again, like oh my god, no, no. And um, just looking at the baby girl just, being with her father, just having fun and being a kid with a loving father. And I [said] like, [he's] just another one. If my dad died, why not him? In like, in my opinion, my dad was a good person. And why him?

The death of Flora's father was unquestionably traumatic. But through her participation with a local nonprofit and through long conversations with her mother, it was also couched in the recognition that this was a too common occurrence. Flora explained how, since Trayvon Martin had been killed by George Zimmerman, she had begun to shift the way her own trauma and loss shaped how she acted: "It just made me change so much about the way I think now. And my mom is like 'Oh you know you're perfect now' and I'm like 'No, I'm not perfect. I'm just trying to change.'" Flora had begun to advocate against violence and for social justice. Her trauma was not just a risk. Trauma undermines beliefs about how the world should work. With the support of her family and facilitators, Flora's loss became a catalyst for her to work to change society and herself.

When I first met Scott, he eagerly and unprompted told me about his pet snakes. He had been largely home-schooled, I was told later, because his mom moved often in order to stay away from an abusive man. When his mom took a job outside of California Scott, eager to maintain the friendships he had built, stayed in Los Angeles in a small apartment with his best friend. In what seems to have been a tragic case of mistaken identity, Scott and his friend were shot leaving their apartment complex to get pizza. His friend died and Scott was badly injured and needed major surgery. He was devastated. He was not able to attend his friend's funeral because he was in the hospital. His mom flew back to town, but did not have a car, so she had difficulty getting back and forth between the hotel and the hospital. She was spending more money than she could afford and had to ride several hours each way on the bus several times while Scott was in the hospital so that she could keep her job. The prevention team at POV rallied around Scott. The day of his friend's funeral, several stayed with Scott in the hospital, and several others went to the funeral and streamed the proceedings to a laptop so that Scott could watch. POV staffers drove Scott's mother back and forth to the hospital and out for errands and raised over $1,000. It would be wrong to draw a straight line between Scott's trauma history and the violence enacted against him. Instead, it was geography and Scott's desire to achieve some normalcy that put him in harm's way and exposed him to still more trauma.

Hoxton's story, while still marked by the symptoms of trauma, was very different from Scott's or Flora's. Hoxton switched schools after experiencing repeated and extensive bullying. He described "an absolutely horrible experience . . . I even got a legitimate rape threat from another student and I was escorted for the last few days, before I was transferred here." He explained that the rape threat came from a "dumb-ass of a guy." Hoxton's performance of gender fell outside the norm at the school and some students took his unwillingness to conform as a reason to harass him. At his new school, a few students who "think they're big shots" made fun of Hoxton in physical education, but he largely brushed it off in our interview. Hoxton talked excitedly about video games; first-person "shooters" were his "main thing." His mother worried that he might consider joining the military, but Hoxton had no plans to enlist. He did, however, want to try shooting an air-powered rifle called an Airsoft and was considering buying a gun for self-defense, which he planned to keep "in, let's say, a secret glove compartment I have in my car just in case I ever needed it." But, the airsoft rifle was "the furthest I'll go to ever shooting an actual person if it wasn't for self-defense." As I listened to Hoxton, I was worried too. While he was doing well in his classes, he also seemed to be struggling to make sense of the threats he received at his previous school and the bullying he was still experiencing. He was, understandably, giving a lot of thought to how he might defend himself. Unlike Flora, Hoxton had no shared connection to other young people who had experienced similar trauma, and that seemed to narrow how he saw his options.

The loss experienced by Flora, the violence enacted upon Scott, and the bullying endured by Hoxton are just three forms, albeit common ones, among the many traumatic events that happened to the young people I spoke with. Trauma left youth questioning their social world. For some, the world seemed uncertain, marked by unpredictable and often overwhelming danger. This view was shaped in large part by a sense that institutions had failed them and would continue to fail them. For others the world looked unjust, as those in power exacted harm with little thought to the consequences. However, the way that trauma impacted youth depended in large part on the resources available to them in their school or community. Young people, when met with some support from an organization or adult, were safeguarded against the forces that can bend trauma into violence.

"Display Aggression toward Peers or Display Other Aggressive Behaviors"

Most of the young people I spoke with at one point or another had displayed some form of aggressive behavior. Aggression, after all, is a broad and often subjective marker. Young people often teased each other or play-fought, some threw a phone or tipped over a chair when they were angry or disappointed. Many played aggressive sports or violent video games. However, the use of these behaviors to mark individuals as at risk often narrowed in on young men of color. Meaning that actions that might otherwise be seen as unfortunate accidents or as youthful roughhousing were more likely to be marked as violent, and, in turn, as a predictor of the future.

When I interviewed Joe Moses, a young Black man, he was 15 years old and already six feet tall, although he bent his neck down, which made him seem smaller. He wore three strings of rosaries around his neck and his arms were dotted with burn marks and scars. We talked at a picnic table in the courtyard of his South Los Angeles high school. Joe was calm and shy, speaking with a slight lisp caused by a metal lip stud, while he told me about his experiences with police. He was arrested in eighth grade after a fight: "The dude was in class, he just kept bothering me, bothering me. So, he pushed me, and so, I socked him, and then I got arrested. They said battery assault, and then I was arrested." Joe was arrested again after a teacher mistook play fighting for a real fight: "[The teacher] said if I didn't go to the office, she was going to call the school police, so I said alright, I'm going to go to the office, and she still called for school police." Even when his friend, the one he was play fighting with, told his parents that they were not actually fighting, they did not believe him. Joe was sent to Los Padrinos Juvenile Hall for two weeks. I asked Joe why he thought people seemed to worry that he was being violent, and he explained that it was because of his size: "Because I'm big, that's why," he said. He felt that he was treated unfairly and that the teacher assumed that because he is the "big one" that he started the problem. The police cuffed Joe, put him into the police car, took him to the police station, booked him into the system, and then took him to Los Padrinos. According to Joe, juvenile hall was "not cool, it was, like, boring in there (laughs). You got no type of freedom, all you do is go to school for, like, three hours, and then we go back and then we just, like, watch movies, and then we go to sleep and stuff." Now, Joe did his "best to stay out of there," he explained, because "it's not a good place to be locked up in. Like, especially, if you're not a violent person, you shouldn't be there. It's not a good place." Joe's experience mirrored the stories of other young Black and Latino men, especially those who are big for their age and are treated as adults and violent offenders, instead of playful teenagers.[17]

Crystal, a Latina young woman with multicolored hair, whose bag displayed a pin for a sexual assault awareness campaign and another that read, "I'm picturing you naked," told a very different story about a fight she had in eighth grade. She explained that while in middle school she was "going through stuff and didn't know how to handle it that well." She had a "low temper" and "would, like, just let it go on people." We talked in a counselor's office at the back of the school office suite:

I had this one girl, she was talking to me and I was like we were fighting, but it was on top of—it was like it was the stairs, and then like I pushed her.

I didn't mean to push her, but she like fell down the stairs, and I got—I got like in big trouble because they like the police took me, and like I got a ticket for like fighting, and my mom was all like in my business, and everything. And then the—the girl, I mean, the girl was OK, but they still saw it as like I tried to harm her.

The police wrote Crystal a ticket, but her repercussions paled in comparison to Joe's: "I had to go to court, but I just paid it off, like, with money, because I don't want to, I don't want to do community service, so I just paid it off." Crystal's light punishment, and her ability to get out of it by paying, was in part a byproduct of her gender, race, and class. In this way, the ubiquity of racialized and gendered crime control both triggered and slowed the social processes that gave rise to aggression. Similar behaviors, such as play fighting, are interpreted differently depending on the social location of the actors. These interpretations are then more likely to be translated into risk data.

By attending to the lived experiences behind the risk factors, we are able to see how this process flattens experience. Structural inequalities along the lines of race, gender, and class were clear parts of the stories that young people told. Economic pressure on immigrant families, pervasive trauma threaded through marginalized communities, and harsh, racialized policing gave rise to the events that would become risk factors. However, risk factors fail to capture this social reality. In addition, the collapsing of risk factors obscures the relationships, agency, and identity that are vital sources of hope and support.

RED FLAGS

In Los Angeles schools, I found teachers, administrators, and implementers who often saw, and discussed, "red flags" in their students. Red flags were everyday expressions of the researched and defined risk factors described in prevention programs. I was surprised at how easily teachers, administrators, and preventionists would mark things as "red flags." Some red flags refer to personality qualities, while others are based on environmental and demographic attributes. Not long after being trained as a facilitator, I felt like I could see red flags too, flashing like alerts over the heads of the students as they flooded out of the classroom and into the hall, their possible futures unspooling in a number of directions.

Ann Ferguson has argued that one way in which public schools criminalize young men of color is to adultify them, depriving them of their social position as children—and all the support for experimenting, learning and growing that it affords—and placing them in a framework of adult rules and regulations.[18] Red flags enact a distinct and parallel process that I call *futurification,* whereby a system of nonprofits and facilitators treat young people not as individuals with specific pasts, but as potential futures. My concern with red flags is not that they are wrong, although they very well might be, but that as they fast-forward the lives of young people, they transform how we make sense of and respond to experiences. Risk requires that we live in a constant "before" of violence. Take for example Paula, a Latina youth, who was 17 years old when I interviewed her at the Peace Over Violence office. She was in jeans and a black cardigan and wore thick-framed glasses. Paula was crisp, relaxed, and professional during our conversation. I have chosen Paula, but I could have picked any youth I talked to.

Early in her life, Paula witnessed a shooting in Koreatown, and the suddenness and proximity stuck with her: "We were just walking down the street and there was like a drive-by and then like it was like right in front of our faces and my mom was super scared. She just like threw us on the floor and she was like 'Get down!'" *Red flag.* This was one of many incidents of violence in Paula's life. When I asked her where she saw violence, she said, "Well, like everywhere. I see it in a lot of places. Not just here in LA, also like the valley. I used to live in [the valley], you know, there was violence there. Violence is everywhere. It's like you can't escape it." *Red flag.* She continued, "Well, like in homes. You see a lot of violence in homes, just in the street with sometimes like moms hitting their child. I mean I don't find it right for a mom to hit their child, even though it's *their* child but, you know, it's like they're not doing—you're not supposed to do that. And it's illegal, too, to smack your kid across the face or something." *Red flag.* With violence seemingly inescapable, Paula valued personal action in the face of uncertainty.

Paula made sense of her experiences largely in relation to the influence of those closest to her. She told me that she was a good student early on, but then things changed when her sister, who had been her "role model," was arrested and sent to juvenile hall. *Red flag:*

> Who was I going to look up to now, you know? . . . There's been a lot of violence in my family, like my brother. I was about to join a gang too but I was like, no, you know, this is bad . . . The people around me they weren't good role models either and then, like my environment, my surroundings, like the park, it was like filled with gangsters, you know.

Red flags. In middle school, Paula fell under the influence of some "older kids" who, like many teenagers, wanted to "try everything." *Red flag.* She became "a big ditcher," began experimenting with drugs, and was "not good in school." *Red flags.*

As a teenager, Paula left home several times, "I've never really ran away from home but I've gone and haven't came back sometimes because I'm mad so I just like sometimes get mad." *Red flag.* "The last time I kind of ran away was like two Thanksgivings ago. So my sister got me really mad so I just left and I didn't come back until like two days later." When Paula looked back on this period in her young life, it wasn't breaking the rules that she regretted; it was how easily others had influenced her.

There are two main ways to understand the meaningful moments and turning points in Paula's life up to this point. There is the one that I have emphasized here, with red flags flashing throughout, highlighting a sense of impending risk. But there is another way of understanding Paula; the way that she preferred to be seen. Throughout our talk, she described her life in active terms, as the product of decisions that she made. Much of Paula's worldview was shaped by broken social ties, which taught her to be independent and often isolated and distrustful. The extensive use of risk data to organize social policy meant that most adults never saw this Paula. And they missed out.

Not long after she ran away, things began to change, but Paula had difficulty explaining why. She started working hard to do well in school: "I'm kind of myself, but like in a productive good way. Not being like, you know, really bad and stuff because—I mean if I do drugs that's going to get me in trouble or if I drink, you know, it's illegal for me to drink and—or sometimes if I ditch school I could just get caught. It's stuff that—you just have to be—it's like logic. Like you know you're not supposed to do that, why do it." Paula's phrase, "I'm kind of myself, but like in a productive good way," aligned with the way other young women who had been once been "really bad" made sense of themselves as active social agents and saw reliance on others as a source of weakness.

Paula's commitment to doing what she was "supposed to do" sometimes meant going to great lengths. Paula's sister was held up at gunpoint for her jewelry while walking home one afternoon. "She just came home crying. She was like super scratched." After her sister's experience, along with several scary incidents walking at night, Paula decided to change her lifestyle:

> I just do everything I have to do during the day. Because during the night sometimes [I get] really scared because like I've experienced, once like somebody just came and they touched my butt, some guy just walking by and I was like, well, this is not going to happen ever again.

Paula's strategies for keeping herself safe excluded police. Instead, she took it as her own responsibility to look out for potential dangers and avoid harassment and armed robbery. When I asked Paula if she still looks up to her older sister, she said no, "I just look up to myself." Among the young women I interviewed, violence, often enacted by men, was a persistent specter as they moved across the city. With little trust in authorities to maintain their safety, women carried the existential anxiety and emotional weight of this violence. In Paula's case, her sister, who would have otherwise been a source of support, was caught up in the same system that Paula had seen fall short. Rather than risk being let down by those closest to her, Paula, like many young women, developed a deeply held belief in personal responsibility as a means of avoiding violence. Even though Paula got back on track, and now holds herself up as her own role model, those around her have kept up their messages about how she should act. She told me,

> My mom's like don't get pregnant. People are like don't get pregnant. It's like I'm not going to get pregnant. And it's just like, oh, you have to do good in school, just don't follow like any, like don't hang out with bad people, or like

bad friends or bad influences and I have friends that are like bad influences but it's also my choice, you know. If I choose to follow them. It's not just like them and, oh, you know they're bad so I'm going to become bad. So my mom sometimes like she puts an order, you know, like you can't hang out with these people because they're bad.

The operative word from Paula's mom was a version of a prevention strategy: *don't.*

Whether we see Paula's story as a tale of systemic inequalities or mounting risk factors will determine how we make sense of the most important moments in her life. Was the horrific violence she witnessed a byproduct of violence and gun laws, or was it the first red flag? Was her persistent anger a warning sign, or was it a way of coping with inequality and harm? Risk factors position us to lose sight of the aspects of young people's lives that they find salient. It made it difficult to see their sparks of agency in the face of daunting uncertainty, as well as the underlying structures that give rise to risk in the first place.

Red flags are a way of telling stories about the future. If risk data could somehow perfectly mirror the social worlds of young people of color in urban environments, this might not be a problem. However, in reality the difference between these two views resembles the difference between Google maps and a late-night stroll under the streetlights: they both tell you about the path between A and B, but they are dramatically different ways of understanding the world. The sliver of lives captured by population-level risk data tells us nothing about what experiences meant to individuals, how their social location shaped those meanings, the social context in which they occurred, who they turned to, or how to support them. This does not mean that risk data is "wrong," but it does narrow our field of vision into the lives of young people.

I understand why policymakers and youth workers alike think in terms of risk. I found that it was a useful shorthand to organize and triage how I engaged with a seemingly endless stream of young people. Noticing a risk factor provided a clear and concrete course of action and a way of interacting. This was particularly helpful because facilitators and other adults spent so little time with so many youth. Red flags worked because it helped to make sense of fleeting interactions in the ephemeral state.

WHERE RISK IS NORMAL

MAX: Have you ever heard the phrase "at risk"?

HENDRIX: At risk? Yeah.

MAX: Yeah, what does it mean? Where have you heard it?

HENDRIX: I mean, I haven't heard it a lot, but I know what it means.

MAX: What does it mean?

HENDRIX: It means, like, something that's, like, you're walking on egg-shells pretty much.

MAX: Do you feel like you know people who are at risk?

HENDRIX: At risk of—of just period?

MAX: Of anything. Yeah.

HENDRIX: Yeah.

MAX: How about at risk of violence?

HENDRIX: At risk of violence, no.

MAX: No, okay.

HENDRIX: I don't know a lot of people. I mean, I know a lot of gang members. That's, like, violence, right?

By formal and informal measures commonly used in the professional violence prevention field, every young person I spent time with was "at risk." Hendrix himself, the young man who pondered the definition of at risk at the start of this section, was undeniably so. Latino, with an easygoing demeanor, he was 16 years old when we talked in an empty classroom after school let out. The small "continuation" high school Hendrix attended was in a storefront on a major thoroughfare, in a predominantly Black and Latinx neighborhood in South Los Angeles. There were 80 total students enrolled, only 50 of whom regularly attended. The school had a reputation for accepting students who had struggled elsewhere, and many of the students were on probation or in foster care and had been pushed out of other schools, which led some students to describe it as a "last-chance school." I expected that of all the youth I talked to, the ones there would have picked up on the language of risk and red flags that swirled around them, but they had not. Most, instead, shared Hendrix's confusion. This was also true of young people that Peace Over Violence recruited into their leadership programs from schools across Los Angeles, many of whom excelled at academic pursuits. Regardless of which young people I talked to, I found that the same narrative of risk that animated troves of research and millions of dollars of funding for prevention programs made little sense to the young people it was supposed to help.[19]

Many facilitators said that *every* youth they worked with was at risk for one reason or another. Ella told me, "In the communities I've worked with, every single [youth] is high-risk just because of the environment that we live in." I asked if she just meant high risk for violence, and she responded: "At risk for anything, drug use, alcohol, pregnancy. It's overall just high-risk." I heard a similar sentiment in my interviews with young people. Several times, when I asked youth where they saw unhealthy or violent behavior, the answer was simply "everywhere." Gina, who at 25 was by far the oldest youth participant I interviewed, was part of a performance-based anti-violence program run out of a dance studio. Gina saw herself as a role model for other participants, some as much as a decade younger than her. We talked in a break room alongside the mirrored space where the group was practicing for an upcoming performance. Gina said that "a lot of the warning signs that one would never think or one is so used to, such as, you know, fighting all the time for example, in my community are a normality. So to [learn] that that's a warning sign for me was, well, I hear [warning signs] all the time." She continued, "You hear ambulances, police, your typical city. So, there have been calls on domestic violence maybe two houses down from me. A child was abused in the house diagonal to mine. There was a juvenile delinquent who actually was a friend of my brother's when we were young. He grew up with the wrong crowd." Gina found it bizarre to make sense of everyday life in her community, among her neighbors, peers, and family, through the lens of risk. As Gina described, in underserved urban communities, risks are multiple and proximal but residents rarely identify them as such because they are attached to specific individuals and embedded in their local social world. It is hard to see your neighbors or your brother as embodiments of risk.

The things that were statistically designated as risk factors felt commonplace. Angel, a 19-year-old Latino young man with deep-set eyes and a level voice, explained how he saw his life compared with other people his age: "I think it's normal, the same thing [as] like every 19-year-old, like certain things we go through, like, uneducated, a lot of 19-year-olds are like that. Not being employed. Like having, like rough things at your house. Things like that." Angel is partly right. Los Angeles has a low high school graduation rate, just 67 percent,[20] and according to a study by the Brookings Institution, one of the lowest rates of teen employment in the country, 16.7 percent.[21] These troubles are byproducts of the social and economic context in which Angel lives, but from his perspective they are simply how life is. As Angel explained, in underserved communities, risks are common and therefore young people develop a locally defined sense of the baseline level of risk. Angel: "I know everything about violence . . . Like that's all I know. Like all I know is about violence. Like everywhere I'm surrounded by, it's like violence everywhere." He continued: "I feel like violence was just there for me." Like Gina and Angel, young people rarely described marginalization and violent events as risk factors, but instead as everyday facts of life. From their perspectives, living in their community, risk was everywhere and therefore in a way, nowhere. The sheer quantity of risk in marginalized communities meant that young people experienced it as embedded in the social ties and structures of daily life, which, in turn, made the predictive logic of risk factors fall apart. In such communities, young people already had ways of making sense of and navigating experiences marked as risk factors.[22]

To be alive is to carry risk. The form and consequence of risks may change, but no one is entirely insulated. For this reason, risk factors might be better described as *increased* risk factors that gauge how a population compares to a baseline "normal" level of risk that is present in the general population. That is, risk is fundamentally a measure of relative inequality. When I asked Hendrix the same question that I had asked Angel, what life was like for men his age in Los Angeles, he echoed this logic. He understood himself and those around him as different from a mainstream definition of normal: "I don't even know what a normal 16-year-old feels like, 'cause I got a lot of friends that are doin' the same thing that I'm doing." It was clear to Hendrix that race and place played a role in what normal meant. He continued, "But I think it leads back to race too. Some 16-year-olds don't deal with this. Like, I mean, I'm not putting you—like, people in a category, but I know, like, people out here in LA, like, they deal with the same thing that I deal with." It was clear to me that when he was talking about "people out here in LA" he was talking about Black and Brown youth in contrast to white people, like me. Hendrix was right—his experience was different from the "normal" category against which risk was measured. He was growing up amidst a mix of structural inequalities that composed daily life for youth in Los Angeles. Hendrix, in fact, was far more normal than he realized. Using endnotes, I have marked some of the moments when the circumstances of Hendrix's life put him in line with broad historical shifts.

Hendrix was younger than his peers and preparing to graduate early. On the first day of a six-week prevention program, he enacted the quintessential performance of "contrived carelessness" common among young men in schools: head down, one earbud in,[23] an orientation that has been associated with the low rates of young men graduating high school. But in the following weeks, he became a vocal contributor to class discussions. He took his pseudonym from Jimi Hendrix and talked effusively about his love of music. He closed his eyes for long stretches while we talked, composing his answers in his head, and he fidgeted with a roll of paper. He planned to devote his time to a career as a music producer once he graduated, and he already spent much of his free time working with a soundboard at a friend's house.

Hendrix's parents worked physically taxing jobs for low wages and were rarely at home. His mother worked in a sweatshop in LA's garment district[24] and he lived with his father, who had worked as a long-haul truck driver[25] since Hendrix was born. His parents were financially stable and he no longer needed to contribute as much to the household as he once had. He was thrilled to have new stylish clothes, bought from money earned at his part-time job. However, his parents' precarious work made his economic future uncertain.

Like many young men marked at risk, Hendrix had been in trouble for most of his educational life. He was skeptical of schooling, but he did well enough to get by when he tried. At a young age, he was pulled into a pattern of suspension and expulsion, a pattern far more common among young men of color. He was suspended in second grade for "poppin' a firework in class."[26] The harsh discipline at the school was disconnected from lessons at home. He explained, "My mom didn't know. She thought that I was just being sent home for some reason. In school I've been suspended sixth grade, seventh grade, eighth grade, ninth grade, tenth grade been suspended. And I've been suspended, like, three times every year."[27] When I asked him what kinds of things he was suspended for, he explained:

> I used to get in a lot of fights with people.[28] I used to do a lot. And my principal didn't like me. She hated me. She hated me so much. She used to try to find little things, she, I guess, I'm pretty sure she sent someone to write "Fuck Ms. Curtis" on the wall, right. And it was the teacher that I had just had a parent-teacher conference with. This principal hated me so much she brought me up to the office, she had a paper of mine—I don't know how she got a paper of mine, right. She was like, "It's the same writing that was on this wall," tryin' a suspend me. She was like here comes one administrator. But I was, I mean, I wasn't stupid. I was like, OK, you can bring them all in, I didn't do it. And do you have proof that I did it? Why are you accusing me that I did it? You know, she didn't like me. And she knew that I was smart, and I wasn't stupid, but that was always her motto, like, tryin' to suspend me, tryin' to take me out of school. So when she found out that I was leaving the school, she was like, "Yay! Thank God he's leaving."

Here, Hendrix's story splits. He begins with a classic marker of at-risk status, constant fights, but then he emphasizes the role that the authorities at the school played. Hendrix's belief that the principal "hated" him, whether it was true or not, significantly impacted his investment and trust in the school institution. After Hendrix left that school, he went to a charter school in the valley, but he was only there for a short while before it was closed down, "'Cause my principal was corrupt. Corrupt principal. And they found, like, a lot of stuff about her. She was keeping the money to herself." The school was supposed to be a "two-story place" with a "big gym" but since the principal had been diverting the money, the school was "real small and it was real ghetto." Hendrix went to another school, but that didn't last either: "I was a bad kid. I moved to [another school]. After there—they didn't want me there—I moved there for a month, and I went to a continuation school . . . I went there and then I came here. Yeah, so I've been at, like, five [high] schools."[29]

Hendrix's experiences of corruption and criminalization in turn put more weight on his social connections with friends. When I asked Hendrix to say more about why he left the previous schools, even though he had said it was because he was a "bad kid" and that they didn't want him, he elaborated, explaining that he "didn't like school" because at his previous school "it wasn't diverse at all.[30] Like, it was just a bunch, a bunch of Latinos." His school, in other words, was segregated, like a growing number of schools today. He went on, explaining, "It's not that I didn't want to fit in with them, it's just that I knew I was gonna move, 'cause I wanted to move. So I was like, no, I'm not about to talk to nobody."[31] After a stint at another school, Hendrix decided that he wanted to join one of his best friends, Michael, at the "last chance" school. Several young men I talked to recounted attending multiple schools, often in response to disciplinary issues, and this had negative repercussions on their view of schooling broadly. For some, such as Hendrix, building and maintaining connections with peers served as a response to the unfair institution.

In his moves between schools, Hendrix learned to navigate institutional authority even as he resented it. This was also true of his interactions with police. He told me that he had learned to avoid the corner and the liquor store and not to be out with "a pack" of his friends. Still, Hendrix had been "pulled over a lot" while out walking in his neighborhood.[32] When I expressed surprise, he laughed it off, "I'm from LA, of course." Hendrix was right, in a way— young men of color are far more likely to be stopped by police. Hendrix told me that he believed that police knew that he was just walking home, but "they try to play with you." According to Hendrix police said they pulled him over because he looked suspicious. He saw this as informed by racial attitudes, explaining: "They can put charges on you, just because they don't like you, period. They see you're a young kid, you're Latino, you're walking at night, they're gonna pull you over. They're gonna do something to you." Hendrix seemed resigned to this pattern of harassment. "I still walk at night. I don't really care about it. I mean, I do care about it, but I'm just one person, you know? It takes a lot to change that," he told me. I asked what he thought it would take: "It would take a lot of people with their same state of mind to change that. But [for] my part, I wouldn't want to. I really wouldn't care about it." I asked if he thought there was anything that could be done. He shrugged, "I'm pretty sure eventually change will come, 'cause change is inevitable. It will come. It always has. So it will come, but I don't think I should do it." Hendrix did not have a clear answer for why he didn't want to be a part of this change, but his story provides clues. Repeatedly, institutions and authorities decided Hendrix's options in ways that seemed to him to be unfair and manipulative. In response, Hendrix had learned how to navigate and move between those institutions by using their disdain for him to his advantage. Instead, he came to prioritize his friendships outside of school as his primary source of meaning and connection. Hendrix's story reveals a common pattern in the way that young men in Los Angeles experienced institutions. From their perspective, schools and the police were a series of poorly run, fickle institutions with corrupt adult leaders. In response, young men distrusted them and disengaged.

The dangers that Hendrix faced, however common where he lives, were real, and even though he had avoided them, he was still faced with risk in very real ways that stretched beyond the everyday risk of being alive. However, the quotidian character of those risks in his life helps explain why he did not experience his life as risky or himself as at risk. Structural inequalities widen the gap between statistical lives and personal lives. In places marked by pervasive risk, danger and closed options come to feel—and in fact are—normal. In an environment fraught with risk, everyone is at risk and risk factors lose their meaning. And, at the same time, in circles of power and policy, the stories that we tell about at-risk young people take on a growing urgency and centrality. This looming gap between policy and experience undermined the shared understanding necessary to build trust.

THE MISSING DISCOURSE OF THE PAST

The driving logic of risk data is that the past matters. What happened to someone before shapes their future. Young people echoed this sentiment, but in a different way. Risk data implies that the consequences of the past should be avoided—that hegemonic notions of gender, trauma, violence, and inequality can and should simply be escaped. But it is not so simple. We need our pasts to make sense of who we are. We do not choose them and they cannot be erased. Risk factors distill robust and complicated experiences that anchor our narratives of who we are and who we are not.

Young people—everyone really—lives, as cultural sociologists like to put it, by narrative.[33] Our identities are shaped through the stories we tell to make sense of the churn of experience, shot through with emotion and power. The statistical story of risk provides little fodder from which to construct a narrative project. Risk is a story without characters or agency; only what happened determining what will happen. It is divorced from the relationships and cultural forces in individual's lives. When young people talk about their lives, they rarely see them in terms of risk.

Young people, caught up in the dueling gravities of autonomy and childhood that come with emerging adulthood, seek meaning with urgency. They struggle to reconcile the narratives of the adults around them and their experiences. Take for example Manny, a Latino young man whose parents emigrated from Guatemala. He was 17 when we met in a prevention program at his high school. We talked in an abandoned counseling room at his school jammed with a small desk, two chairs, and an old computer, the floor riddled with scraps of paper that looked like confetti. He hugged his backpack against his chest for most of the interview. Manny, like all of the young people I talked to, lived with risk. His experiences with violence, his economic position, a history of aggression, and more had made him that way. Manny, like Hendrix, did not understand himself as at risk; instead he strove to construct a narrative that reconciled his past and present.

Manny explained that his notions of gender were shaped by his parents' culture: "It affects me as a male, because we're seen as the head of the house. You have to, if something goes down, you're responsible for it, like, you have to take care of everything, you have to provide for the family, support the family." Beyond defining his responsibilities in a patriarchal family, Manny felt like the notions of gender that he learned from his parents limited how he could express himself:

> Crying is seen as weakness, so you don't, you just don't cry. So growing up, you're just, something hurts you and you don't show it, or if something offends you, you don't show it, or someone hurts you, or someone breaks your heart, and you just don't—you just let it go, but inside you know it hurts you . . . it's a lot of conflictions, because there's—there's a point where a man just breaks . . . I bottle up a bunch of feelings that I'm—I'm maybe not supposed to bottle up and that just turns into—it just ends up being, like, anger.

So I'll have anger in my heart, and then I won't—I won't let it out, and I just keep putting things in, and then it's—it's—you just—you just dying inside, and you keep adding more things, and—and it affects you real bad. Well, it has affected me really bad.

Manny's explanation of the stresses he felt as a man were bound up with his family's notion of manhood, and how he was viewed in society. He explained that people saw young Latino men like himself as "drug dealers or gangsters" who "aren't going to amount to anything and they can't go any-where in life."[34] Money "comes and goes," Manny told me, and he "learned to live with that." Still, he hoped that he would have money someday so that he could give "to those so they don't have to re-live, like, something that I lived." He also hopes that through hard work and responsibility, he will be able to relieve the economic pressure on his mom, who "brought up six kids in, like, a screwed-up environment" and "took the role of a father and a mom at the same time." For many young people, stepping in to clear-cut gender roles, even as they recognized the potential for negative ramifica-tions, fit within a story of a path through economic uncertainty and family strains. In many families, in particular those with parents who were recent immigrants, idealized notions of gender roles helped young people to recon-cile the tensions of poverty, violence, and criminalization in the stories of their lives. However, for some this meant sacrificing the opportunity to cul-tivate a distinct sense of self as an adult on one's own.

Manny felt like he owed it to his mother to do well in school. His mother had left school after second grade, and his father only made it to sixth grade. Manny wanted to make the most of his opportunity to get an edu-cation and had a 4.0 GPA through ninth grade. However, during his sophomore year in high school, "things started to get complicated at home" and school became "a rollercoaster ride" as he struggled with "depression, anxiety, and insomnia." Manny explained, "It was something I didn't have a hold of, and that was kind of a curveball to me, because it was—it just came out of nowhere. It was, like, a slap in the face, because I was trying to understand something that was not at my level of under-standing yet." This undermined Manny's focus at school, and his teachers were troubled at his fall from being an A student. These expectations weighed heavily.

I look at myself and I'm like, well, I was that person in ninth grade, and now I'm this person. And it's hard to—to focus when, I guess you got some sort of spotlight on you because of your background, and because—because I'm really hostile, and because I'm very, I guess very secretive of what my past has been. It has—it has conflicted with—with me getting help of what I need.

Manny made sense of the dramatic and unexpected changes in his life— the twists and turns of his narrative—in deeply personal and emotional terms. He felt caught between the pressures of a particular cultural formation of masculinity and the repercussions they were having on his life. His father had been "unfaithful" to his mother and that reverberated through his home life, as his parents nearly stopped speaking to one another entirely, save for arguments, that "always result in oh, man, the kids this, or the stressing out." Manny felt that he had to grow up quickly in order to face the uncertainty and dysfunction in his family life. "I snapped out of my childhood real, real quick, because I started to understand things more . . . I guess that was part of growing up that I—I snapped out of my childhood, and part of that also deprived me of myself. I was deprived of myself." Manny, like all of the young people I spoke to, sought out a way to make sense of the past in order to construct his identity. The narrative of risk, one of the main ways that adults understand youth, lacks a way of talking about the complexity of the past, and therefore keeps adults from grappling with the fullness of young people's lived experience.[35]

Risk data presents more than a mathematics of associated moments: it reverberates through identities, narratives, and forms of social connection. It does this by narrowing the stories we tell about young people and creating statistical lives. To put this more concretely, we can look at Joe Moses's violence, or Hendrix's disengagement, or Paula's isolation not as risks for their futures, but as responses to—perhaps even coping mechanisms for—systemic racism, economic deprivation, and cultural pressures. Without understanding young people's experience, we not only ignore the structure of risk, but we are in danger of obscuring the sparks of hope and resilience that are shot through lived experience.

4 Familiar Strangers

Before Presentation:
Wear appropriate attire. Feel free to wear denim as an education tool.
Get the logistical information (location, time, audience size, room #)
Make sure you have your contact's information
Know your audience and speak to them based on this knowledge
Prepare your presentation and practice
Have an outline
Bring sign-in sheets, handouts

During Presentation:
Pass out sign-in-sheets
Write hotline number on the board
Set ground rules
State objectives and goals of the presentation
Acknowledge / validate participants' contributions
Use participants' names if possible
Make the presentation interactive
Make sure to wait after you ask questions to give participants a chance to generate
    responses (at least 5 seconds)
Keep it simple (use accessible language)
Be sensitive and use appropriate language
Have a beginning, middle, and end to the presentation
Use visuals
Provide incentives for participation (i.e., buttons, posters, etc.; if you want to offer
    food, ask teacher / contact's permission first)

After Presentation:
Submit sign-in sheets to Trainers
Complete a presentation evaluation to Trainers
Notify Trainers of any issues, concerns, etc. with the presentation

[Note: Handout from a facilitator training program]

. . . . .

It is a hot Tuesday morning in September. The GPS delivers me through
construction and haze to a high school north of Los Angeles, a sprawling
complex of concrete wrapped in twelve-foot-tall chain-link with no clear
way in. I can hear the school bustle rising. A woman points me through a
twist of buildings toward the office. There, the woman behind the counter
nods over to a sign-in sheet, gives me a visitor tag, and I go in. Kids give
me skeptical glances, or look through me. I ask an adult, walking briskly,
for directions. "You have to go the wrong way to go the right way," she says.
There is an elevated walkway over the street; on the other side, in the middle of the teachers' parking lot sits a prefabricated one-room building.
Students meet at the locked chain-link gate at the edge of campus at the
bell and a teacher leads them over the quiet street.

The flickering halogen inside the square trailer is no match for the
blinding sun outside and my eyes squint to adjust. The box is small and
cramped and hot. The desks packed in nine dense rows. Scraps of the previous class remain—worksheets and Gatorade bottles litter the desks and
floor. A whiteboard runs the full length of the long wall, and there is a
small wood-veneer table and a metal projector in the corner. I slide into a
desk by the near wall and pull the heavy white curriculum binder out of
my bag, crisp and barely used. I shuffle through the hundreds of sheets of
the curriculum and do a last-minute review of the day's unit: *Healthy
Relationships*. The students squeak and thud in now, filling every seat.
Against the far wall the AC strains to whir out 72 degrees.

Over the course of seven weeks POV will present seven 50-minute
"doses" of a teen dating violence prevention program to all of the school's
freshmen, over seven hundred students. It is a herculean task presenting
to a parade of twitching, addled teens for five classes a day, so it has been
"all hands on deck." Jennifer backs through the door of the permanent
trailer, dragging a rolling plastic bin in after her. It is pressure-cooker hot
outside and the kids are in all states: vibrating, faces pressed against cool
desks, lazily chewing taffy candy, screeching their chairs across the tile,
tapping pens like snare drums. In the back, framed by the window, a
young woman curls away from the room; another girl has a comforting
hand on her back. Jennifer arranges worksheets into neat stacks on

the desk at the front of the room. With a nub of a marker, she squeaks *Healthy Relationships* across the whiteboard. The PE teacher and baseball coach, Mr. A., a middle-aged white man in sweats with a whistle swinging from his neck, rigorously marches through the attendance, "gum in the trash, Powerade on the desk" as the students settle into their seats. When he finishes, Jennifer rubs her hands together, steals a glance at the clock, and begins: *I'm here to talk about violence.* The weight of this, that her job as a violence prevention specialist is to explain the legal—and in a way, the moral—edges of one of the most terrifying and puzzling of human experiences to a brimming classroom of teenagers does not phase her, not anymore. If anything, a sliver of weariness escapes her set smile as she looks out at the audience of familiar strangers. Jennifer already feels behind from yesterday and skips the check-in, diving straight into the curriculum.

An hour later, it is my turn to facilitate. The students flood in. I don't even remember the last group leaving. I ask them to go around the room and "check in": say their name and how they feel. It is slow. They stare off, dragging out an "ummm" before shrugging out "fine." It takes 10 minutes. I stick to the curriculum as best I can. When chaos or confusion rises, I fall back on it, turning to a new exercise or example. I try to make sure that the students will do well on the post-test. I bristle when they misunderstand a concept. I can feel whispers compete for air. At any given time, I figure that between one quarter and half of the class pays attention. A boy sits in the front and likes to watch the air conditioner vent pull on a sheet of paper. I will write later in my field notes that I was trying hard to care about them because that is what I believe in, and they don't know me from the rest and maybe they are right about me anyway. I get through the lesson for the day with a few minutes left. I've been talking too fast. I keep checking the clock and now I am deliberately speaking slowly to burn time. When the bell rings I feel myself breathe. The students rumble out and I'm not sure how, if at all, I figured into their day. I am exhausted and I gather up the sheets scattered around the class. I look over the agenda and make a note of what I covered and the section I am pretty sure that I skipped, so I can tell the others how to make up for it later. I collect my things and dash off field notes in my hot car outside. Then I slog through traffic back across the city to the office where Jennifer has her plastic bin parked beside her desk and, one by one, she enters the responses to the post-survey used to evaluate the program.

STREET LEVEL IN THE EPHEMERAL STATE

When I entered the field, the thing that struck me most was the strange pace and rhythm of the everyday for the women and men who implemented programs: the off-kilter swings of time and emotion and power that often caught me off guard. Coming and going; never staying. Sometimes, this was the shrugging banality of doing good in the nonprofit world. Early in my fieldwork, one lunch stretched into its second hour, and Lisa joked, "This is Friday at a nonprofit." However, what at times felt like an endless stream of "boring desk work" also sporadically overflowed with meaning. One day, while talking about YouTube videos, Eleanor mentioned a video of a spoken-word poet talking about rape called "blue blanket." Jennifer closed the shared Google calendar and pulled it up. Four facilitators stood around the computer and watched this video, eyes watering.[1]

Not long after I started in the field I watched Eleanor, a lively and engaging facilitator, work a coed class through a healthy relationship curriculum. On the first day a Black female student, maybe 16, with her backpack on and arms folded, was "not having it" as Eleanor put it. The next week the student did not say anything at all. By the fifth week she laughed at a bad joke. And by week 9, she told the class, with no pretense, that she was abused and she cried for a second and Eleanor thanked her for sharing. After week 12, I never saw her again.

After the first sessions of another program Michael, 17 and Latino, who always had white headphones tucked behind his ears, gave me a hearty pat on the back and a big smile as he walked out. Every week, he was engaged, and he often tried to poke holes in the logic of the program even as he seemed to really appreciate it. A few weeks in, he pushed back against the descriptions of consent given in the class, not rudely, but earnestly, saying that while he understood the law, "that's not how it works" in regular teenage relationships. He was pulled aside by his teacher, maybe because she thought he was out of line. Then he didn't show up weeks 6, 7, and 8. When I saw him again in week 9 and asked where he had been, he was cold and explained that he "just didn't feel like coming to class." He barely engaged over the next three weeks and then the program moved on.

These stories are not particularly noteworthy in the world of prevention programs.[2] They have the hallmarks of the work—brief spikes of emotion and connection, tempered by distance, confusion, and uncertainty. In programs, conversations about intimate encounters and painful experiences occur between strangers who never see each other again. Reeling from the vacillations of prevention programs, I turned to micro-level theories of the state.[3] Rather than think about the state as a monolithic and coherent actor, this scholarship has emphasized how representatives of the state—teachers, police officers, welfare administrators, and the like—actively construct state policy on the ground as well as shape citizens' understanding of the state through their interactions.[4]

Facilitators are at the forefront of the grinding and whirring policy apparatus of the ephemeral state.[5] This collection of social policies, designed to be fleeting and transformative, reorganizes interactions across time and space between the state—in this case facilitators who act as street-level representatives of policy—and youth. Unlike the slow state, which is marked by looming bureaucracies and domination through waiting, I found that the ephemeral state produced alienation and social distance through its temporariness. In order to draw out contrasts with the slow state, this chapter elaborates on several seemingly simple questions: Who represents the state? How do individuals and groups come to be marked for state intervention? What is produced through state action? What are the lessons taught by the state?

WHO FACILITATORS AND YOUTH WERE TO EACH OTHER

Robert's white two-door sedan was sputtering, back from a "one-shot wonder" presentation in South Los Angeles, and gearing up to head to the San Gabriel Valley. Robert, a white facilitator in his forties—in a Hawaiian shirt, a red, yellow, green, and black cap, and faded denim jeans, he looked like a sort of tourist—had his arms stretched out to the steering wheel, and JJ, a Black part-time facilitator in his early 20s, was leaning back in the passenger seat, nodding and laughing in a jersey and matching hat.

JJ often relied on public transportation, by way of considerable coordinating and planning, to get to the schools and community centers across the city where programming was running, so he was happy to have a ride and company. Most of the facilitators had cars, and much of the daily work of prevention occurred in them, often alone: Streaking back and forth across the city on a tight timeline, parked in front of a school rushing to review a unit, taking a break between periods to eat a sandwich in the passenger seat, scuffling through the console for a sign-in sheet. Implementation in practice was a string of ad hoc and fleeting performances for shifting audiences of young people. At street level, the ephemeral state was carried on the backs of low-wage facilitators and volunteers. Facilitators lived out the words of Rose, O'Malley, and Valverde as "workers in the twilight world of the marginalized" who "deploy the logics of normalization, social skills, self-esteem and so forth in order to 'empower' their clients at the same time as they contest the politics which has made these the organizing principles of 'social' policy."[6] These workers were facilitators like Robert and JJ. The twilight world of the marginalized was an audience of distracted students that one would find in a health classroom in East Los Angeles on a Tuesday.

Although their formal titles varied—for example, some were "youth outreach coordinators," others "violence prevention specialists"—the people who do the work of implementation talked about themselves in a few consistent ways. The language they used sheds light on how they related to their audience. When they were being blunt and feeling cynical about their work they called themselves implementers, which implied a cog-in-the-machine regurgitation of program content. In professional settings some would call themselves preventionists, a title I also heard from those who did not do direct service, but still worked in the prevention field. Most, however, called themselves facilitators, which is the term that I use, and which points to a more interactive and dynamic role than the one defined by program funders. Robert, for example, related what he does to the work of radical education scholar Paulo Freire and said that "I think of myself as a facilitator, not a teacher" because "teaching is a crappy form of education . . . We're not trying to get youth to follow directions, we're trying to get them to think." However, facilitators often felt hard-pressed to live up to this dictum given the litany of requirements in their job.

Longtime facilitators told new trainees, "You are a franchise," meaning not only that they should dress, speak, and act accordingly, but that their own individuality should be downplayed in place of representing the brand. Facilitators consistently found themselves pulled between the formal requirements of their work and the emotionally-stirring possibilities of it.[7]

The facilitators at POV, a scattershot collection of feminists fresh from college, former program youth, and transplants from other corners of the nonprofit sector, shared in their hope to change young people's lives. Facilitators' passion often ran counter to their grant-mandated responsibilities. Jose, a facilitator for high-risk youth, told me, six months after starting his job, "I am not really thinking about the numbers because to me numbers are numbers." He cited Stalin's statement that one death is a tragedy, but a million is a statistic. With a conspiratorial glint, he continued:

> I feel like changing people's lives. I'm not here because of the grant and I'm not here because the grant says to do it. I took on this job so I can help, so I can help kids . . . I try to put space in their brain so they can say, "Hey, I can make it to college. I don't have to be a dropout. I don't have to end up in jail or be a nobody." I believe the youth, you can mold them and then they can take it from there.

Many facilitators came in with similar aspirations and found them repeatedly blunted. Although they struggled to form the meaningful connections they aspired to, the sheer amount of time facilitators spent implementing programming enabled them to interact with young people at an unprecedented scale. At POV, a full-time implementer would facilitate over 600 sessions in a year. They would run as many as three or four programs in a day and they could be miles apart.

In JJ's case Robert or another facilitator would call the week or even the day before and tell him where he needed to be and he would catch a ride or string together a series of bus routes. On this day, something had come up at the school. A teacher overheard racial slurs used in the class. Robert decided to ditch the planned lesson and, 15 minutes out, planned a new lesson about racial violence. JJ was not familiar with the unit Robert was planning to use and read from a xeroxed page that Robert had dug up and handed to him as they pulled away from the office.

JJ and Robert both signal the extent to which the ephemeral state is de-professionalized.[8] JJ was first introduced to POV because someone at his school had reached out to the organization and Robert brought a program to his high school health class: "If I wasn't at the school I was at, if I wasn't talking to the certain people I was talking to, I probably wouldn't know nothing." The program, he says, resonated with him despite his lack of experience with that kind of thinking because it provided support during a difficult time. "When I was going through certain things they were like, 'it's going to be alright,' and I got through it. It was something that I wanted to teach others, other guys and other young males about. Letting them know it's okay, what you're doing is wrong, ask for help." JJ told the facilitator of the program that he was looking for a job and asked that they keep him in mind. After JJ graduated from high school, he enrolled in the required training and soon after began working part-time as "a youth violence counselor . . . I try to prevent as much abuse or violence that I can." JJ did not see this work as a long-term career though: "It could be something that I take with me along the road, but it's not something that I can just settle for because I think that there is much more, another purpose for me, but it's cool to know that I have something to fall back on, someplace I can go and call home basically." JJ's path into the work, and his closeness with the organization, was uncommon but not unprecedented.

While he did not have much training or professional experience, JJ's time on the other side of the program gave him credibility and narrative fodder. He told me that he felt like he not only had knowledge about what was going on in young people's lives but, having grown up in a lower-income Los Angeles neighborhood, he had been through it. "When you know something you just know of it, you have no clue, no deeper emotion about it. I feel like I've been fortunate enough to have been through and get through those things so that I can show other people that I've been gotten through it and it's okay." For this reason, POV sought out facilitators from the parts of Los Angeles where they did most of their programming, and when they were able to arrange it, they placed facilitators in schools where the students had similar racial identities. But shared social location only achieved so much, and the fleeting timeline of the programs limited the ability of facilitators to make connections. At the school, Robert and JJ asked about the incident, but no one would tell the full story. Robert showed a dated video about racial tensions in a school in another part of Los Angeles and the students giggled and repeated the most charged content back under their breaths.

As a way of bringing social policy into the lives of people, facilitation is distinct. Facilitators show up in large institutions with visitor stickers on their chests. They are more like tourists than bureaucrats and their position was often illegible to youth. They would introduce themselves by their job title and organizational affiliation—"Hi, I'm a violence prevention specialist from Peace Over Violence"—but what this meant to young people was not straightforward. They were strangers, just like many of the adults who careened through young people's lives.[9] But it was clear that young people were not surprised to see them. Some did not even raise their heads off their desks. Because facilitators lacked an institutional affiliation or clear role, young people, like anyone else, used visible identity markers to determine how to interact with facilitators. On at least three occasions, I witnessed students ask Robert, a tall white facilitator with close-cropped hair and a broad build, if he was a police officer. While I am also a white man, I was received differently. I am shorter and I grew out my hair and a beard while in the field. One Latino young man called me "homie Max with the Jesus beard." Students I had never met before would approach me in the hallways and ask who I was and what I was doing there: "Are you a psych? A lawyer? Social worker?" This represented a pervasive pattern of misrecognition between youth and facilitators, multiplied by the arrangement of their interactions.[10]

Sometimes, it was apparent that a student was struggling to figure out how best to engage with the facilitators who came into his or her classroom. During the implementation of a pre-survey one student, a large and round-faced young man with dark fuzz on his lip, bounced his way over to me in the back of the room and said, apropos of nothing, that he used to be violent in the fourth grade, but then, he explained, he "went through some things," trailing off. When I asked if he finished the survey he said that he did as much as he felt like. Then, as the thought struck him, he chopped at the air and explained that he had learned mixed martial arts from playing video games. He vacillated between thoughtful and exaggeratedly masculine interactions for a couple of minutes, at one point proclaiming, "I could break your arm if you mess with me" and "I will give you

a three-ring slap." He seemed to want to signal his relationship to my position, but could not figure if I should be seen as a social worker or a rule
enforcer. Other times, students quickly assessed facilitators and decided
not to engage.

Young people seemed to use a phenotypical shorthand to make sense of
facilitators, as they drew on intersectional stock images of various state
representatives. Broadly, men tended to be perceived as authorities and
technical experts while women were approached as care workers. About
halfway through a presentation to a multiracial group of students at a
small charter school in West Los Angeles led by two experienced female
facilitators, I stepped up to run a short exercise on the definitions of violence. As I stood up, one student called out, "Oh good, an expert." I was
quick to reply, "No, I'm not an expert," and a facilitator named Sarah
jumped in to say, "None of us are experts." The young man, catching on in
a way, said, "We're all experts." Sarah responded, "Yes, we're all experts"
while Janet nodded. Sarah and Janet were far more experienced and
skilled facilitators, but as was often the case, they were perceived as less
knowledgeable. When men presented the more emotional or relationship-
focused aspects, they experienced pushback. For example, one survey
response included answers saying that the survey was a waste of time, that
dating violence did not happen at the school, and that facilitators were
"stupid sad single men." Donna, a Latina facilitator, told me that students
often tried to determine her age in order to decide "if they can hit on me
or if they can't hit on me." She explained: "Once they find out my age, then
they step back and their attitude or performance around me changes . . . I
remember one time this young man asked me, he said, 'Miss, do you have
a boyfriend?' I said, 'No.' He said, 'Are you married?' I said, 'No.' 'Do you
have any kids.' 'No.' He said, 'What's wrong with you?' and I said, 'Nothing.'"
The cultural misrecognition on the part of students, which Donna and the
other facilitators worked to manage, was multiplied by the fractured and
fleeting arrangements of the ephemeral state. From the perspective of
young people, facilitators arrived out of thin air, which made it difficult to
understand who they were and what they wanted.

In order to undercut these dynamics, facilitators took pains to present
themselves as distinct individuals with experiences that paralleled young
peoples' own; not as a franchise. When Robert, who was regularly mistaken

for a police officer, introduced himself on the first day, he often recounted the violence he experienced in his youth, the bad part of town he grew up in, and his single mother. Joseph, a twenty-something Latino facilitator who had come up through the program, explained that he always told students about himself first:

> I let them know about what I used to do and what I do now. They could tell me, like, "you don't know what you're talking about" and I go up to them and tell them 'well, I was in this position, I know what I'm saying' . . . I mean, Hispanics and African Americans, they're hurt because sometimes Robert, he is white, they see it as, you know, a cop that was white treated me bad and I think that Robert is going to treat me bad as well. And I'm like okay, well I'm Hispanic. They think [I'm] not going to do anything because [I'm their] race.

Joseph cultivated moments where he could show that he was more like the young people than they might imagine. At one point, he pulled up a list from the internet of terrible things to do in a relationship and ticked off all the numbers that he had done. He explained that he would make a girl fall in love with him and then break up with her. He was not always the person they saw in front of them: "I've done bad things, all the people in this job have bad pasts. Back then I wasn't a good guy," he said.

Jennifer, a white, 24-year-old facilitator, told me how she worried that students would not "take her seriously" because her experiences were so different from their own:

> We have Black students, Latino and a whole mix—and I'm just this happy white girl, it's like, "What the fuck do you have to say to us?" I didn't think that would be an issue until I was actually in front of them and I'm like, "Wow, okay." This isn't as comfortable . . . I feel like I try to make them still feel like we are kind of part of the same peer group. Make the pop culture references whatever it might be. "I'm living in the same world as you, I'm not some sort of total outside government official."

Jennifer had experience doing prevention work with her peers on college campuses, so while she felt somewhat connected to youth, she was "still kind of out of that scene, so I had to reintegrate myself back into thinking as a teenager and how to talk to them." One strategy she picked up was using the song "Love the Way You Lie" by Eminem featuring Rihanna, to illustrate the patterns of an unhealthy relationship. "I try and make it informative and fun. Part of why it's fun is because I'll stand up there and rap to them and they think it's hilarious to see me rap. That kind of hooks them and then I can get them like to talk about it." Facilitators often resorted to "hooks" to incite interest and engagement on a tight timeline. However, despite all the tactics deployed by facilitators, they often struggled to make connections. This was not simply because youth were resistant. When I interviewed young people, they explained that they wanted, often badly, to find a meaningful connection and support in adults. And yet, far more often, when facilitators and youth met, the result was a jumble of misunderstanding and misrecognition, punctuated by moments of heightened meaning. Within the fleeting arrangements of the ephemeral state, a parade of tourists in the lives of youth, social location and difference were heightened and the gaps that facilitators hoped to bridge were widened.

HOW YOUTH ENDED UP THERE

At risk, high risk, the rowdies, those kids, youth with trauma histories, system-involved youth, future leaders. These were just some of the seemingly incompatible ways adults described the young people in programming. These labels were tied to the ways various institutions engaged with youth, such as the probation department, the school administration, campus police, or school psychologist, and aligned youth with prescribed tracks that organized their physical movements, educational opportunities, and access to resources. These labels also shaped how young people understood themselves. One representative class of students, when asked why they had been selected to participate in a program, variously described their enrollment as retribution for a disagreement with a teacher, a therapeutic intervention suggested by a counselor for a personal issue, or a demonstration of their role as a campus leader. Sociologists have detailed how institutions apply labels and attach stigma, which can end up becoming identities.[11] However, across the scattered institutions of the ephemeral state, labeling worked differently.

Not once did a young person say they were there because they were "at risk." The fact that young people did not use the term was all the more surprising given the fact that—away from the classrooms—grants, teachers, administrators, the organization, and the facilitators themselves all regularly described the audience for prevention as at-risk youth. Lauren, a manager at Peace Over Violence, explained:

> A lot of our focus has been on working with those most at risk.[12] They might not be most at risk for teen dating violence, we really don't know that. We do know they're at higher risk of not finishing high school, of being poor, or of involving violence . . . We do it based on like school lunch subsidies. We do it based on where they live in a community. We really have focused in the public-school system for sure and we focused in the communities that have needed us, we felt needed us more . . . We know that our kids are trauma-exposed, from infancy a lot of them. We're dealing with a real—something much bigger than just one issue.

As Lauren's explanation shows, "at risk" was a pliable label, not directly tied to any one system or problem, and a diverse set of processes marked youth as at risk and enrolled them in prevention programming. The term itself was a consequence of a multifactor risk analysis that was largely invisible in the course of lived experience. This made it easy for most adults to apply the at-risk mark and also to remove and replace it with other labels, such as criminal, troublemaker, or even leader. Risk, in this way, facilitated a kind of status laundering, whereby the hand of the institution that applied the mark was erased and replaced with the vague and free-floating label of at risk.

The loose enrollment mechanisms and status laundering that marked youth as at risk took place within a broader system that circulated young people between interventions depending on available resources.[13] Schools and community centers in Los Angeles were often understaffed, crowded, scattered places, full of adults with divergent institutional goals: police officers, school administrators, teachers, and program facilitators. Programming—largely free and operated by outsiders—was a boon for schools that hoped to navigate the tensions of dwindling funding and mandates that were both increasingly fervent and vague. One teacher told me, "I sign up for everything, I don't look at what it is." Counselors were stretched thin and many reached to outside programs to support their students, hoping to ease their load while providing services and assistance.

This shuffling was not reliant on case files, criteria, paperwork, or intake interviews. It was the accomplishment of scattered, often arbitrary institutional actors. There was no rationalized approach to who was labeled as at risk.

According to facilitators, schools often asked for programming in order to do "damage control" for an ongoing issue, such as sexual harassment or fighting on campus. "It's a lot of word of mouth and it's a lot of people like, oh my god, I'm having an issue, let me Google something," Eleanor told me. Jennifer explained that schools "may reach out because they've been carrying a lot of disclosures from students." In addition to this crisis-driven outreach, POV relied on sustained, largely informal ties, with school counselors, teachers, social workers, probation officers, and others in schools in order to arrange for programming and determine which students to enroll. The person who worked with them on the ground to bring the program to a given school was referred to as the sponsor. Eleanor told me about an incident when, after a counselor who had been POV's sponsor left the school, they set out to formalize a relationship with the principal through a memorandum of understanding, "The principal had no idea who we were and was like, 'why do I need this?'" They were not asked back.

Eleanor explained how the sponsor at one school, a social worker, managed the school bureaucracy in order to enable the program to run smoothly. This person made sure to call students out from classes ahead of time and sought out new students who might benefit:

> When there is a student who is having a lot of issues either with violence or trauma or there is DV [domestic violence] in the home or they have been sexually abused or they need something of substance he will send them over. Sometimes they stick, sometimes they don't. It really depends on the young person and it really depends on what day [of the curriculum] they are coming in to.

As Eleanor points out, there was a wide latitude as to who was enrolled in programs. Once administrators had requested programming from Peace Over Violence and the organization determined the source of funding for implementing the program, then probation officers, school counselors, teachers, and administrators drew on existing perceptions in order to decide which students would participate. This could be an entire grade level or a small, hand-picked group. Jose explained how this process worked for the high risk program he facilitated. While he would receive a list of students on probation, there were other, less clearly defined paths to being placed in the high risk program:

> They don't necessarily end up there because they're on probation. The probation officer could be working with counselors or the principals within those schools and say, 'Hey, this kid, or this young woman or man, they might need some type of extracurricular education on violence.' Then they come into his or her caseload, and then my list therefore expands.

Jose's expanding list illustrates how school officials not only used formal labels by institutions and officials to enroll youth in programs, such as being on probation, but also informal labels, such as students who are deemed to "need" education on violence, due to a perception of aggression, defiance, or trauma.

While school officials used informal and formal labels in regular interaction with young people, including as a means to explain why students were enrolled in programming, I never observed facilitators using stigmatizing labels or institutional markings with students. Facilitators believed labeling young people would stigmatize and "isolate" students. Jose explained how he looked at youth differently from the way they were viewed by school officials:

> Maybe they did stuff wrong, but that doesn't mean that that label should be put on their foreheads, and that's it. Their label in society is "probation youth" or "high risk kids." I don't even see that. I see them as first-name basis, so I know them as "Oscar," "Michele." Whatever their names are, I want to see them as that.

As Jose makes clear, facilitators resisted labeling by ignoring the very institutional labels that framed their work and instead sought to refer to the youth as individuals. However, despite Jose's description, facilitators rarely knew students' names. This was due in part to the overwhelming volume of youth they encountered in programming, as well as poor communication from school staff, many of whom were overworked and sometimes failed to provide a list of enrolled students. But, even when they had a list of student names, facilitators rarely took attendance. While they often passed around a sign-in sheet, many facilitators described feeling resentment for the task and downplayed its importance even though it was often central to their grant funding.

For many young people in underfunded schools, the prevention program was one stop in an ongoing series of ricochets between interventions and fractured institutions. They would be bounced between suspension, the school counselor, outside nonprofits, policing, and so on. Along the way, adults could lose sight of the initial incident and the path that the student had taken to them. To be marked at risk was to have one's institutional world splintered into a churn of temporary interactions with specialists and counselors and nonprofit facilitators and educators. Within this fractured system, individuals and organizations tried to meet the social and emotional challenges of youth through multiplying and condensing interactions with institutionally situated adults. So, while being marked as at risk increased the number of adults in a young person's life, those adults were often more temporary and less reliable.

In contrast, violence prevention was situated differently in the few higher SES (socioeconomic status) or more privileged schools that received such programming. Just twice in my time at POV did I experience programs in schools where the population was not mostly Black or Latinx students.[14] The first was at a small, environmentally focused private school where one of the administrators had volunteered at POV. The other time was at a large and diverse public school in the suburbs north of downtown. I never saw or heard of programs enacted in an upper-income area. Schools with a "higher socioeconomic status" did sometimes request programs, "but those kids and those administrators view it differently," Eleanor, an experienced facilitator, told me. Those schools were more likely to request a program on "bullying or something," and when Eleanor would raise the issue of teen dating violence, the school would respond, "No, no, no, that's, that's not our problem." Instead, Eleanor told me, they wanted programming "coming in so that [students] can put this on their college application or like they want skills so that they can help support kids out there, but they don't *need* it." In these schools, institutional actors did not treat programming as one of multiple interventions for students marked as at risk, but as a skill to be incorporated into their path to college success.

In a concrete way, if any of the youth in this project had been able to move to Beverly Hills, even while he or she would remain the same person with the same history, his or her geography would significantly distance them from the institutional mechanisms for enrollment in prevention programs. They would almost certainly no longer be marked as at risk. Programs, in line with school officials, frame young people in working-class and poor neighborhoods or school districts as at risk, without having to say that these young people are disproportionately Black and Latinx and in schools and communities deprived of resources.

Kim, a program manager at Peace Over Violence, explained a stance I heard from many facilitators: "We're trying to provide [programming] to at-risk youth, and not to say that kids in Beverly Hills aren't at-risk, because they are at-risk for all kinds of things. Money doesn't really protect you from violence." However, programs were "grant funded to support low-income schools; to provide resources where there aren't resources . . . In Beverly Hills they can pay for somebody to do some classes." In this, facilitators' views echoed the logic of grants: prevention programs were intended as a remedy for the risks posed by limited school and community resources. As one preventionist put it while leading a webinar: "This is about a toxic environment, more toxic than lead." To facilitators working at street level, the notion that they were doing some small part to remedy structural inequality motivated their daily work. However, taking a step back, we should question this presumption. In fact, programs were often funded by the same local, state, federal, and private institutions that underserve their youth. Instead of acting as a remedy for a lack of resources, prevention seems designed as a replacement for sustained investment.

WHAT MATTERED ABOUT PROGRAMMING

Jennifer charged into the East Los Angeles classroom 15 minutes late, towing her plastic cart of handouts. She had printer trouble while running off copies of certificates for a volunteer training graduation that night. Then there was traffic. When a student asked about the sign-in sheet, she said, "It is for my boss so they know that I didn't just take off for the day. It is also so we can show the state that we are reaching people—not just the number but the kinds of people—so they can give us money. Yeah right." One woman made an "ooo" sound and wiggled both hands in the air to symbolize a sort of big deal gesture. Another young boy in the front simply said "money" and chuckled to himself. Jennifer introduced herself as a rape prevention educator, saying, "It's a long title, I know. I say that the longer the title, the less they pay us." When she passed around the sign-in sheet and a student raised her hand and asked if they needed to fill it out if they did not want anything. Jennifer clarified that the sign-in sheet is "to show that I did my work." At some point, the paperwork got to everyone.

For most facilitators, prevention was not what they had expected. Facilitators came into POV full of energy and ready to change lives, a belief echoed in the rhetoric of marketing materials put out by Peace Over Violence. And yet, few facilitators lasted more than 18 months. All of the people working in prevention when I started had left the organization in the three and a half years I was in the field, many for other nonprofit organizations. Experiences piled up. Where once they would bound in to classrooms early to set up, they eventually squeezed out every minute before going in, pausing to breathe or play on their phone in their car. They found themselves drifting into a sort of trance during presentations and skipping entire parts of the curriculum without a thought. Some facilitators talked about their work as a calling or a dream, but they were the new ones.

When I first met Jennifer, she was prone to love-conquers-all Hallmark lines. In regular conversation, she would say things like, "If you aren't including yourself, your compassion is incomplete." But when we talked several months after she started, her idealized narrative had begun to fade. Joseph had told her when she first came on that presentations could get boring and she had been surprised, thinking, she recounted to me, that "this is what we do, this is what we love," but now she realized that he was right, that she could easily go on autopilot. Jennifer was disconnected from the economics of her work as well. She made "about 33 and that's before taxes" out of the $120,000 that was paid out on her grant. "I don't try to make the math work in my head," she told me. She put together a nearly 50-page report detailing her efforts: "I have about seven goals and about three objectives in each of those goals. It's a lot of work." She paused and looked away before changing the subject, "Anyhoo." Several other implementers knew little or nothing about the grant that provided their funding. Sarah said that she "didn't even have a copy of the grant I was funded with." Most implementers, most of the time, were worn down and frustrated by the long hours, low pay (every implementer I asked made less than $40,000 per year), and the repetition of facilitation. The last time I saw Jennifer, she was exhausted and saw no end in sight. She was doing better at self-care, she said. But there's "a lot, always a lot." Not long after, Jennifer left.

The paperwork that took its toll on Jennifer makes up the technical substance of prevention: the concrete evidence that programs do what they claim—change behaviors and cultural norms. As a form of social policy, prevention functions as a mechanism for people-changing. This makes it quite different from welfare bureaucracies, which work to process people, sorting and providing for them. Rather than counts of people incarcerated, fed, employed, or so on, facilitators must count behavioral and attitudinal changes. In several ways, this looks similar to the street-level work of teachers in that they provide education and assessments, but in prevention, the timeline is fleeting, the messages are unabashedly cultural and normative, and the programs are driven by a market incentive to show significant evidence of change.

One argument for the creation of a market for programs is efficiency. But the creation of a market for programs did not limit the paperwork or the bureaucracy in the world of prevention; it might even multiply it. Nonprofit organizations construct the evidence of programming effectiveness in two ways: process-based evidence and evaluative approaches. Process-based evidence relies on tracking bodies in places: the numbers of meetings held, attendance at those meetings, volunteers recruited, and so on. In programs, this was accomplished by passing around a sign-in sheet. I once arrived at the office to find the prevention team crowded around a table in the middle of the youth center, heads low, surrounded by at least a dozen stacks of paper, some half a foot high. Eleanor explained that one of their funders was being audited for their last three months and because of that audit, POV was hustling to find and count old sheets or to recreate missing ones. Ella was upset because, by her rough calculations, they were missing sign-ins for at least 3,000 individuals. I could understand how this happened. Sign-in sheets were fragile material objects, often crumpled behind desks, in foot-tall stacks of mixed paper, in the backs of cars, tucked into classroom desks, or lost. Eleanor did the math and found out that her presentations between January and August reached at least 1,500 students.

Evaluative approaches were based on comparing the results of identical surveys administered on the first and last days of the program, often called pre- and post-surveys, to look for positive changes to answers. Take these questions from one survey as an example, which would be given twice and the answers compared: "1. List three examples of emotional dating abuse. 2. List three examples of physical dating abuse. 3. List two warning signs, or 'Red Flags,' that a person may be a victim of dating abuse." The evidence-based "gold standard" would entail random control trials of the curriculum, but the time and resources required means that most curricula would never be evaluated that way.[15] Lauren, a manager at POV, told me that as the organization competed on a larger scale, "funders are looking at the data" and the organization was working to get better at measuring what she calls "impact": changes in knowledge, attitudes, and behaviors caused by the curricula. It is a facilitator's job to show a 25 percent increase in "awareness" and "attitude change." This is a stunning, and yet rarely questioned, claim: that evaluations accurately represent a simple, 20-minute measure of cultural transformation. Jose, a facilitator, once remarked, in reference to how youth might experience the program evaluations: "They're like, 'Am I being a subject, am I being studied?'" They would be right to think that. They were, in fact, the subject of a massive experiment in cultural transformation.

Facilitators often described their resistance to the quantification of change. They told me that evaluations failed to tell the full story about their work. Kim explained: "I understand from a fiscal perspective the importance of evaluation because you have to prove that your program works and that's how you get funded to do the work." But Kim was skeptical that those surveys really told them anything. She continued,

> Forced answers on filling out a blank or fill in a bubble doesn't really get to the changes at the individual level, which is how this program really works. These programs work in changing ideas and thoughts and actions. It's not only about knowledge. You can know something because you memorized it, but it doesn't mean that you actually applied [it] to your life.

Most facilitators echoed Kim's sentiment and believed that evaluations said little about their work and tended to be ambivalent about the evaluation process. The evaluation system was set up so that the only thing that gets counted, even if facilitators are engaging, caring, and make lasting connections, is what students answer on the post-test.

It is difficult to know what youth made of the evaluations. It is clear that there was a diverse array of countervailing forces at work. Oftentimes, institutional and personal forces undermined the fidelity of post-tests. As students would fill in the survey, some would chat and read questions out loud, while other students laughed. In one class, a young man whistled quietly and then pointed at each blank line, gesturing for his friend to give him the answer. Another student exclaimed that it was really hard and that he had skipped a lot, but that he did the second page, because it was easy. A few students would push it to the side and put their head down, but also some would apologize for not getting to all the questions. One time, a student raised his hand to say that they already filled this out, missing that that was the point. On a few occasions, students proclaimed loudly, "This is boring." Students who had missed several classes happened to be there on the final day or those who had been consistently engaged failed to show up. At one school, the substitute was never given keys and several students were left on the other side of a locked gate, so they missed the post-test. By the last session, twelve weeks had passed since the pre-test, a lifetime in the tribulations of a high school student. All of this noise went into the data.

The metrics of prevention programming—like all scientific knowledge—are produced by social actors, and therefore open to the pressures and tensions of social life.[16] There is an adage, referred to as Campbell's Law: "The more any quantitative social indicator is used for social decision-making, the more subject it will be to corruption pressures and the more apt it will be to distort and corrupt the social processes it is intended to monitor." That is, when weight is placed on a measurement, as occurs with program evaluations, social life will distort around that metric. The distortions around evaluations were extensive.

Evaluations did not simply jump from the minds of youth into data analysis. Instead, they were filtered by facilitators, who, in the search for something that could be made intelligible as evidence of transformation, used a range of strategies to produce strong results on the post-survey. One was to provide as little clarification on the initial survey as possible, letting most any question go unanswered so as to encourage a larger improvement down the line. Sometimes facilitators squeezed in reviews on the last day. Jennifer would recap key concepts and preview questions as she handed out the survey and she would say things like "do we remember the word for this?" or "what were the six kinds of violence?" If no one knew the answer, she would provide increasingly detailed hints at the answer while avoiding explicitly stating it. At one point, trying to get a class to say "warning signs," she asked, "What might you call a signal for something bad?" When there was no answer, she said, "Like a big flashing light." "Camera," one student said. She gave up after that and just told them. Jennifer was not the only one. Many facilitators, in their own ways, helped students on the post-test. When I asked about this, they often explained that they were confident that students had learned a lot, but they worried that they had not have picked up on the jargon and that the survey was not the best mechanism for capturing changes. From a pedagogical standpoint, reminding students of the central lessons of the program makes sense. Joseph took a different tact and often spent the last day making sure that youth liked him, telling jokes and showing pictures of his dog, so that students would invest time in the post-survey. Eleanor walked around and answered questions during the test. Facilitators often let students help each other on answers.

Completed pre- and post-surveys were material objects, loaded into backpacks and bins and trunks, where they stayed until things slowed down enough for someone to enter them into the computer at the office, at which point they were entered one by one. Sometimes it was a paid facilitator who entered the contents of the surveys, but sometimes it was a volunteer or an intern. There were dozens of total fields to fill in for each survey and entering them was slow, mind-numbing work. Sometimes after steadily working for three hours, a reasonable expectation would be to have only entered 12 of them. Of the paper evaluations that I looked at, maybe several hundred in total, many showed students who tried to answer at least some of the questions thoughtfully and honestly. They had circled answers to multiple-choice questions with intention and provided answers to fill-ins that were not insulting or non sequiturs. Still, very few answered all or even the majority of the questions and most of the surveys were at least half empty. Most students only filled in the circle scale and true/false answers at the start, but then their commitment appeared to wane. The social life around the evaluations was warped again when facilitators entered the surveys into the system.

Facilitators and volunteers made difficult decisions about what counted and what did not. For example, they had to determine if a sheet with one question answered counted toward the overall response rate. There was often word-choice confusion: "blackmale" instead of blackmail; "dictator signs" instead of warning signs. Those could either be solid answers that show some confusion or deliberate attempts to challenge the curricula. In the section that asked if the respondent had ever felt threatened, one student wrote that sometimes Armenians try to run him over. One post-test had "penis" written across the top of every page but was otherwise meticulously completed. In the blank where they were to fill in their sex, someone wrote, "yes please." Under "What to do if a friend is sexually assaulted?" they wrote, "Call Max." "That's actually a good answer, from my perspective," Lauren, who directed the evaluation and policy work at POV, explained. "You want to get what they really meant as much as you can without reading too much into things. When they say, 'Call Max,' I see them reaching out to a trusted adult, I see them actually calling someone that's affiliated with the resource agency, or the direct services agency. I see that as like even better than just calling the police." Ultimately, we cannot know what that student intended. A small number were full of intentionally wrong and sometimes harsh language. One survey was particularly memorable. Question 16 was: *If your friend told you she/he was being abused by her/his boyfriend/girlfriend, what would you do?* In the box for the answer, a student wrote "Please enjoy this drawing!" and next to that was a pencil sketch of a person shooting a handgun at a T-Rex, which was saying "RAWR." The next question asked: *What three things can you do to prevent dating violence and sexual violence?* Here, the student had enumerated: "1. talk 2. talk 3. talk." These answers do not fit neatly into the narrow metrics of evaluation and the demand for simple net-positive change, but it would be wrong to contend, therefore, that they show no engagement with the program.

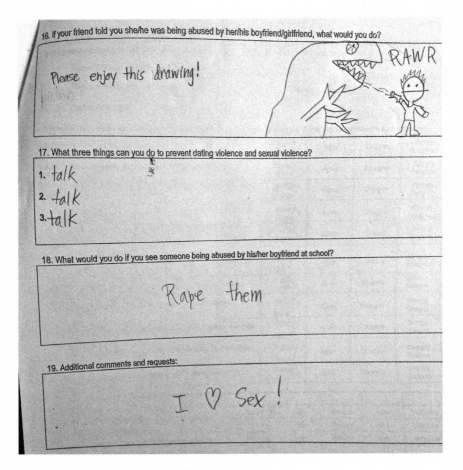

16. If your friend told you she/he was being abused by her/his boyfriend/girlfriend, what would you do?

Please enjoy this drawing!

RAWR

17. What three things can you do to prevent dating violence and sexual violence?

1. talk
2. talk
3. talk

18. What would you do if you see someone being abused by his/her boyfriend at school?

Rape them

19. Additional comments and requests:

I ♡ Sex !

Figure 2. Evaluation form. Photo by author.

The pursuit of evidence-based change was concerning on a practical level, as it showed how evidence of effectiveness was at best opaque and at worst false. And yet, it was perpetuated by facilitators, who found ways to show change, even while they questioned its validity. In this way, they were like shop floor workers who use tricks to produce more goods with less work: they gained a sense of agency but at the same time propped up a system they often resented.[17]

WHAT HAPPENED BEFORE TODAY AND WHAT
IT MEANS FOR TOMORROW

Eleanor and Mark were in a small classroom in a storefront charter school in South Los Angeles, light pouring through the big window that looked out on the main street. It was the first time Mark gave the mandated reporting explanation that started every program.[18] Nervous to get the wording right, he began "We want this to be a safe place, safety is our priority, but we are mandated reporters." Violet, a Black female student in the front row laughed, shook her head and finished his statement in a stiff voice, "which means that if we hear that you or someone else is getting hurt, then we have to inform the authorities." For Violet, like most youth, mandated reporting was part of the background noise of her life in institutions. Before hearing Violet's comment, I had given little thought to the role that mandated reporting played in violence prevention work. It seemed like an inconvenient but necessary disclaimer. In classrooms, implementers talked about violence and relationships and it would be reasonable for young people to see it as a chance to talk about something they had experienced. Facilitators were not trained for that, so it made sense to pass the information on to authorities. But as Violet repeated it perfectly, it became clear that she had heard it many times before. I began to ask youth about mandated reporting and nearly all of the young people I spoke with had heard the explanation multiple times. They had heard it not only from Peace Over Violence facilitators, but from representatives of other organizations. It was a way that the slow state slipped into the work of ephemeral programs.

Prevention, as the name implies, proposes to change the future, but it is directed by the past. Funding places prevention programs in particular schools and communities because the youth there are likely to have experienced some form of trauma, which statistically ties them to future violence. Sarah, a young white implementer critical of the tensions she experienced when facilitating programs with youth, explained that in prevention programs, "you're never just talking about [prevention]." She continued: "These kids, especially the kids in inner cities, are openly talking about experiencing [violence]. If they're not talking about experiencing it, they know exactly what you're talking [about] . . . it's too late to start from the beginning [of the] discussion." According to a 2012 study from the Department of Justice, at least one third of youth, and even more in poor marginalized neighborhoods, have some experience of violence.[19]And yet, during my entire time in the field, including observations of hundreds of conversations with young people about relationships, trauma, and violence, I never saw an incident that led to a mandated report being filed.

Facilitators wanted the program to be a place where young people could be honest and open and they made a promise, describing the program context to students not only as a permissible environment for talking about feelings, but one that was set aside from systems of institutional surveillance. On multiple occasions, facilitators described the class to students using a variation of the descriptor, "Like in Vegas, what happens here, stays here." This was a promise that they would inevitably struggle to keep as rules around mandated reporting threatened to trigger a process that would bring any disclosures of violence to authorities, setting in motion a series of consequences certain to reach beyond the room. In this way, facilitators strove to construct "safe spaces" free from fear or criticism. However, because this was impossible within the institutional setting, facilitators told youth they can talk about things they wouldn't otherwise, but taught them to do so in distant, vague ways. A safe space is not a free space.[20]

Many of the formal curricula included guidelines on how to deal with and avoid disclosures. One curriculum stated: "Make sure students do not use real names or too many details when talking about other people." "Be aware that some students in your class may be experiencing dating abuse or other abuse, perhaps at home. Don't force students to answer questions if they're uncomfortable doing so." "It's difficult in a class environment to guarantee complete confidentiality. Warn students of this fact, so they don't reveal too much." That the formal guidelines of a curriculum designed to help youth navigate unhealthy and abusive relationships discouraged the use of real names and details is telling. Organizational trainings reinforced this perspective. As Kim put it during a training for new volunteers, "It's not counseling. It's just education." Facilitators were taught that if a young person starts to tell a story which might lead to a disclosure, the facilitator should "pause" the conversation. The facilitator should thank them for what they have said and encourage them to speak after class. This happened on multiple occasions. During a training session on mandated reporting, Amy, a longtime facilitator, said, "Don't worry about it," then paused and added, "Just kidding, I'll get someone sued." Then, she said slowly and with authority, "You can't report someone unless we know all of the relevant information—name, birthday, address."

Facilitators often talked about the challenges of balancing the betrayal of trust on one hand and the real threat to health and safety on the other posed by reporting something a student said. During one class session, after the explanation of mandated reporting, one student called out, "The authorities can give a rat's ass." Sarah validated this point, saying that authorities may not always be the best ones to contact because "sometimes they let us down." Donna, a Latina facilitator, was one of the few to have filed a mandated report, and as a former youth participant in programming, she had an insightful perspective. I have provided her full quote here, unbroken, as it encapsulates the internal tensions and contradictions that facilitators faced in relation to mandated reporting:

> The adult of me understands that it's there to protect the youth and to help them and to make sure that whatever unspeakable act that's happening, try to resolve, try to stop it and I understand all that. The part that I don't like about it is the fact that here's this young person who is confiding in me to tell me this secret or tell me this problem and that now has to turn around and go tell some other adult and who's now going to go tell another adult, who's going to tell another adult and then now it's going to come back to their parents and their parents are going to be super-pissed at them.
>
> There's all this internal trauma and drama that happens in your home that [they feel like] "fuck, I wish I never would have told you" kind of happens with them. So, that initial anger that happens from young people towards you when you have to do that, it really sucks. The idea is that the proper agencies can step in and do their work, right? But when it comes to DCFS, they suck (laughs) and so sometimes I feel like is this going to do more harm than it is good and then I'm like required by law to report this and I'm just like, mmm, do I really have to?
>
> Those are my inner struggles with it of breaking the trust that this young person is now building in me that I can never regain, which most of the time that's what happens. Of then having an entity step in that I know historically and presently doesn't do a very good job of doing what they're supposed to do, even though that is the only thing that exists that's supposed to help or knowing the fact that now I have this information and this young person is going to continue to go through this dreadful thing. Either way, it sucks.

As Donna makes clear, in addition to joining the list of adults who had broken the trust of youth, many facilitators, alongside teachers and school counselors, were deeply skeptical of the capacity of the state to handle the situation with care and support. In fact, a distrust of the supportive arm of the state on the part of adults posed a significant dilemma: to report or not to report. In this way, adults interested in supporting youth found themselves caught between the processes that enabled meaningful connection and the institutional mechanisms for protecting youth.

Eleanor, a former youth participant turned implementer, put it this way: "We're like this weird in-between. We're an adult so we can help them but we also are not like in this crazy position of power that it's like they can't talk to us or they can't trust us." This put them in a position to talk to young people about their lives in ways teachers and administrators could not. She explained how she saw informing young people about their mandated reporting requirements was an important part of building trust. As opposed to youth thinking they could talk and then finding out that something they had said led to a report: "We're pretty clear with the students of what they can say or not say and we try and be really open about it because with us a really huge component is the trust with the students . . . I'm always afraid of it, like I'm like what are you going to tell me right now." Like Eleanor, Jennifer was afraid of what would happen if a youth disclosed something that mandated she report it: "I've never had to make a report at this point which I'm glad. It freaks me out, I'm not going to lie."

It's not that facilitators did not care, far from it. The most moving and serious part of the way that they described their work was the stories of youth. Robert explained that the story of a young man he met while implementing a program in a juvenile program had a lasting impact: "And this one young man shared a really, I won't tell his story, but a very gripping, frightening, dramatic story. And I was so shook by his story that when I left, driving home I cried, and when I got home I could not shake this visual image that had come to my mind when this guy told his experience and it haunted me, it still haunts me." But, as Robert makes clear, while he was profoundly impacted by the story, it was not his to share.

Facilitators often struggled to walk the line between building connection and providing safety. During one session, Marvin, a junior in high school, joked that a female classmate should say that she abuses her boyfriend; he said, "Come on, be honest, we are all family." Eleanor, a facilitator, interjected: "I know you said we are all family, and this is your class and we can talk about whatever you want and I want this to be a safe space, but I want to remind you that all of the adults in here are mandated reporters, which means that if we hear something that has to do with your safety we have to report it." Marvin responded, laughing, "Aw no, you're not family no more. I don't trust you now." Eleanor replied, "I'm just telling you how it is, you can talk about 'a friend' but if we get the sense that your safety is in danger, we have to say something." Marvin said that "parents don't snitch though" and Eleanor tried to explain that it was not snitching, it was looking out for their safety. Variations on this scene played out regularly and revealed the tightrope walked by facilitators as they struggled to create a safe space while abiding by the rules of the institution.

Borderline disclosures happened frequently during programming. For example, when giving a lesson on how to help a friend, a young woman whose name I never learned raised her hand and said, "I don't usually tell anyone this, but I was molested when I was younger, like eight. I don't like to tell people because I'm worried they are going to use it against me." The room was quiet for a few seconds before the facilitator, Eleanor, spoke. She thanked the young women for sharing and validated her fear. The young woman explained that she had not talked to her school counselors about it because she did not trust them. Eleanor thanked her again and returned to the scenario at hand. The young woman continued, this time with less confidence in her voice, and explained that she thinks about it every day, that it has a big impact on her life. Eleanor again validated the young women's statement and gave an explanation of post-traumatic stress disorder, then moved back to the scenario. This, while difficult both practically and emotionally for Eleanor, was exactly the way facilitators were trained to deal with these situations. Eleanor explained afterward that she wanted to be able to talk to the young woman, but not in front of the whole class, where other students could hear or interject. While Eleanor suggested that the young woman stay to talk afterwards, as was often the case, she did not show up.

At a predominantly white school, one student gave a detached and detailed story about how his dad has scars from where his stepmom stabbed him. He talked about how the authorities only care if there is money to be made. Sarah responded with an uncharacteristically brief "thank you" and moved on. When the next student raised his hand, Sarah pointed to him and asked, "Is this a personal story?" with a hesitant tone. When the student shook his head no, Sarah nodded at him to continue. Given the mandated reporting rules, and the emotional volatility of the moment, facilitators felt it hazardous to engage in such conversations.

One strategy that facilitators used to avoid disclosures while assessing the situation was to encourage youth to frame their experiences as those of friends or a third party, explaining, "Just don't give us too many details, tell us about your *friend*." This led facilitators to disrupt young people's narratives. If students were trying to determine if something was abusive, facilitators encouraged them to "use hypotheticals," and to say "what if" before asking their question, instead of describing lived experiences. In one instance, a high school student asked if hitting someone with a ruler counted as abuse. When the facilitator explained that technically it did, the high schooler began, "Well, my dad . . ." but the facilitator interjected, asking if the student was about to tell a personal story. When the student shook his head no, Sarah nodded at him to continue and he began again, "What if my friend's dad . . ." By teaching strategies for sidestepping the formal policy of mandated reporting, facilitators were able to provide some limited advice to youth without enmeshing them in distant, fractured, and untrustworthy state surveillance and management. As a result, within a fractured and impermanent system of adult–youth relations, mandated reporting in part served to undermine the goals of support as it pushed young people away from trusted adults and taught them to speak in vague and detached ways so as not to trigger the intervention of institutional authorities. The formal and informal rules of the slow state, intended to provided care and support, often constrained the efforts of programs.

In my time in the field, I saw dozens of last days. They often went like this one, from a school north of downtown Los Angeles: "Today is my last day," JJ said as he put his hands together, "so I won't ever see you again." The 25 eleventh graders let out a ritualized chorus of "awww," which I came to recognize after a half-dozen last days with facilitators. Most young people seemed accustomed to last days. Still, this class appeared genuinely sad to see Joseph go. One young woman asked if he would be her friend on Facebook and he smiled, "Of course." A few young men stopped on their way out to shake his hand or thank him. This scene played out often, not just with Joseph, but with all the facilitators. It was a reminder of a casual fact of life for many young people: often, adults are temporary. The hall flooded with a long, flat tone and then the thunder of zippers and hinges. Students unspooled into the hallway and as they came together they came to life. They parted around Joseph as he moved down the hall. Joseph pushed through the front office, phones clanging nonstop, and out to the heavy gates at the edge of the campus. Once he got to the sidewalk he peeled off the neon yellow badge proclaiming "VISITOR," checked his phone, and blinked into the sun. Off to another school, another first day, another room full of familiar strangers.

The celebratory story about programs goes like this: At-risk youth are found and picked out of the crowd and met with the well-trained facilitation of a program, which transforms their attitudes and behaviors in ways that are reflected onto evaluations. If the program stirs up some buried trauma, the facilitators pass it along to the relevant authorities. But beneath that story a more complicated reality can be found, one in which labels obscure experience, the representatives of programs are strangers, programs make meaning out of unclear narratives, and no one trusts the authorities. While these are all the case for interpersonal violence prevention programs, they also likely represent wider patterns within the ephemeral state. For those on the front lines, life in the ephemeral state is often profoundly lonely. Programs, for all their noble goals, function as a distancing apparatus. Even as they bring people into closer physical proximity, they increase social distance. This is produced not by propaganda from some distance source or by dividing physical space, but close up, eye to eye.

5 Stories Come Apart

Carissa: Emily, I want you to do what is right for you, and only you know that answer. You know I can't stand to see you get hurt physically and emotionally. Well, maybe you need to take a break from Jason for a while and see how that goes.

Emily: Maybe you're right, but I'd really like to talk to him and ask him why he—

Elizabeth: Why he pushes you around and slaps you? Emily, no one should have to put up with that, but you're the only one who can do this; and you can change it. You're smart and you've got lots of friends who want you to be happy and safe. We'll be there for you and for Jason, too, if he'll let us.

Emily: We'll probably need all of you guys. Listen, can you stay with me tonight? My parents will be home soon, but I can't talk to them about this right now and I really don't want to be alone.

Carissa: Sure, let us call our folks and then we can just talk or chill or whatever you feel like.

Emily: Thanks, you're great friends!

(All hug. Scene fades.)

—THE END—

[Note: Excerpt from the Safe Dates curriculum]

·　　·　　·　　·　　·

The purpose of a violence prevention curriculum is to explain and transform the legal and cultural edges of one of the most terrifying and puzzling of human experiences to a brimming classroom of teenagers. On the back of evidence-based research and broad cultural acceptance, we have come to believe that this is a simple goal: a matter of the right message, well told.[1] We have lost sight of the fact that, to young people, interpersonal violence is not academic, nor is it an issue of norms or attitudes or behaviors: it is friends and family and loved ones, and it is commonplace threats and consequences.[2] It was into the morass of emotion and lived experience, and the notion that violence is simply a personal problem, that change programs dove headlong.

Change programs put stories into motion as social policy.[3] In interpersonal violence prevention, these stories may include notions of how better communication leads to healthier relationships, or how beliefs in gender equality decrease violence.[4] Violence prevention programs attempt to provide new characters and plot points for stories of violence. They are intended to act on groups in order to transform attitudes and behaviors close up and, at the same time, shift statistical rates on a population scale. A new story, change programs imply, can change a life, and in aggregate, change culture. This seemingly audacious idea, given a second look, belies history, as policy has often been as much about sending moral and cultural messages as the practical distribution of support and sanction. All social policies are discursive and rhetorical acts. In this way programs are an evolution: cut out the support and punishment and leave just the story.[5]

Ella, who had worked at POV for over a decade, believed deeply in the ability of curricula to change people. "The greatest tool that we have is In Touch With Teens," she said, and then explained:

> You begin to challenge those beliefs that these young boys and girls have [had] for many years, but you are still catching them at a very vulnerable age. You can, you have the ability to shift something so that this kid will make healthier choices, perhaps. Not that we're saying we'd reach every single one, no.

To do so, programs mobilized narratives of healthy relationships.[6] Although the particulars differed, curricula told stories intended to transform how young people moved through the world. Eleanor, who first became involved with POV as a youth and now worked as a facilitator, explained that everyone in the prevention department works on "different projects which require different outcomes, but the curriculums make up the core values" of the work.

Curricula are the physical manifestation of this narrative social policy. *Safe Dates: An Adolescent Dating Abuse Prevention Curriculum,* available for $245 from Hazelden, comes in a white three-ring binder; on the cover is a photo of a multiracial group of smiling teenagers beneath the red and green Safe Dates logo and the names of the authors. Where the first edition had a line of text at the top right that read "research based," the second edition has a small gold emblem that says "evidence based." "A ten-session program that targets attitudes and behaviors associated with dating abuse and violence" intended to "change norms," the curriculum explains its goals thusly: "identify key ways of preventing dating abuse including changing gender stereotypes, promoting healthy communication and equal power in relationships and dealing with feelings, particularly anger, in healthy, non-violent ways."[7] Safe Dates is among the most evaluated and implemented interpersonal violence prevention programs in the United States.[8] The first randomized-control evaluation, which set the stage for its sustained use, was conducted in rural North Carolina schools in 1994 with a mostly white population.[9] Hazelden, which was founded as an addiction treatment center in 1949, has made a business out of curricula over the last 20 years. Today, according to their website, they host "the nation's largest addiction recovery publishing house," "an influential institute for recovery advocacy and public policy," and "[a] renowned addiction prevention program for children and families."

In public health parlance, Safe Dates has shown effectiveness at changing attitudes and norms. One evaluation stated: "Program activities were designed to alter dating violence norms by increasing the adolescent's perception of negative consequences associated with dating violence and altering peer responses to dating violence." Another: "Norms related to gender-roles provide a framework for selecting future behaviors. According to cognitive-developmental theories, children form gender-role norms and then, as adolescents, they strive to become like the categories they created." In association with the curriculum, norms—and in turn, norms change—were assessed by asking adolescents how strongly they agreed or disagreed with a series of statements. For example, the eight dating violence norms statements assessed acceptance of dating violence under certain situations, such as "It is ok for a boy to hit his girlfriend if she did something to make him mad," "It is ok for a girl to hit a boyfriend if he hit her first," and "A girl who makes her boyfriend jealous on purpose deserves to be hit." There were also 11 statements designed to assess "acceptance of traditional gender-role norms," such as "In a dating relationship, the boy should be smarter than the girl" and "In general, the father should have greater authority than the mother in making decisions." Safe Dates moves the needle on these norms.

Crack open to most any page of Safe Dates and you will find a detailed plan. Content aside, the structure of each session is tightly managed. Plastic tabs mark each of the units. The first page of each lays out a straightforward plan "at a glance" for 50 minutes, with each minute accounted for and a list of "learner outcomes." The curriculum explains that rigidity is important to the "fidelity of the product and the accompanying outcomes." The curriculum includes step-by-step guides for every task, from how to introduce oneself, to how to build trust, to how to describe each exercise. This can make things easier for facilitators, who show up with a wide range of experiences and training to implement programming across diverse sites.

Peace Over Violence's own curriculum, In Touch With Teens, was on the other end of a relatively short spectrum of formalization. ITWT was also arranged into units with clear breakdowns, but the exercises themselves allowed for more creativity and less evidence-based prescriptiveness. The lessons were built on a tradition of feminist scholarship that has shown how dominant narratives of masculinity, such as the idea that "boys will be boys," undergird men's violence and assault and included lessons about social justice, including oppression and racism.[10] While the kinds of stories that ITWT and Safe Dates told were different—and to be sure, the outcomes often echoed these differences—the underlying narrative mechanisms and the social organization of their implementation were similar. In other words, the differences between ITWT and Safe Dates were of degree, not type. Both laid out narratives intended to counter existing gender norms. They told stories to change lives.

As Ken Plummer has said, "stories are social actions, embedded in social worlds."[11] Stories are social and political objects, with texture and force: they organize thought and shape action. Recent research tends to conceptualize narratives as limited in number and occupying a kind of limited cognitive space. Most of us, so the theory goes, have a small cache of stories in our heads and we use one or another to figure out how to make sense of situations.[12] Decisions are, in part, a byproduct of the stories we tell. One may, for example, go to school because one believes in a story about how school leads to a brighter future.[13] From this angle, curricula are a rational policy apparatus: encourage new behaviors by telling new stories.[14] However, this theory does little to explain how new narratives are experienced and why the stories of policy often fall apart.

This chapter trails the healthy relationship narratives from the pages of the curriculum, into Los Angeles classrooms, and then out into the stories of youth.[15] I call this an ethnography of stories: I follow a story around and see how it moves and shifts. Observing narrative across multiple sites provides an opportunity to test theories about how stories function as policy. In particular, I am interested in a paradox of change programs: If programs do in fact signal a transformation in narrative and norms, then cultural forms are stunningly unstable—alterable in one hour a week for 12 weeks—and the deeply held narratives that give us meaning are fleeting. If not, however, then we must reckon with why evaluations show a change that is not there.

In classrooms, I found that the healthy relationship narratives of programs did not simply slip into young people's heads.[16] Instead, curricular narratives collided with the preexisting stories held by youth, then fractured or fell apart.[17] This was not the end of the curricular narratives though. Young people put them back together but did so based on their experiences, rooted in social location and institutional incentives.[18] In this way, I found that curricula narratives were incorporated into *gendered narratives of the state*: overarching stories told in policy and practice about what kind of citizen-subjects women and men should be—in this case Black and Latinx youth—which shape the way that individuals talk about their relationship to social support, the criminal system, and politics. Marginalized young men and women incorporated shards of the curricular narratives into ongoing gendered narratives that situated them relative to the state, effectively jamming unrefined chunks of content into an existing plot. Young women told a story of empowerment and resisted describing themselves as being changed, while young men placed themselves within a story of transformation. There were, however, some young people who consistently and creatively took up and applied the curricular narrative in dynamic, situational, and at times contradictory ways: youth who had participated in sustained programs. These programs were more successful in changing narratives in ways that echoed beyond the scope of evaluations, but not in the ways that they intended.

A DISTANT NARRATIVE

Facilitators and funders expected the narrative of healthy relationships to be new to youth. Lauren, a program manager at POV, told me that, for example, most students coming into the program "won't even identify their behavior as being abusive. Like, jealousy is romantic." At one of my first sessions, I watched as Michael, a young and energetic Latino facilitator, wrapped up the day's lesson by explaining to students: "You need to check yourself, the other person doesn't know, you know because we told you." During a first-day ice-breaker, Jennifer would often ask the class to split up into groups of two, with one student in each pair making a fist. When she said *go,* the other student had 30 seconds to open their partner's fist. Students commanded, pried, jammed, tickled, and offered cash. Most failed. It was difficult unless you knew the trick. Maybe three times out of hundreds of pairs did I witness a student *ask* their partner to open their fist.

One exercise from ITWT, called "red lights," provides an example of how the healthy relationship narrative was intended to shape action. Facilitators gave clusters of two-to-four students three squares of construction paper; red to signal "unhealthy behavior," green to signal "healthy behavior," and yellow to signal "depends." The exercise was also described sometimes as "stop, slow, or go." Facilitators would ask the class a series of questions, and each group would respond with a signal. Then the facilitators would talk through the responses and the correct answer. Questions included: "If your boyfriend or girlfriend is drunk or high, can you have sexual relations with them?" or "Your boyfriend or girlfriend has been acting strangely; can you sign into their computer and check their email?" In exercises like this, complex moments, interactions, and relationships were sorted into categories: harmful or not harmful, or more often: healthy or unhealthy. As a facilitator named Joseph said to a classroom full of tenth graders: "If it's not healthy, it's unhealthy, right?"[19]

Exercises like red lights set out to change the stories associated with those closest to young people, including friends, family, and loved ones. Red lights marked everyday behaviors, such as lying or jealousy, and made them part of an ongoing story that led to harm and abuse. The exercise also marked protective factors, such as open communication and emotional support as green lights, and tied them to future health. Thus, the exercise, like many of the ones in change programs, created a narrative through-line that linked up seemingly disparate and often commonplace experiences in the present to violence or health in the future.

Narratives, by definition, emphasize some things and leave out others. What is missing from the healthy relationship story? Let's take, as an example, a story from Safe Dates: Tony and Jennifer were once insepara- ble, but as their relationship went on, Tony restricted what Jennifer could do and became increasingly abusive. Jennifer ended the relationship, and with her parents' help, got a restraining order against Tony. But, the story explains, school officials did not enforce the order: "Dating abuse isn't a big issue for teens, or so school officials thought." Tony stabbed and killed Jennifer at school. The story ends with this line: "But how could they have known? After all, Tony and Jennifer were only teens."

This story reflects two characteristics of Safe Dates, as well as other cur- ricula I looked at. First, the story was hollowed out of any detail about the characters' lives, identities, or social locations. Who these people are and what matters to them outside of their relationship do not factor in. The goal of stories like this, it seems, is to provide a blank slate onto which youth of various social locations can project themselves or people they know into the roles. Race, if signaled at all, was marked through names in most curricula (e.g., Chan, Tyrone, Pablo). Class was largely absent.[20] Sometimes, gender could be inferred by pronouns or the terms boyfriend and girlfriend and the majority of stories were explicitly focused on heterosexual relationships, although one character in many stories had a name that could be read as a man's or woman's name, such as Alex. This hollowing-out of identity meant that program stories took place in an eternal present, without the pasts that give meaning to action. Often students would respond to these stories by asking why the characters would do that.[21] In addition to stripping out the lived experience of social location, the story of Tony and Jennifer, although it gestured to structural and institutional failures, narrowed the scope to the choices of individual young people. In the vast majority of the stories and exercises, scenes took place between friends, largely away from adults.[22] It seemed that when it came to the stories that curricula wanted young people to take up, adults were never around.

The contrast between the content of curricula and the institutions that surrounded young people was often stark.[23] I could not help think as

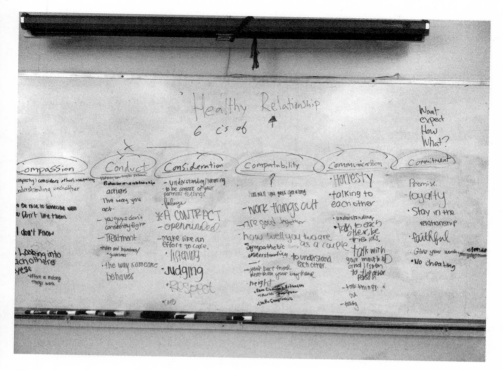

Figure 3. Whiteboard. Photo by author.

much while looking over the "teen relationship equality wheel," a list of traits that "promote good relationships." The wheel includes a number of laudable qualities for relationships—honesty and accountability, communication, shared responsibility, negotiation and fairness, nonthreatening behavior, trust and support, and others. The first time I read it, I thought about its applications for the relationships in my life. And if one imagines interpersonal relationships as free-floating dyads, it is helpful. But when we used the relationship equality wheel in classes, I wondered how students understood their relationship to the school and wider systems of authority. Those relationships, which structured their lives, included few if any of the traits laid out on the relationship equality wheel.[24] Curricula often imagined a story for youth in which they were empowered actors, but, in practice, they made their decisions within institutions.

NARRATIVE ENTROPY

Classrooms are not places where one story wins out easily. They are contested spaces.[25] Students want to be heard and teachers want to get their message out. At a school on the east side of the city, I observed a teacher with a novel way of minimizing this narrative clash. All of her students had whiteboards and erasable markers and when she would ask a question, they would write their answers on the boards and lift them up above their heads.[26]

Curricula often narrowed the voices of young people to prescribed responses. For example, in one exercise Safe Dates directed facilitators in this way: "Ask: What activities are examples of dating?" but never asked about young peoples' own experiences of dating. Even when curricula engaged with trite topics, it avoided asking students to talk about themselves. In another exercise, Safe Dates had facilitators tell students to list people who had made them feel good about themselves, but without including specifics. "No one will see this list except you," it explained.

Facilitators, however, rarely treated their work like a straight-line process of forcing new narratives. I saw a unit facilitated "down the line" on only two occasions. Once, by a first-time volunteer, who was overwhelmed and raced through the session while the audience ignored them. The other time was early on in Jennifer's career, when she was dismayed that a group of students had not understood the lesson on sexual assault. In response, she gave a detailed lesson, meticulously moving from concept to concept. Some students began to whisper to each other and others fidgeted in their seats. Jennifer made "shh" noises every few seconds as she wrote on the board, dedicated to completing the lesson. At several points, Jennifer asked for students to engage, but they did not. "How could you help a friend?" she asked, arm pointing up at the POV hotline number. No one mustered an answer. "Where do I work?" she followed up; still no answer. Eventually she just explained it. Facilitators tended to be more rigid if they were less experienced or when deadlines for evaluations came up. They did this by repeating ideas, quizzing youth, and doing more educational exercises. This was the closest to the formal curriculum that facilitators got, but it still required a great deal of skill to identify and work through pedagogical challenges.[27]

This did not mean facilitators ignored the curriculum. I only heard one story of a time that a facilitator went totally off script. A volunteer, brought in to help with a daunting series of implementations at a high school, told me, proudly, that the class had become "a bit of a therapy session." One woman had explained that she was bisexual and that her parents were upset at her. The volunteer had let her talk and then said "We all support you" and everyone clapped. A full-time facilitator who heard the story was concerned, and said that her next session should be "a bit more presentation-y." The volunteer explained that she did not want to cut students off when they were sharing. The facilitator told her to say "thanks for sharing, we can talk about that more after class, but it isn't what we are talking about now." Jennifer, a full-time facilitator, explained the "push and pull" between getting the curriculum done and giving young people a chance to speak:

> I just, I don't let it become that type of a space. I want it to be a safe space and I want them to feel comfortable and to feel connected to each other and all those things. But at the same time, I'm not about to lead a group counseling session with like 40 students. It's more like I'll say "Thank you for sharing. I think that's really great, if you want to talk with me after a class. I'd love to talk more with you about this. But I want to get through some more of this presentation so I can give you guys the information I came to give you today."

This can sound cold and facilitators often felt conflicted or guilty about it. But this tension was built in to the mission of the curriculum. Their job was to create a new narrative, not to engage with the ones that were already there.

What happens in that key moment when narratives collide? In order to get inside this question, which has been a black box—unexplored and unexplained—I draw on recent work on cultural entropy, which describes the way that tightly bound and structured cultural messages devolve and transform as they move across contexts. McDonnell, who coined the term, used it to understand how public health media campaigns—on billboards and ribbon campaigns for example—transformed in the messy context of the material environment. As a consequence, meanings would transform too and shift in novel and unexpected ways, dissolving into disarray. In the close-up give and take of interaction one can see how narratives are propelled into one another, and what happens as they fracture and splinter and recombine.[28] The curricular healthy relationship narrative carried by facilitators, despite their best efforts, collided with the lived narratives of youth and fractured in a kind of narrative entropy. In fact, it seemed that the tighter facilitators held to their stories, the more brittle they were. At first glance, young people's responses looked like scattershot pushback and non sequiturs that shot through programming, much to the annoyance of facilitators. However, these sparks, counters, and playbacks were lived stories crackling through.

Sparks

Despite all the ways that the content of prevention curricula avoided and obscured social location, race, class, and gender were constantly reasserted in the classroom. Content often sparked questions, realizations, and tangents from youth, which arose when the health narrative fleetingly aligned with an existing narrative of a student. This sent the conversation, and with it the narrative, flaring off into unexpected directions, before fizzling. These sparks were common, but fleeting, leaving possibilities and narratives unexplored.

A few minutes into the first unit of ITWT, facilitators would stand at the front and ask the roomful of students, "What is violence?" The answers would be surprising, in large part because it seemed like it was an easy question. One time, a young woman called out, "Like, dead people." "Drive-bys!" shouted a boy. The facilitator wrote "relationship violence" on the board and underneath it wrote "physical violence." "What else?" "Mental violence." "Shanking" was called out and two boys at the side mimicked a stabbing scene. "Yelling" was written under a heading of verbal abuse. A student in the back quietly said "Rape" and then the facilitator added a third category, "sexual violence," to the board. Sometimes youth caught a thread they had heard and gave an explanation of a technical term, such as psychological violence. Other students provided odd or disturbingly specific examples, such as "getting your head chopped off." While some of these answers echo media and music, many were anchored in experiences. Drive-bys, shanking, and yelling were, if not part of their lived experience, then at least part of the narrative world through which many young people understood violence and relationships. Programs set out to take those meanings and reframe them without unspooling the stories that animated them.

Young people were eager to talk about relationships, love, fighting, and identity. They rarely had the chance to do that with adults. This was clear when, on occasion, a facilitator let personal stories take center stage. Franklin, a Black high school senior in a *Star Trek* T-shirt, paused during an emotional discussion about arguments in relationships, and then said, shaking his head, "We can't talk like this usually." Some young people actively pushed their narrative forward even when the exercise had a different goal. However, these sparks were temporary and fragile, as challenges from other students or facilitators often pushed young people to recant or stop talking. During one check-in Ben, an eager sophomore in a small group of young men on school probation, described how he "cried buckets" the night before with his mom and dad when they explained that they were worried that they could not get married even though they wanted to. After a couple minutes of Ben's story, one of the other young men called out "Man, stop crying" and others laughed. Ben stopped, said that he was finished, and barely spoke for the rest of the day.

These sparks turned the narratives in unexpected directions, but facilitators, eager to get back to the content, often left them dangling. During a discussion about issues that can arise in relationships, one student exclaimed, without clear connection, that "some guys act like bitches." Rather than agree or ignore this statement, Sean the facilitator asked him what he meant, feeding a spark. After the student explained that he meant that some guys act overly emotional, Sean explained, "That demeans that man by saying he is a woman and that demeans women." The student, nodded, then countered, "Not all women are bitches though." Sean decided that the tangent had gone on long enough and left it at that, leaving the students with a complex chunk of narrative to parse, with no clear message.

It would be wrong to assume that these sparks left young people simply confused. Instead, it is more apt to think of how sparks opened up ways to rearrange portions of the curricular narrative. On multiple occasions when asked about the most important parts of the program, young people described things that were not in the curriculum, but were part of a spark. For example, I asked Misty, a Latina young woman, about her favorite part of the curriculum:

MISTY: I like doing the skits too. I don't know, I just feel like I'm in shoes and I can think like them so I can understand them better. It's sort of like being an outsider and be like, "Oh, why did they do that?"

MAX: So, can you give me an example of whose shoes you feel like you were in?

MISTY: Yesterday we were doing about what was that, the abuser? Why do they abuse, sort of? So, I was the abuser's friend and I had to turn a blind eye to what he was doing. Before, I was always like, "Oh, why did they even support that friend, he's like no friend at all." But when I put myself in their place, now I'm like, "Oh, he's my friend, so I have to support him." and I can feel sort of power? Kind of? It's bad, but I kind of feel powerful like, "Oh, I can make them feel inferior." Sort of.

MAX: So, you were saying you could understand sort of why they would do that.

MISTY: Mm-hmm. Why they would do that. And I felt so guilty afterwards. It made me sort of feel guilty, I was also worried that, "Oh, I actually like can understand them." So, I was worried if I, if I will become like them one day maybe. I don't know.

Relating to an abuser's friend was not the goal of the exercise and no evaluation would attempt to measure that as a positive outcome. And yet, Misty's experience enabled a powerful statement about empathy that we should not simply ignore. In this way, as the curricular narrative and the lived stories collided, the resulting sparks created new possibilities of understanding and sent them streaking out of view.

Counters

For a small but vocal number of students, the cultural ideas in the curriculum did not connect with any narratives they had. Sometimes these students struggled to pronounce the words and phrases on worksheets, did not know their meanings, or resisted their applications. A student asked, "What is making light?" A young woman, reading the word malicious, had trouble; a young man jumped in to help, pronouncing it "male-icious." One young woman stopped reading when she reached the word "homophobic" and asked to read a different example. A young man, one of the few white students enrolled in programming, did not recognize "socioeconomic." When a facilitator asked a crowd of tenth graders, "What is sexism?" one young man earnestly replied, "Who's sexier." A discussion of the "acute stage of abuse" lead a young woman to sigh, "Aww, a cute stage." These responses were not simply "acting out," although sometimes teachers perceived it that way. One young woman explained that sometimes she felt uncomfortable talking about some of the subjects in the curriculum and that would lead her and other students to laugh: "I find myself feeling bad for laughing. Because I feel like maybe I'm not being as understanding to that person or that situation. But at the same time, I know that I'm laughing because that's just not normal to me." Unlike sparks, which propelled the conversation in unexpected directions, counters blunted aspects of the curricular narrative and made it difficult for the new narrative to take hold.

Students often spoke up when the narrative did not accurately represent their understanding of the world. In response to a question about whether it was acceptable to search a partner's bag, students often stated a version of the sentiment "if you weren't doing anything wrong you got nothing to worry about." Many said that jealousy was bad, but not a big deal and that everyone experiences it. Young people often pushed against universalized statements with specific cases of exception. For example, a student argued that a boyfriend following his girlfriend around might be justified if both partners consent to it. Controlling what someone wears may be okay, some youth suggested, because, "what if they are wearing something really inappropriate"; isolating may be acceptable if they are "hanging out with meth dealers"; throwing things may be okay if that is their "way of relieving stress." When counters occurred, I vacillated between dismayed and impressed by the ways that youth added nuance to the generalized messages of the curriculum.

When students had more room to create their own stories, it was even clearer that they differed from the curriculum narrative. Marcus and Shawna were tasked with performing an unhealthy relationship in front of their peers. Marcus was to play a distracted boyfriend to Shawna's controlling girlfriend. From the front of the room she held her thumb and pinky to her ear and mouth like a phone, in the back Marcus answered. He mimicked playing video games, eyes locked on the imaginary screen, feigning interest in Shawna's words. The audience got into it. "Damn, that's cold," one student called out. Others started to encourage Mark and Shawna to do one thing or another. She screamed at him through the phone and then hung up. Mark smirked. The audience laughed. Afterwards, when Shad asked the students in the audience what was wrong with that relationship, the students responded that she was controlling, that she seemed not to trust him or communicate well, that she was isolating and being mean. What Mark did was fine, they said. Shawna and Mark were then asked to "show us healthy" and perform a role-play of what a healthy relationship "should" look like. This time, Shawna explained that she is okay with him not explaining where he is going. When the facilitator asked the students what type of relationship the second performance showed, "healthy" and "boring" were both called out. Some students said that she was acting "too suspicious" although she said almost everything the way the program would describe it. It felt scripted, while the first felt realistic.

Sometimes, counters arose because of who was telling the stories. Two facilitators, Mark and Eleanor, both white, were facilitating at a small school in South Los Angeles. On the first day, I noticed the young man in a crisp red baseball hat, head down on his desk and earbuds curled behind his ears. I figured that he just tired or distracted, which happened often. The next day, when they returned to facilitate a unit on the roots of violence, the young man was absent. The teacher pulled the facilitators aside during a break and explained that after the first class he had come to her and said, "I'm not coming to your class. I'm not being lectured at by a bunch of white people about what I should do in life."

Playback

While sparks showed fleeting alignment, but pulled facilitators off topic, and counters questioned the authenticity of stories, there was one narrative pattern that facilitators were excited about: when students repeated the stories of the curriculum as fact. Kim explained how she saw the stories of the curriculum translate into real life:

When you hear a kid talking and they sound like you, you know you did a good job. When you see a kid call another kid out on something like, "That's sexist." When you hear it in their natural conversations you overhear that they'll call each other out on things. They're like, "That's not healthy" or "That's not cool." Then you know, they really got that. They really believe it. It's a lifestyle change, not just information.

I did hear youth in the program do this on multiple occasions. Students repeated the core content, often word for word, from the curriculum. Few other actions provided such clear and tangible evidence of content translating into action.

However, in the room, the interactional dynamics of playback shut down personal stories, as the language of the curriculum took on the practiced structure of a script. During a presentation on healthy relationships, a young man called out, to no one in particular in his best deep radio voice, "Don't drink and drive kids!" While it seemed to come out of nowhere, I understood why he made that connection. Curricula, especially when implemented as written, can have the feeling of top-down health campaigns, the kind that attempted to tell young people to "just say no." Take for instance a performance group, who I observed as they ran their lines for a brief skit. They had two scripts: the first was technical, with conceptual details from the curriculum, the second, which they had written themselves, was about violence and relationships in their lives. These young people, lively and engaged as they performed the script that they had written, struggled with the curriculum language. Donna quizzed the group, who were stretched out on the floor of the gym. "What are warning signs of an unhealthy relationship?" One student gave a long and twisting answer about "irritability and fighting." At the end, Donna laughed and said that he was really reaching for it, but he did not get there. Another young woman gave a correct answer but, as Donna pointed out, she was clearly thinking while she said it. Donna explained that they needed to study, that "this is as important as learning your lines." It seemed like she was onto something. This was a second set of lines that they had to learn: lines about stats and concepts, lines with no "I" in them, no race or class or institutions. The "learn your lines" approach to violence prevention was what ended up measured on evaluations. In contrast, the stories that youth told were complicated, heartfelt, and unresolved.

Many young people did seem to learn the lines of the curricular narrative. However, they rarely used them to make sense of their own experiences. Instead, I mostly heard narratives from the curriculum when a comment or example reminded a participant of something they had learned about unhealthy relationships, like someone joking that they would "smack" someone else. In these instances, a young person would reply with short, verbatim phrases from the curriculum, calling out "that's not cool" or "that's an unhealthy relationship" or "peace over violence." These call-outs successfully marked specific behaviors in public settings. However, they also ended the conversation and crowded out true stories. After leveling one of these challenges, the original speaker would shut down, laugh it off, or change the subject.

In a kind of code-switching, when young people used the language of the curriculum, their posture and tone changed and they moved into a mode of interaction outside of their lived experiences. They would go from laughing and play fighting with friends as they waited for the class to start, to talking about "verbal abuse" in the class, and then back again to insulting each other after the bell. For example, after the final session at a high school on the edge of Los Angeles County, a young man with a shaggy haircut paused on his way out the door, handed me his post-survey, shook my hand, and thanked me earnestly, saying "I wish we had more time to talk about this stuff." As the bell rang and he was a few steps down the corridor, I overheard him as he smacked his friend on his backside and chuckled, "I just raped you." I glanced down at the boy's evaluation: it was nearly all "correct" answers. He may have been trying to salvage a masculine identity, or he was faking it for his friend. Regardless, he switched between the narratives with ease.

On several occasions, youth stated that their own behaviors were warning signs or risks. One student summed up what he took away from the program: "We learned that a lot of what we do is actually violent and we don't even know it." He was right, this was a version of the message of the curriculum, but I was not sure what to make of it: was it a valuable moment of insight, a hollow chunk of narrative, or a brutal piece of self-critique? The answer, at least when it comes to determining the effectiveness of the program, is unknowable. On paper, they all look the same.

One implication is that playback—spoken out loud or on evaluations—may simply be temporary narratives untethered from experience. We do not know what evaluations signal beyond the ability to play back narratives on a piece of paper. That is, paper evidence of learning a new narrative tells us little about how young people deploy that narrative in daily life. However, the fact that playback so tightly hewed to formalized narrative should not be a source of confidence, it should be a concern.

Taken together, playback, sparks, and counters fractured the healthy relationship narrative in interaction. In the process, the temporal logic that linked events and people, and emphasized certain moments over others, came apart in a process of narrative entropy. As a result, students experienced narratives that were varied, novel, and often unexpected. Entropy was just the beginning of the story though. In the next section, I explore the afterlife of curricular narratives, when young people picked up the pieces and stitched them together.

NARRATIVE PROJECTS

Even though narratives fractured in the room, it is difficult to argue that programs did not change young people.[29] Some changes were small, like the young man who spent the first day of the program staring out the barred windows and occasionally shaking his head in disagreement, but who, by the end of the program, was nodding affirmatively and engaged. Some seemed larger, like a young man on probation for fighting who pulled Robert aside after the bell rang and proudly explained that he was doing some of the things he learned in the class with his new girlfriend and that he was happier. Or the young woman who began crying and said that she had never talked about what a healthy relationship meant before. Others were disappointing, like a young woman who began the program engaged, but by week three kept her head down, and by week four abruptly walked out of the class and never returned. Or the young man who seemed to be opening up and engaging but then, on the day I was scheduled to interview him, was suspended for fighting. Many young people transformed in the ways that the program hoped, developing new ways of thinking about relationships and new ways to manage conflict with loved ones or strangers. Somehow, even as curricular narratives fractured and fell apart, they still produced sweeping changes evident not only on evaluations, but in person.[30] The stories told in change programs were not transplanted fully formed into the heads of participants. Instead, young people incorporated policy stories into ongoing narratives under construction.[31]

Social location and personal experiences dramatically shape the stories we tell about ourselves.[32] Curricula meet youth in the course of their lives in overlapping systems of power and privilege, which Collins describes as the "matrix of domination," within which violence is a "saturated site" of meaning.[33] New narratives mix with a universe of contextual lived experiences within an architecture of race, class, gender, and other aspects of social location. The past is durable. Narrative is more like a renovation than a new house: adding rooms and doors, tearing down a section to rebuild it, keeping the bones of the structure but shifting the layout. I describe the ongoing effort to build a story of oneself that reconciles the messy past with new stories as a *narrative project*.[34] Whereas narrative entropy describes how stories fall apart, narrative projects explain how individuals put them together. Our task, then, is to understand how new narratives are incorporated into existing ones. Specifically, in relation to interpersonal violence, new narratives must be reconciled with lifetimes of experience in a society shaped by heteronormativity and sexism and, in the case of many young people enrolled in violence prevention programming, with systemic racial and class inequalities; at the same time, I found that young people talked about the program using the plot points of the gendered narratives of the state. Most women I interviewed made sense of the program through the lens of an ongoing narrative project of empowerment: the program did not change them, and they largely described the program as a means to bolster skills to help others in ways that they already saw themselves doing. In contrast, the majority of men recounted a powerful and transformative experience in change programs. However, they were rarely able to point to specific lessons that they had learned or concrete ways they had applied them. In this way, their ongoing narrative project was built around change. A third group, made up of both young men and women, revealed how, under certain circumstances, new narrative projects emerged.

"We Just Like a Man, But We More Empowered"

Kashmir explained that she learned from the curriculum how to recognize unhealthy behavior in others, but she was hesitant to act on it: "My mom and my stepdad, you know, they get into it and I see it and I see the stages, how my stepdad do it, yeah, I saw it all. So [the program] brought it to my attention and I'm like oh, those, there's stages to it so I get it." I asked Kashmir what she was going to do with that information. "Well, I told [my mom] about it, but you know, she going do her. She's going to figure it out on her own, so you can't do anything about it." Kashmir was not familiar with the word feminism. Still, she explained that her mom taught her that women are empowered. "We have the power to do what we want because we want it and I guess we can do more than a man can do. That's what I've been told. We take care of kids, we clean, we do work, we just like a man, but we more empowered." Scholars have pointed to the way that discourses of empowerment have entered the mainstream, and as a result, young women repeatedly receive the message that they can do anything they want if they set their mind to it. As Ray has argued, this is multiplied and mobilized for marginalized young women at the same time it is detached from feminism.[35] As a narrative, empowerment plots a story about women making their own choices with little concern for institutional demands. This story was one that the young women I interviewed absorbed into their narrative project and it shaped how they responded to programming.

On some occasions, empowerment messages were carried by facilitators. Leah Aldridge, one of the original authors of ITWT, explained how, while talking to a group of young women of color, she would say:

> I'm telling you that these things will deter you. You need to understand that you are not a victim here but that you have choices that you make, and the choices determine whether you become a perpetrator or not. How much are you a victim? where do you have power? not where you are disempowered, where you do have power? . . . which incorporates neoliberalism, I admit it.

Most of the programs I looked at were coeducational, but two were gender-specific. BeStrong, a "comprehensive empowerment curriculum," was a "female counterpart" to MyStrength, a men-focused program. Kim, one of the creators of BeStrong, explained that while "MyStrength is really about defining masculinity and redefining it or exploring it," BeStrong was concerned with "building girls' capacity to assess themselves as individuals and then in relation to others . . . It is not only defining femininity for them, it's about defining what it is for them and then having them navigate themselves through those different relationships." Kim's description illustrates a discourse that sees young women as navigating a "socially contextualized field of choices."[36] Whereas young men were told to use their inherent strength differently, women were encouraged to *choose* to be strong.

In order to tell a story about themselves as empowered, young women described their choices as always part of who they essentially are. To be empowered meant that everything you did was exactly what you meant to do and outside forces could not act on you. When I asked young women if the program changed them, most said no. Take Valeria. She was 18 and Latina like most of the students in her downtown school. Her hair was blonde and shot through with orange. She would blink hard before answering, composing her answers in her head. She loved understanding other people's worlds, spoke Spanish and English, and was learning Tagalog for fun. Valeria told me that she had chosen to participate in the program at the urging of her guidance counselor, who told her: "'You've experienced so many things. You've seen so many things.' She's like, 'This class will be great for you.' I told her, 'OK, I'll give it a try.' I told her, 'If I don't like it, I'll change.'" Valeria stayed in the program. I asked her, "Is violence in society an important issue for you?" She told me:

> To be honest, no. It's not. Because I've not experienced so much violence in my life, just with my mother, which was temporary. So, nothing major has happened to me that I can say, "Wow, I need counseling because of this issue, because of violence and stuff." No, but I would like to help other people.

This echoed what I heard from other students, nearly entirely young women, many of whom did not incorporate the narrative of the program into their own narrative project but wanted to pass on what they learned to others. Crystal, for example, also wanted to apply some of what she learned to other people's relationships: "I didn't know what to do, to like, help them. But now I, like, I do know. So I could make a difference."

When I talked with Cleo, I could hear her shifting into the empowerment narrative when I asked if the program changed her: "It opened my eyes more to the world." She paused, then continued: "Like, I always had my eyes opened to, like, worldly views and how everything is happening." She explained that the program did not change how she saw things, but "made me stronger on what I believe." Later in our interview, when I asked Cleo if she used anything from the program in her relationship, she explained: "Well, actually, I'm just naturally a loving person . . . we both went to church together and we both really had things, but I know that actually this— actually this helped me with just look at warning signs. We haven't had a problem. We haven't had an argument. We haven't had an argument at all."

Most young women avoided saying that they had *ever* changed. In this way, Valeria was an exception. She had changed recently in a dramatic way. How that happened tells us about how change programs fall short. The change Valeria went through was rooted in her moving to a new school. Valeria said:

> It's changed me. I grew up in the ghetto, in the hood type of stuff. And [school] changed me from bad to good. Because I started to see other students in this school, and they were not into the same things I was. So I guess they made me feel lower class . . . So I think you could say that when I came here, none— nobody was like me. And everybody was different. I met a girl who was the same way as me. And when I saw her and I looked at myself, I was like, "I look like that?" So that made me change. And I just started to be different. I started to get into more stuff, talking to people. And that book that I'm telling you about I made, we actually got to express our feelings in there, about our life stories. And hearing all those stories about how girls have been raped, have been abused, have been damaged, it's like it made me feel at home. I'm not the only one. So I'm like, "All right." So I got more comfortable. And I just, it's—it changed me, you could say. And I got more comfortable and I just changed my personality to someone outgoing and more outstanding.

Throughout her story Valeria emphasized how her experience with new people—different from her and similar—led her to reassess how she thought of herself. Valeria feuded with the woman who she looked like for a year. Eventually she changed too: "She changed her style. She's a pretty girl now. And I'm just like, I guess problems could change you."

For most young women, admitting to being changed by a program threatened their narrative of already being empowered. After all, if you are empowered, some outside force cannot come in and change you: you are the one who changes the world. For this reason, many young women resisted describing a program that was trying to change them as successful. Instead, the narrative of empowerment cast them in the agentic lead role, capable of using the lessons of the curriculum to help others, as it encouraged them to downplay their own histories of harm.

"I Answered the Questions Nicely"

Q: *What do you think was the goal of the program?*
A: Just to show people how violence like—what violence can do and that violence shouldn't be the only result.

Q: *What did you think of it? Did you like it?*
A: I liked it. It helped out a lot.

Q: *How did it help?*
A: Like—like in relationship things, it helped me out a lot 'cause like it showed me like how to—how to make a relationship better. And how to have a good relationship with somebody.

Q: *Do you feel like you're going to use some of the things you learned?*
A: Yeah.

Q: *Like what? Can you think of anything in particular?*
A: Like the respect. What else? They deserve respect, then like all the—how else can I say it? They deserve respect. It taught me a lot . . .

Q: *Was there anything else that you wanted to see people talk about in a program like that and you thought was missing?*
A: No, I feel like they—they talked about every topic.

Q: *Was there—how did you feel while you were in there?*
A: Oh, I liked it. It like—it taught me like things like—it taught me a lot. But I should have took down my notes and I would have—I would have remembered some of it.

Q: *Yeah. You felt like it connected to your life, like you could sort of relate it to what we were talking about?*
A: Yeah. It did.

Q: *How so?*

A: Because like—I don't know. Like—like—like the violence. Like I'm all—like I'm all—like I'm all about that—like I know like everything about violence. So like when it come to—like when it came down to peace, like, I really didn't know a lot about it. So this was like—it was kind of like just changing my mentality about the violence.

Q: *What did you learn about peace?*
A: Like—man. (Shakes head).

I was unsure what to make of this interaction when it happened. Part of me was excited; after all, Angel was clearly telling me that the program had a positive impact on him. But I was also skeptical. I had asked Angel in at least ten ways about what he took away from the program and, while he was insistent on the fact of its transformational power, he had difficulty articulating what exactly had transformed.[37]

While young women drew on empowerment to explain that the program did not change the way they thought of themselves and their lives, young men constructed a narrative of change, marked by a plot of uncertainty turning to epiphany. They incorporated scattered phrases and concepts from the program, but the ways they applied ideas from the curriculum were often inaccurate, fleeting, or immediately contradicted. Young men would emphasize personal change, using a variety of terms I heard repeatedly, but these narratives were overly generalized, without clear connection to personal stories or relationships. Some young men were both vague and positive about nearly every aspect of their lives, including their sad and traumatic experiences. One young man named Ariel provides a fitting example.

In a gray polo buttoned to the top and khaki shorts, Ariel moved like he was still growing into his body. Plus, he had hurt his leg on a diving board the day before our interview and was trying to cover his limp with lopsided purposeful gait. A 17-year-old sophomore when we talked beneath a metal umbrella in the expansive courtyard of his large public school after a session with a group of young people on probation, he spoke in an even and crisp tone, and spent the interview furrowing his thick eyebrows and glancing up at other students passing by.

Early on in the interview, I asked Ariel to describe how he would talk to his friends about the healthy relationship program he was in, and his response had an intentional quality that I heard often from young men. He told me, "I'll tell them it's a nice program. That they should join. Because the stuff that we talk about is really, just makes people think about it, about the violent stuff and about the racial stuff that happens." I followed up, asking if there was anything that he did not like or that he was unsure about and he responded without hesitation, "No, I like everything. It's making me learn more stuff about, like, not to be violent, and, like, about, like, girls, about everything." I heard answers like this from other young men. For example, Joe Moses explained how he would describe the program to a friend: "I would tell a friend, well, you should take this because it's going to teach you how to stop violence, and, like, to help, like, women not get sexually assaulted by men and stuff, and teach you, like, the right path." Joe Moses insisted that the program had changed him in several ways. He said that now he would intervene if he saw someone being bullied, which he says would not have been the case before.

These were the kind of answers that facilitators liked to hear and the type of cultural change that public health strove for. It showed a shift away from violence and toward a new definition of masculinity. As I listened, I was excited to hear how this transformation had occurred, but something was strange. Ariel's tone was upbeat, but also vague and distant.

Ariel saw supportive messages beyond the program. He seemed to see them everywhere he looked. While I talked with Ariel in the courtyard of his school, the mascot, painted on a massive wall across the courtyard, caught my eye. He was a giant muscular man with a raccoon cap and a beard. Every student I had seen on campus was nonwhite and the mascot, while his skin was shaded gray, was clearly white. I asked Ariel about this: "It's not that it's a white dude, it don't make a difference if it's a white or a Black, because it's just all the same thing. It's like, be a person, find the pride. He went to school. Think about, like, that we got power and that we could do it." "He's really muscular," I said. "That's just to give us the sign that we could do it and we could make it somewhere." Ariel told me that "there's a lady one too" who is not as muscular.

When I asked Ariel about times he had seen unhealthy relationships, he recounted a traumatic public scene: "There was a car flying so fast down the street, like, when they stopped, he [the driver] just, like, threw the girl out of the car and he got out [of] the passenger and started hitting her." Ariel explained what he was thinking as he watched: "He's doing that to a girl for what reason? It don't matter if she make you mad. It's a girl. Girls will do that. Girls, like, want that to happen, and then the dumb boys that lead to the violent stuff start hitting them." Ariel seemed eager to show me that he knew that what he had seen was wrong, but his rationale revealed the complicated role of violence and masculinity in his life. Needless to say, "girls, like, want that to happen" was not the message about relationships that the curriculum set out to send. In fact, this was perhaps the most victim-blaming response I heard during my interviews. But it was one of several discordant messages I heard from young men who proclaimed that the program had changed them. Joe Moses described where he saw unhealthy relationships: "Sometimes, like, these dudes, they try to force their girlfriends to give them kisses and stuff, and the girl be like, 'Nah, like, I'm in a bad mood or something,' and they be like, 'You better give me a kiss, or I'll break up with you or something.' And the girl be like, 'Ah, I don't want to break up wit' you,' so she just gives him kisses and stuff."

Ariel's life story was a familiar one. He grew up in a difficult part of the city with two brothers and two sisters. He described his youth this way: "I've been through a lot, like, going to elementary, I had stitches, falling, like, a lot of violent stuff. Falling off bikes, fighting and all that. I grew out of it because I noticed that fighting is not a good thing. Fighting is not good at all. It's just, to just [do that] for no reason. When I realized that, I changed. I changed as a man." I was struck by the way Ariel narrated his childhood, which had been marked by violence and loss, with relentless, albeit discordant, positivity. He told me, "My mom passed away, so, you know, my dad worked as a parking enforcer. Yeah, and we'd be going out to eat, having family fun, he'd buy me stuff. We'd just be having family fun." This continued as he explained how he came to be on probation for robbery: "I regret that I did that, because I was, I wasn't supposed to be the robber. Why would I rob stuff that I could get? I noticed that when I, 'cause I was little and I wasn't thinking. But now that I got older, I started thinking about it, like, I don't need to be stealing when I could get the stuff that I want." This was, on its surface, a rational response from a 17-year-old, but one that made little sense to me. Not only can I imagine a number of reasons why a young person would steal something, but also his argument seemed to justify stealing if the thing you steal is something that you could not otherwise get, making his statement of regret more complicated. Ariel's responses followed this arc, from negative to positive, even when it did not fit with the story he was telling.

Like most young men I talked with, it was clear that Ariel had regular interactions with adults who tried to change him. Some of these were disciplinary authorities, including police officers and administrators. While on probation, he often interacted with his probation officer. He explained, "He helps me with stuff, he writes good reports, writes stuff that I do good, the stuff that I do bad. Like, it all combines. And when they see that I'm doing better, they see that I'm trying to help myself, and when they see that I'm trying to help myself, they provide me with stuff to, like, for the programs to provide me to not be a violent person and to succeed in life." Ariel was practiced in the logic of juvenile control. He knew that he had to demonstrate that he was working to help himself in order to be provided with programs, which would then help him further. And while he was up to the task, it could be daunting. He told me, "You have to do everything right. I do everything right but, like, they want you to do everything right. You gotta stay on task." Ariel explained that several of his teachers used the threat of reporting him to his probation officer, which could lead to jail time, to make sure he did as they said. Given this pressure, I could imagine why Ariel seemed so positive and dedicated to convincing me that he was doing "everything right." Maybe he imagined that his probation officer's reach included me. Or maybe he was just so practiced at it, that this is how he learned to interact with adults.

The tension between the person that Ariel talked about being and the way others reacted to him came up often as we talked. He told me about a scenario that often plays out when he enters a store at the same time as other young Black men.

> I seen it before plenty of times. Like, say I didn't know the people, but they walked in a store and I walk in behind, and they'd [the store owner would] be, like, "Oh, are they coming . . ." but I'm just buying stuff. I'm not even with the violent people. I'm just coming to buy my stuff to get at the store. I'm going to get no problems, no problems with nobody. I just want to be a friendly person.

This dichotomy was central to the way Ariel interacted with others. He explained:

> I switch my attitude a lot, like, it depends on, like, if we chilling, and then if somebody say something dumb. I'm not a soft person, but I don't like people talking stuff to me, like, "Oh, you this . . ." I don't like people who do that. I tell people, like, don't do that because I would get mad fast, 'cause I don't like people talking to me.

The version of himself Ariel described here seemed miles away from the professional, charmingly awkward person I was talking to. Ariel told me, "I don't like to fight, but if people push me, I would fight. But I just love making new friends." This was a sentiment that I heard from several young men. That they wanted to be kind, but often felt like they had to use violence.

After we finished the interview, Ariel told me, with a proud smile on his face, "I answered the questions nicely." It was not clear if he meant that he answered the questions well, or with a friendly affect. Both were true. Several young men I met, when we concluded the interview, asked me how they did. They told me they were interested in being interviewed, in part, so that they could practice their interviewing skills. And it showed. Many of them were practiced, focused, and professional. Several of the young men, in particular young Black men, talked about their personal qualities during the interviews even though I did not ask. They described how friendly they were or how much they loved talking to people.

I walked away from my conversation with Ariel content to see him "on a good path" as he put it, but ultimately, unsure if I knew Ariel at all. He had managed to talk for nearly 45 minutes about himself and give little personal detail and avoided saying anything overtly critical. If I had been an adult with any authority in his life, I would have felt like Ariel's good path was maybe a bit narrower than he let on. But I was not an adult in his life, not in any consistent way. I, like many others, was a visitor and he had done exactly enough to send me on my way without questioning him or his future. It is difficult to know how intentional this was. If it was a strategy, it was an effective one. But regardless of intention, many young men pulled the narrative of healthy relationships into existing plots of positivity, friendliness, and transformation. To facilitators and on evaluations, and likely to administrators and probation officers, as well as other temporary adults, this certainly looked like meaningful change.

"Someone Is Bound to Hear My Story"

Alex and Arianna, two youth participants in a month-long intensive summer program, talked about the message of short-term programs they had participated in, giving the example of an anti-drug programs. Arianna said: "The other ones, just [say], 'Oh, be drug free!' You know, that's it. I'm like, talk to us more about it. Like, see what we have to say." Alex agreed: "They'll read off the book and then be like, 'Here you go. Any more facts?' And we're like, 'Really? Really, man?'" Arianna: "All they say is, 'Just don't do drugs.' 'Why?' ''Cause they're bad.'" According to Alex and Arianna, short-term programs discouraged young people from talking about their own experiences. Alex worried that young people would come to believe that no one wanted to hear their stories, which he believed could cause a string of problems: "Some of them won't tell their parents or nobody. So they'll keep it in. So they'll consider themselves worthless." This, Alex told me, would lead to depression, and disconnection from school. He continued, "They're pushed out, then. That's when she's like, 'Oh you know, screw this. They think of me this way. I might as well give them what they think.'"[38]

In contrast to the young people who experienced the new narrative of the curriculum in short-term programs, several of my interviews were with young men and women like Alex and Arianna who had participated in more extended programs with the organization, such as a year-long lunch club, or an intensive month-long summer institute. The young people in long-term programs were less likely to subsume the narrative of healthy relationships into gendered narrative projects of empowerment or change. Instead, they put the new narrative into motion in specific stories that they already had, and, more significantly, used them to make new stories. In these contexts, the forces of narrative entropy were limited and slowed. Rather than narratives colliding at high speeds, and fracturing, the narratives were consistently negotiated.

When I asked the youth in long-term programs if they were changed by participating, most gave clear and concrete examples of ways that they used something they had learned in the program in their lives. Arianna explained that she used to feel like there was nothing she could do when she saw abusive relationships. She recalls that a friend of hers was being stalked by her ex-boyfriend:

> I was like, "Oh you know, he loves you. Just don't worry about it." And she was like, "OK." And then when I did the—when I went through the POV thing, I—that's the first thing that I thought of. I was like, "Wow, I could have helped my friend." I don't know what's happening with her now. I was really scared for her. And I seen her again and it just kept—she told me that it was—it just kept going on and I was able to help her. And she got a restraining order against him because he was stalking her. And I just feel that POV has really opened my eyes to what I wasn't aware of. And it's really helped me help other people, and educate people at my school, teens, on what they can do to have a healthy relationship and maintain it.

Alex also described using the narrative to support his friends: "A lot of them are like, 'Oh, my mama's like that, so I might as well just . . .' I'm like, 'No, no, no, whoa, no, you're supposed to be better.' . . . I tell them, 'This is healthy and [that is] unhealthy.' If anything is happening, you better sit 'em down and talk to them and be like, 'This has to change.' So it's been a real help, because I felt useless."

Manny, who participated in a semester-long course led by POV facilitators at his school, told me about how the long-term program made a difference for him. Manny was not, in his words, a "guy that expresses what he feels and things like that," but simply having adults ask about his life— "how was your day, how do you feel, you know"—went a long way. He had tried psychiatrists and counselors, but never connected: "I wouldn't feel that that person was interested in hearing what I wanted to say—or that person really wasn't understanding me." The class was different though: "The words just flow, like, you don't have to hesitate to say things because you know that you're with people that understand you, and you're with people that can get you help, or you're with people that will try to understand you." This led Manny to reassess his own narrative, hoping it could help someone else: "Someone's bound to hear my story, or someone's bound to hear my name, and maybe who knows, to an extreme extent, [maybe] that can help them, and help them speak out, or help them feel that they're not alone." Manny had felt "real alone" when he was going through struggles at home and at school and he "wouldn't want someone to go through that." For Manny, this all helped him not just work through his own struggles, but to take the messages from the curriculum out into the world.

This narrative project required rewriting past stories. Take, for example, Arianna. Even though the program had given her confidence and led her to support friends, she still believed that the definition of harassment in the program was too narrow because it meant that her one-time boyfriend had harassed her. They were "on and off for a long time" and he texted her "constantly" asking to hang out. She would say no, and he would continue texting her. "I found out that that's like harassment and I didn't know that. But I was like, 'Wait, but he just wants to talk to me.' And—but they're like, 'No, that's harassment.' So little things like that can be labeled as harassment. And I'm like, 'Well, like, just little things like that?'" Disagreements like this, over whether or not some real-life event counted or not under the technical terms of the curricula, were common among this group. These were moments when they worked to make sense of the stories of the past through the new narrative of healthy relationships.

Randy, who had been in a violence prevention club for a couple of years, was 17 when I interviewed him fresh from football practice. He shook my hand, tightly, before and after the interview. Randy, in particular, had taken many of the messages of the program to heart and as a result, he explained, he was behaving differently and encouraging others to do the same. In particular, the program gave Randy the security and perspective to come out as bisexual to his football team: "I've been more open to people. I remember back in the summer institute we did this healthy sexual day or something like that, healthy sexuality. That was my realization that it was okay." One year later, he came out to his football team, who were "very supportive actually" and since then, Randy has been working to promote some of the central ideas of the curriculum on his campus and beyond. When I asked Randy what it meant, in his view, to be a real man, he explained: "There's no definition of a man any more. I guess, I'm a football player. Is that enough for me to be a man? I don't know. If people look at me in a different way because when I came out and stuff, that's on you, I really don't care."

However, Randy's understanding of violence was still complicated by his own story. While he worked against interpersonal violence with a club on campus, being a football player was a central part of his identity. I asked Randy how he reconciled his work against violence with his love of football. He explained that football is a form of violence, "but the thing is, there's consent. That's the nature of the sport." In this way, Randy rewrote one of the key themes of the program, that consent determines what counts as violence, and applied it to football.

Time and again, the young people in long-term programs worked through the program content and in doing so reconciled the struggles between the new narrative and their own lives. Alice, a campus club leader, for example, explained that the program helped "you understand how your relationship is unhealthy, when it's going." She noted the "red lights" game in particular: "They used to do visuals for, like, one is at yellow, one is at red you should stop . . . I felt POV helped me in a lot of ways about knowing how my relationship is going, things like that, when I'm in the yellow light of what I need to be fixing, what am I not doing right?" This even led Alice to apologize to her boyfriend for going through his computer. "I would do that, but I felt that I'm not doing right. And then I saw a lot of things that I say to him that's kind of abusing, and then I apologized. That's what I see in myself. And I said sorry to him later on. I said, 'Oh, you know, I joined this new POV thing, and I felt that I have done so many things wrong to you.'" However, when I asked Alice to say more, she revealed the limits of this discourse:

> I know my relationship is a red light, but I—but I love him so much, but it's a red light also . . . because we get like we have a lot of fights, I mean because I know, 'cause I'm trying to get it—to get it together. I know people telling me oh—we stayed in a long-distance relationship—don't be in it. You don't tell me what to do, OK, it's my relationship. I'm trying to, like, get it together. Like, it's been four and a half years, I'm here. I'm still trying to get a hold of it, and I know we have fights and things and, you know, I know we—you know, fight over phone and [do our] relationship over phone and that's hard, I know, but I'm still trying to have, like, the ending to be good.

Even as Alice showed a deep understanding of the narrative of healthy relationships and applied some of its lessons, she still struggled to reconcile it with her actual relationship. Her story was a work in progress.

. . . . .

It is alluring to believe, as programs often contend, that if given access to new and perhaps more effective cultural narratives, people will simply take them up and live by them. However, if we take stock of the narratives told by curricula within the social world of the stories we tell about ourselves and our institutions, such hopes cannot hold up. Instead, evidence of cultural change through short-term programs represents the incorporation of pieces of the program narrative into ongoing narrative projects that young people tell about themselves in relation to adults and the state. Despite our hopes, pervasive social problems cannot be met with a narrative cure. If you explain to someone how to live a better life, that will not cause them to take that story on as their own. It is, however, for the best that culture does not work this way. If narrative was as fleeting as curricula make it out to be, then new stories could come in, from basically anywhere, and in the course of a dozen hours change how people thought about themselves and the ones they love. Day-to-day life would be an endless volley played out at the whims of new narratives crashing into people and sending them off in unpredictable new directions.

Narratives can change, however, and power has a say in how they do. The state, as well as other institutions, can, with time and effort, nudge narratives one way or another. But they cannot do so with the flip of a switch or the turn of a phrase and they cannot change the past. It takes sustained engagement in people's lives to create narrative change. For this reason, even if one recognizes a behavior as unhealthy in the present, it seems unlikely to change one's narrative unless one is able to reconcile past experiences of that behavior in a new light. New narratives need not be rooted in lived experience, nor must they serve some rational function in order for them to stick. Instead, to persist, they must be incorporated into ongoing narrative projects.

Just because the healthy relationship narrative was undermined did not mean that the young people in my study were all in unhealthy relationships. Instead, they had to write their own stories about how to stay safe, happy, supported, and in love. We know very little about those narratives.[39] For many young people, violence was part of their story,[40] and out of everyday violence, a narrative began to emerge in the stories of youth.[41] When I asked young people where they believed violence came from, they told me that love and emotional support deterred violence and a lack of personal control over "negative emotions" caused it. Kashmir, for example, told me that most young people were not violent, and those who were needed more love and care: "It's some young people that's not getting love. That's what I think most violence comes from, not getting love, and nobody showing care for the person, so they're going to be violent, and not care about nobody else's feelings." I also often heard that violence was caused by young people not knowing how to manage the violence or trauma they were experiencing. Crystal said, of people who were violent, "They have problems, family problems or something, and just let it go on other people, and they don't know how to control their, they don't have anybody to, like, help them out." Manny, talking about other people his age, said: "A lot of times we think that it's just, I guess, me against the world, you know, it's like us taking on a bunch of problems that we have no control over. And we just think that oh, you know, well, we're stuck in here." Love, support, and agency—these were the key points of the story that young people told about preventing violence.

According to Finkelhor, the most common message in violence prevention curricula is to tell an adult if you or someone you know is experiencing violence. Eighty-eight percent of young people who had participated in violence prevention recalled that their program encouraged them to tell an adult.[42] However, just over a third (37 percent) of youth who participated in programming said they could think of a time they decided to tell an adult something "because of what they learned in the program." This gap points to a larger question: What is it about young people's experiences that leads them not to trust adults? The next chapter takes up that question.

6 The State of Adults

Hi, my name is Kelvin, and I'm 18 years old. At the start of my freshman year in high school I didn't feel close to anyone but my best friend. As we became closer, I soon realized our relationship grew unhealthy as I let him take advantage of me, both physically and mentally. I was psychologically damaged to the point where I felt suicidal and ended up in the hospital. If only someone had seen the signs: my grades declining and my constant depression. If only someone had talked to me I would have felt comfortable expressing myself so others could truly know and understand me.

I believe that a daughter's first role model should always be her mother. Mom, I needed you. I wish I had your presence in my life as a little girl to be aware of all the dangers in life. You were supposed to protect me. You needed to tell and show me the value in myself. To know how to let go of all the pain that life brings me. We were supposed to fight all of these battles together. The minute you decided to neglect me was the day I knew I was in this all alone, when it should have never been like that. Because of you I am now fragile but learning to grow thick skin. Not being able to ask for help or know the difference between right or wrong, your presence was strongly needed. My name is Shirley and I'm 16 years old.

For adults not to assume. For you to take us seriously. To not ignore the problem when it's right in front of your faces. For we are affected by the violence. We learn from it, it's all around us. We urge you to guide us. To listen. To act. For this is our world, too. And if you don't want to make change, then we will. But we're stronger if we stand together.

[Note: Transcribed from a YouTube video: Digital Storytelling, Youth Institute, Summer 2016]

·   ·   ·   ·   ·

To thrive, it helps when young people have a caring adult they can trust.[1] These connections can do a lot: stabilize an identity in the face of uncertainty, serve as a guide star in challenging times, ground one's long-term goals against more fleeting pursuits, and build up a reserve of self-worth to counter institutions that deny it.[2] Many young people, particularly in marginalized urban communities, do not have such a relationship. Not even one.[3] Prior research has looked to families and communities for these connections and found them wanting. Adults in marginalized communities hope to be there for the young people in their lives, but in the face of the time drains of inequality and precarious work and poor health, they fall short.[4] Rarely considered, however, are the adults with whom young people have their most substantial and frequent interactions: representatives of the state.[5]

The state looks different depending on where you are standing. For many adults the state is often experienced as faceless bureaucracies: voting booths, taxes, courtrooms, or the DMV.[6] Young people, however, rarely see the state from this angle. Instead, they experience the state in the form of individuals with whom they have regular contact: their teachers, school resource officers, administrators, and school counselors. On a strictly numerical basis, public education, even more than the legal system, is the most significant institution in which young people learn about their role in the state.[7] However, schools are not monotonous and monolithic bureaucratic institutions.[8] They contain heterogeneous cultural forms and meanings.[9] Adults in schools, accountable to a cacophony of distant mandates, carry out a complex and often contradictory mix of discipline, support, and apathy within close physical and temporal proximity. Young men and women who are marked as at risk may face disparate adults in even greater numbers, not only as the ephemeral state works away at reshaping them, but as police officers, specialists, and other adults churn through their lives in an endless cascade of interventions. While students that I encountered knew dozens of adults, few could name a person in their school that they felt connected to. When I asked about people who they could trust, some named older siblings. Most students I talked with did not name anyone. They often felt alone in places crowded with adults who insisted that they cared.

In this final empirical chapter, I step back from the ephemeral state and explore young people's interactions with the adults who represent the myriad pieces of the contemporary slow state. Even as the ephemeral state has taken over pockets of social policy, the slow state remains, albeit fractured and fragmented. Whereas most adults encounter street-level bureaucrats sporadically and thus as fickle and unfair representations of slow state authority, young people, particularly those marked as at risk, were in repeated close contact with specific adults acting as arbiters of different corners of the state.[10] Youth knew the state personally rather than interactionally.[11] This led them to make sense of the state not as a bureaucratic morass of rules and waiting, but as a series of fraught relationships and ties, shot through with disappointments, miscommunications, and long-simmering feuds. In an age of fracture, individual adults (and all their whims) carried with them whole systems of power, but the institutions they represented faded into the distance. As young people made sense of state systems of power, inequalities, and social control mechanisms through the lens of interpersonal relationships, institutional failures and fractures felt, intractably, like interpersonal troubles.[12] The meaning of governmental power took shape in the patterns of repeated interactions over time with individuals. I call this *policy in person*.

In the pages that follow, I recount the overlapping and often confounding messages of discipline, support, and personal responsibility in the lives of young people in a fractured state. In the daily social world of young people, discipline was ubiquitous, while support was distant. However, while they seemed to be everywhere, representatives of punitive power were also unpredictable; young people came to make sense of them through the lens of interpersonal relationships. They took policing personally. At the same time, although several individuals felt close with their school counselors, who represented support, young people were anxious about the role of supportive state institutions, and the interpersonalized surveillance they signaled. As a result, they avoided forming meaningful connections with supportive adults. Lastly, the logic of responsibility was pervasive, threaded through countless interactions and policies.[13] The

Figure 4. Schoolyard. Photo by author.

way that teachers and other adults talked about responsibility echoed through young people's interpersonal relationships with friends and family, often in gendered ways.

"HE DOESN'T SEEM TO CARE ABOUT US": DISCIPLINE

One glittering fall morning in a science class outside of downtown Los Angeles, junior and senior high school students banged their palms on their desks. One of their classmates, a young Latina woman in a large sweatshirt, was standing as she gave a fiery, often funny excoriation of the new principal. She explained that he showed no investment in the students, "He doesn't seem to care about us," then built to a crescendo, "He has to go!" Other students joined in, detailing the lack of working water fountains in the school and the perpetual absence of toilet paper. They were confident that this was intentional, but why was a mystery. The principal's logic of discipline and punishment in the school was so obscure and manipulative that they believed a lack of toilet paper and nonfunctional water fountains were penalties for some unexplained actions on their part. The facilitator nodded along throughout the discussion and, at the end, thanked the young woman for speaking up and asked what the class could do to raise awareness and make a change. "Nothing," sighed a boy, feet up on a chair at the edge of the room. Several others shook their heads in resignation. Nothing was ever done. The students could not think of a way to challenge the principal.

At a small charter school on the other side of town, students also dealt with the day-to-day frustrations of vague school disciplinary action. The security guard, a Black man in his 60s who used to be in the LAPD, mostly stood in one spot, but he would trail certain students in and out of the building. He would duck in and out of rooms, often silent with a fixed stare. One day, he watched me give out several bags of chips to young people. Several students I had never met had seen their friend with a bag and asked if they could have some and I obliged. The school officer walked with me through the front door and out to the sidewalk. "You see that lab rat mentality?" he asked, equating young people to animals responding to stimuli. "They're always looking for stuff," he told me. I shrugged and he continued, antipathy in his voice. He told me that students would hang around asking teachers for money for weed after school. He said the staff would not give it to them, but they waited around anyway. When he was a kid, his parents worked, and he "never took food from nobody," that was not how he was brought up, he told me. He sees these kids as having a "take what you can get" attitude, a laziness, and an unwillingness to work. I was confused by his description, and fairly sure he had missed something. I doubt that youth would seriously ask teachers for money for drugs. These two people—the principal and the school police officer—are fitting illustrations of the adults who represented discipline in schools. They were powerful and inconsistent actors in the lives of youth, often glimpsed briefly but persistently, in passing or across a large space. A principal over the loudspeaker, a school resource officer at the gate.

Los Angeles public schools are the kinds of places we talk about when we talk about how policing has spread into the daily life of communities and the institutions of civil society.[14] The Los Angeles School Police Department (LASPD) is one of the largest in the country, with over 470 on-site officers and a budget of $52 million.[15] During the 2011–12 school year, while I was in the field, LASPD police ticketed, cited, or arrested one out of every 100 students—8,993 in total—the highest rate in the country. Ninety-three percent of those tickets went to Black and Latinx youth. In addition to the documented statistics, students in LAUSD reported "widespread, random, and targeted searches of their person and bags, many schools going so far as to bring drug-sniffing dogs on campus. Intimidating posturing by officers in the halls. Handcuffing in front of peers, even for truancy. And . . . an ongoing form of profiling of the 'bad' students." When I first entered public schools in Los Angeles, these mechanisms of punitive discipline and surveillance stood out to me: the pervasive sense of being observed by security cameras, school resource officers with their arms folded, metal detectors looming over the entryway.[16]

Research on crime control in the lives of youth paints a picture of an overarching system of disciplinary control that is so embedded and synchronized that it reverberates beyond the youth who are disciplined, as the "ubiquity of the threat" of punishment dominates the daily life in schools.[17] In conversations with youth and facilitators, more than anything, the schools in Los Angeles were compared to prisons. Rob, a facilitator, described the impact of school policies this way: "We are invited in to classrooms where kids are basically prisoners, so we get to talk to the prisoners and that is very helpful actually." Rob's comment echoed the analysis levied by scholars—that urban schools are increasingly constructed in ways that parallel prisons. However, while schools borrowed architectural and disciplinary approaches from prisons, they were far from being overarching and all-powerful total institutions. Scholars often see the incursions of crime control into daily life as the broad overreach of a massive institution, which they certainly are. But they are also—from the perspective of young people at least—sporadic infringements and disruptions of the pleasures and trepidations of life as usual. Incidents of harsh school discipline were traumatic for students and families and happened far more often than necessary, but they were fundamentally fleeting and sporadic occurrences. Data on school discipline supports this. Although one percent of students were cited or arrested in a given year, in a school of 2,000 students, that works out to 20 students per year feeling the direct force of the legal system. The rest of young people took collateral impacts.[18] The lasting echoes of discipline could be found in stories that ricocheted through the halls and absences as the student at issue disappeared from the daily life of the school.

In all my time in schools across Los Angeles, I never witnessed police, administrators, or teachers using exclusionary punishment, issuing citations, or arresting students, nor did I witness any incidents that escalated to physical police involvement. This is not because the schools were models of calm and obedience. Youth, predominantly young men, often disrupted class time. Students called out "bullshit" during presentations. On multiple occasions, students advocated that sexual assault was justifiable or enjoyable. Others put their heads down, swung their backpacks at friends, or abruptly walked in and out of the room. Sometimes emotional events outside of class carried over into class and students were sad or angry. A half-dozen times during classes, small groups of young women gathered around an upset peer, seeming to provide support and ignoring the teacher. Other times, students were angry at their teacher or a classmate and made a show of acting out. While I saw multiple teachers take students into the hall and on a few occasions send them to the principal's office, I never saw a police officer engaging with a student as a criminal or suspect. This is not to say that this does not happen, but that it was rare to witness in daily life. In fact, school discipline, whether meted out by police officers or school officials, was largely invisible to me, as I imagine it would be to most outsiders. It is not surprising that school personnel would be on their best behavior while outsiders were present, a fact that highlights why it is important to listen to young people's accounts of discipline.

Outside of school, police interactions are regular parts of the lives of marginalized young people.[19] However, when we look closely, we see that the transformation of crime control in recent years is not a tidal wave of ubiquitous punitive control, but rather the multiplication and fracturing of crime control approaches within daily life. The young people in this study were consistently aware of the police, and they passed policing in pieces throughout their day: the patrol car on the corner on the way to school, the school resource officer approaching them on their way to the bathroom, or transit police on the metrolink bus to work after school.

When they came into contact with crime control, however, it was more likely to be confusing and frustrating than violent and dangerous, although they knew both were possible. This makes the spread of crime control no less concerning, but it does change how we should think about the consequences and interpret young people's responses to it. Most young people experienced discipline as ubiquitous only in that it felt like it happened in a wide range of places and synchronized only in that it felt like all adults were a part of it, but it did not feel cohesive, consistent, or logical.[20]

In schools, disciplinary representatives, such as school administrators and police officers, were more consistently present and socially closer than patrol officers in neighborhoods. Unlike police officers in community life, interactions between disciplinary authorities and youth in schools were persistent and often personal, but relatively few rose to the level of arrest or citation. While the threat of punishment was common, the enactment of it was sporadic. In this way, discipline in schools was personal in that the adults who enacted it were present in daily life, and they rarely felt like "police" or authorities as much as individuals with a badge or power, some of whom young people knew well. They also represented, albeit only in a limited way, additional mandates of support and safety, not just control. To put it another way: many young people knew the name and face of the representative of institutional discipline who was most present in their lives. They saw them nearly every day.

Rates of arrests and citations at schools populated by Black and Latinx students, while stunning markers of criminalization of young men of color, only tell us part of the story of policing. Police action in schools largely took the form of intimidating posturing and profiling or a persistent if vaguely detached presence. During one class at a sprawling concrete campus, a teacher read a statement from the principal following a fire alarm. The letter emphasized how great the students are at the school, except for the "one bad apple" who set a fire. After reading it aloud, the teacher added his own addendum: "So if you did it, they will find you. You will be arrested. They have cameras now." Despite pervasive threats, I found that in most schools, aggressive teasing, pushing, sexual harassment, bullying, and play fighting were rarely met with clear or consistent disciplinary action. Many students knew well how to avoid discipline, seeking out hidden spaces on campus, evading adults' questions and investigations, and expressing persistent confusion over rules and laws. In addition, many school officials dreaded and resisted the incursion of crime control into schools.

Young people's interactions with disciplinary adults diverged along gender lines. In schools and neighborhoods, young men were more likely to interact with police officers in the course of their daily lives. Young women, on the other hand, were funneled toward the offices of school administrators and, on occasion, police. Even though these interactions did not always lead to punitive disciplinary action, they informed how young people understood institutional authority.

Young Men, Crime Control, and School Police

Alan, 16 and Latino, was in a Reebok T-shirt and khakis, hair dappled with product and pushed back. As we talked he wriggled in his chair, bouncing his leg, smiling and nodding. Alan told me about his first run-in with the police and how that changed the way he related to officers. He was out with a few friends who were spray-painting graffiti. "I was a good boy at that time," he explained, so when the police came, and his friends ran, he stayed. One officer, "he was a dick," handcuffed him and one of his friends who is Black. They were rough on both of them. They dropped Alan's friend to the ground, "kneed him to the floor." The police told the young men that they knew they had a knife and later, weed, and they pressured them to come clean. Alan was confused; they only had the spray cans. They were arrested and Alan spent two days in jail. Since then, Alan has distrusted police officers: "I don't hate them—but it's just, I just felt like that shouldn't be happening to kids, you know . . . they can't be abusing us the way they did . . . even if I was with a group that was doing something bad." The week before we talked, Alan had gotten in a fight and the school police officer was there but had not gotten involved. Alan was suspended, but the police officer did not touch him. He had to spend increased time with the school counselor, who encouraged him to pursue an internship with Peace Over Violence. Alan's two run-ins with the police highlight how discipline could be experienced differently within and outside of schools.

Sociologist Carla Shedd has described the paradox of policing in many urban schools, marked simultaneously by criminalization and protection.[21] Angel, a young Latino man, provided a clear example as he explained how his experiences with police impacted how he related to them across spaces: "Sometimes you feel like a little crumb and sometimes they like give you a reason not to like them. Like, well, like last time at my house, like they just came, just got us, red lights, put handcuffs on us in front of, in front of my mom for no reason." I asked him how he felt about that. "It makes you feel like you got no protection and you can't call nobody for it," he responded. A few minutes later, in a seemingly paradoxical turn, Angel told me that the only place he really felt safe was at school because of the police presence: "There's security so that you always have somebody to watch your back or to do something about this or that situation going on." Young men appreciated the modicum of protection afforded by police and endured the profiling and intimidation that sometimes came with it.

For many young men, their experiences with policing occurred along a continuum of harassment and abuse that had no clear connection to legal concerns and instead felt personal. Outside of the school, policing was often enacted as a flashpoint system of sporadic physical and verbal harassment, backed by the implied threat of violence and incarceration. Several of the young Black and Latino men I spoke with described instances of abusive and violent police encounters outside of school. Joe, who was on probation after a teacher called the police while he was play fighting at school, was stopped by police a few days before our interview. He and his brother had heard there was going to be a fight and went to watch. The fight never happened because the police showed up. They knew Joe and his brother:

> The police talked to my brother, and then they put our hands on our head, and we're talking and the dude asks me, "Am I still on probation?" "Yes, I'm still on probation." The dude said, "I'll violate your ass and send you back to jail." And my brother was like, "Don't you say that to my brother." He said, "You got no evidence, so you shouldn't be threatening him so you can violate him for nothing." And so they put my brother back in the police car, and then, they was just talking to him and they let me go, then I was waiting for him, for the police, and it was like, "If we catch you guys, like, going to any kind of fight or anything, we're just going to lock you up." We said, "Well, how you goin' to lock us up, it's our right to do whatever we want." . . . And the dude, he was all like, "You're going to jail." We said, "OK, you know, you're not going to catch us, we're not doing nothing."

This back and forth illustrates how interactions with police, though tinged with threats and lopsided power, could take on the tone of interpersonal arguments, rather than the force of law and policy. When I asked Joe, who is Black, if he would call the police in the event of an emergency, he said no. "I can't trust the LAPD, I can't trust the school police, because the school police, they're just, like, trying to set you up for anything." In this way, interactions with police outside of school echoed through social interactions with adults and friends in school. Joe's mother and brother helped him navigate the tricky terrain: "My mom, she tells me, don't do certain things, like, there's people watching you." His older brother would stand up for Joe if he felt like people were "messing with" him, concerned that if Joe were to "fight and get caught," he would "go to jail for three years, and that's not right, because that's just taking away [my] freedom." In order to avoid these risks, Joe told me, "I just kick it with my brother, because mostly I know, if I'm with my brother, I'm safe." But Joe's concerns went beyond police and peers. He told me that he could not trust most teachers: "Like, every teacher, like, when I get in trouble they [say they will call my] probation officer, and I'll be like, 'Why you got to tell my probation officer, that's threatening me, basically, like, you're trying to get me locked up.'" When Joe's mother confronted the teacher about this tactic, the teacher said, "Well, I just tell him that so he can actually do better in class." It seemed that everywhere Joe went, he was met with adults who not only threatened him, but knew him.

One of the most significant distinctions between police inside and outside of school was that in school young men had sustained interactions with the same law enforcement officials over time. The school police officers in young people's lives often knew them, their friends and families, their courses and habits. But while this changed the way youth experienced police, it rarely improved the relationship. John, a Latino youth with a thick build, explained that a school police officer whom he saw daily at the metal detector consistently harassed him. John told me that, recently, the same officer suspended him for talking back after accusing him of tagging:

I'm like, "Whoa, whoa, bro, I just got out of the bathroom. Are you serious?" Then he's like, "Oh, you're giving me attitude." I'm like, "Dude, I'm not doing

[that]." And then that's when he comes over, "Detention." Then he was like, "Oh, I'm suspending you." I'm like, "What? What? Why? I just got out of the bathroom, man." [It was] for talking back, they take it as willful defiance.

John believed that the presence of police for so-called random searches enabled them to profile and police specific individuals. He explained, "He knows I'm coming through that gate. So he pulls me aside. Random, sure, 50 people just passed and automatically you stop me? Smart. Then I'm like, 'Dude, I don't want to go to school and get searched every freaking week.'" Because interactions with school police were persistent and personal, filled with exchanges over time about the ongoing nature of one's life, they did not feel like the actions of monolithic institutions of social control.

During one classroom discussion about forms of power and control in their lives, a small group of Black and Latino young men on probation for various crimes, including robbery and assault, listed parents, teachers, the president, the principal, and police. One Black young man, Wayne, shook his head vigorously at the mention of police and said forcefully, "The police don't have power." Wayne's argument, that police lack power because they lack respect, was surprising coming from a young man embedded in the probationary wing of the juvenile criminal system. Two other students nodded and several spoke up to disagree. Another young man, Oscar, tried to clarify, saying, "No one *respects* them, but they still have that *badge*." This formulation, which satisfied Wayne and the others, boils down to a tension between interpersonal relationships and institutional ones, and the blurry overlap between them in the worlds of youth. For most of the young men I talked to, they made sense of school police using what they knew about interpersonal relationships. Police were fickle and petty, demeaning and disrespectful, and sometimes, caring. Police officers were rarely, however, seen as representatives of social institutions or enforcers of hierarchy or symbols of state power.

Young Women and Administrators

Few young women had the types of interactions with police officers that young men had, and as a result, they had more trust and respect for them. Take, for example, Valeria, who told me that she had been "acting up" in middle school but was turned around by a police officer: "I was just being a rebel. And I got into the gang life. I got into all that wannabe chola stuff. It was just a bad experience. I actually got caught in Rite Aid stealing." Valeria's mother took Valeria to a police officer for an intervention. Valeria recounted what the officer said:

> "If you really want to be a rebel and you think you got balls, then act it. If you really want to do this, you know, I could put you behind bars at this instant, if you really think you're gangster enough." So I thought about my future. And I thought about my mother. And I told her, "I do not want that life. I want something better."

Many young women were ambivalent about police. Ceil, who had not interacted with police, was "suspicious": "I'm not necessarily like, oh, I completely trust them or I don't trust them at all . . . I like them only when they come in time to help." Ciel's friend Rose expressed a similar sentiment, weighing various encounters with police:

> I mean, I've definitely met police officers that I can really like. I really like them and they're genuine good people, but . . . I think it has to do with the fact that people with power scare me, but it's just giving so much power to people . . . I've only met, like I said, a few officers who haven't taken it to such levels where they think that they're better than everybody else.

However, while Rose liked most police officers even though she had heard stories of police abusing their power, she had what felt like countless negative personal interactions with administrators and teachers: "At my old school it was really like, literally, I would ask a question in school, and I would get kicked out. And I'm saying that as being, like, truthful."

While male students described their interactions with police officers, female students were far more likely to talk about their interactions with school administrators. Young women of color in schools and educational organizations across Los Angeles faced a different social landscape than young men of color. They were less likely to be surveilled, policed, and disciplined, and instead were more often ignored or lectured, seen as helpless, dependent, or at risk for teen pregnancy.[22] Still, some aspects of the experience were similar: the whims of administrators did not feel like

institutional forces; instead, to youth, they felt like the actions of specific,
petty adults who they saw briefly every day.

Encounters with administrators rarely led to interactions with police,
and instead often took the form of futile investigations and circular
debates. When young women fought, bullied, or otherwise broke school
policy, they largely did so away from administrators.[23] This put administrators in the position of needing informants and interrogations in order
to discipline students. In eighth grade, Flora's friend was "trying to bully a
sixth grader" and Flora was there. Several days later, the dean called Flora
and her friend to the office and threatened to call their parents. Flora
explained to the dean that she "didn't do anything" and asked the dean to
respond to the bullying that she herself was experiencing. From there, the
conversation quickly fell apart.

> I'm like, "I'm not doing it and I'm being bullied and you're not doing any-
> thing to them." And he started like telling me like, "You know what? You
> should learn English." I'm like, "I just came, how am I supposed to like speak
> English if I just came here?" [He said,] "Like, well I have a cousin that just
> came and in 30 days he just speaks English."

The conversation with the dean, in Flora's telling, quickly descended into
taunts and counterclaims. Often, young women experienced this kind of
language and harassment from administrators. I never witnessed this
behavior directly, but it was a frequent aspect of young women's stories,
signaling a persistent pattern of gendered and raced misrecognition.
These incidents were rarely joined with punishment, and far more often
the insults served as the end of the interaction. This story and others like
it made administrators look less like a concerted and powerful system and
more like a group of people justifying institutional failures with appeals to
personal responsibility and reactive disciplinary policies.

Young women often experienced—and navigated—these interactions
as marked by race and gender. Take for example the story recounted by
Misty, a Bangladeshi young woman. Because graffiti is heavily policed,
when Misty brought paint to school to decorate T-shirts with handprints,
she found herself in the line of discipline, as school administrators questioned her about the paint. She told me, "I had it and I was like, 'I don't

know about that.' And they're like, 'You're gonna get in big trouble.' And these girls lied for me, they're like, 'Oh, it's this little Black boy running around.'" Misty avoided punishment relatively easily. Young women learned that blaming others, particularly by calling up racialized and gendered anxieties and stereotypes, was a way to protect themselves from discipline. Young men of color, unsurprisingly, did not experience discipline in the same way. Young men were consistently worried that they would be blamed and punished for things they had not done.

The young women who had multiple interactions with administrators and the young men who had frequent interactions with the police were toward the far end of a continuum of contact with school discipline. Most young people were at the other end and had fleeting disciplinary interactions or none at all. But all young people were familiar with, and to a large extent accustomed to, the presence of disciplinary control in their lives. However, as I have shown, these forms of discipline were largely experienced as the actions of petty and power-hungry individuals. This undercut any meaningful institutional message that adult authorities may have hoped their actions would send to youth.

"AUTOMATICALLY SHE'S GOING TO GO, YOU KNOW, SNITCH": SUPPORT

School counselors—the most visible representatives of state support in schools—seemed to be everywhere at once and nowhere for very long. I interacted with one counselor nearly two dozen times—I could recognize her walk around the corner—but we never said more than two sentences to each other while trying to track down a particular young person or find an open room. Despite this impermanence, the few youth who knew their counselors described them as reliable and trustworthy.[24] Steven, a shy and consistently frustrated Latino junior, told me who he trusted at school: "At school, my counselor. She knows a lot about me." I asked Valeria one thing she would do to reduce violence in her school and she told me: "I would recommend a lot of counseling. A lot of people to talk to." The role of school counselors has changed over the last several decades, from social-emotional support to college counseling and program management. And there are far fewer of them. In 2013, there was just one school counselor for every 1,016 students in Los Angeles schools.[25]

In place of school counselors, a parallel system of support at a distance has taken hold. Mandated reporting laws govern most adults who work with youth, including all school employees, law enforcement officials, any certified health professional, religious leaders, and more. These rules require them to report to appropriate authorities if they suspect abuse or neglect so that youth can be guided toward the appropriate therapeutic support. The by-product of this system was an evolving, personalized surveillance record much like Foucault described, as it "places individuals in a field of surveillance [and] also situates them in a network of writing; it engages them in a whole mass of documents that capture and fix them" intended to mark students' status in relation to a standard of conduct in order to normalize behaviors.[26] What makes this system different from the one Foucault described, though, was that it was carried out by the adults responsible for caring for youth, the ones they saw every day.

Mandated reporting and surveillance was glaring to students as an institutional policy and it sent messages to young people, many of whom were already distrustful of authority. First, it signaled that the person in front of them was not trusted to handle situations on their own, and second, that most nondisciplinary adults' loyalty rested with institutional authorities. To students, this positioned mandated reporters as neither a trustworthy adult, nor as representatives of a supportive institution. One school counselor told students that if a friend was experiencing violence, they should go to an authority figure. But then she paused, and clarified that sometimes that may lead to more violence. Then she paused again before moving on, leaving that paradox unresolved. Ms. F, a veteran gym teacher with spiky blonde hair, spoke with authority as she emphasized the gravity of sexual violence, focusing on the fact that "someone in this room definitely has experienced it." Then she paused and explained that as a mandated reporter she has had to report violence, and one time that led to a child being "taken away from his or her family on Thanksgiving," implying that students should not disclose unless they want a similar fate. She seemed to repeatedly get caught in a bind, saying both that she knew someone was experiencing violence and that she did not want to know if they were, because then she would have to report it, but also, that reporting was always good. Another teacher explained to me: "I don't think that mandated reporting is benign. I think that it does suck people up in particular ways but I also think that there are real moments where we need something bigger than what a teacher or a school or family can figure out. For me, it's not a particularly clean answer." Young people picked up on this ambivalence.

The majority of young women I interviewed were worried that the adults with whom they interacted most frequently would talk to others about their personal lives. Young men rarely seemed to care, perhaps because they felt pressure not to discuss their feelings or because they already felt watched. Young women felt this way despite the fact that very few reported that they had been implicated in the mandated reporting process. Leah, for example, was frustrated by the possible ramifications of mandated reporting rules: "Like, you know, the person is going to feel kind of like, whoa, like I just told her this. It was really hard for me to tell her this and automatically she's going to go, you know, snitch. So it makes you feel like I'm not going to tell anyone anything anymore."[27] Leah was adamantly against "snitching" except in extreme circumstances, like murder. I pushed Leah to explain how mandated reporting was like snitching, and she explained it using another example of institutionalized monitoring often felt by marginalized youth:

> I don't like when I walk into a store and because I'm Black they think I'm going to steal something and they like walk around and be like, you know, like that's annoying. Like that's the kind of monitoring that I feel like automatically, oh, you're assuming, you know. And that makes me feel some kind of way because I'm far from that ... There's a way that you can monitor people where they don't feel uncomfortable and they feel like you're not discriminating against them or like, you know, making them feel little, less than.

At the time, I could not see the connection Leah was making. Following a young Black woman around a store seemed clearly an act of racial profiling enacted by a stranger, while mandated reporting was, in my mind, an act of protection by a trusted adult. But I came to see things from Leah's perspective. To her, both were forms of intensive monitoring by authorities based in part on assumptions about her race. In both cases, she

distrusted the institutions involved to make fair reports. And in both, surveillance observed, recorded, and analyzed what, to her, were personal
matters.

I came to realize that the full scope of the challenge posed by the distance to social support was not only that it threatened to show young people, often not for the first time, that institutions would predictably fail
them. It also posed a powerful threat to their conception of self. Leah was
not primarily concerned about being arrested. It was the racialized injury
to her identity that was the heart of her analogy. She felt like she was being
watched because she was Black and was made to feel less-than. In this
way, personal surveillance differs in its impact from punitive surveillance.
To be watched is to risk injuries to one's identity.

In order to understand young people's anxiety around telling about
their lives, it is necessary to understand how it is distinct from their fear of
being caught breaking a rule. Glenn Greenwald, a journalist who writes
about governmental surveillance programs, has argued that surveillance
matters not only because it can catch individuals doing something wrong,
but because it brings much of the hidden work of constructing a sense of
self into the open to be judged and critiqued.[28] This is particularly important for young people, who are testing out versions of themselves. I call the
monitoring of individuals over time and across contexts by people who
one knows, *interpersonalized surveillance*.[29] Understanding the impact
of and resistance to interpersonalized surveillance is vital to understand
what is happening in schools.

The majority of students I interviewed were far more anxious about the
prospect of adults they knew reporting things told in confidence about
their personal lives, even in order to gain access to support, than about the
securitized legal-system approach to surveillance. As Ciel put it, "I don't
think it's right that they can, like, just like look you up and they know everything about you." To some extent, young people feared that disclosing
opened them up to disappointment. Kashmir, a young Black woman, captured this general sentiment when she explained, "A lot of people might
have stuff done to them and nothing changed about the situation. [So]
they're scared to tell [authorities] about it." This disappointment was
rooted in the fact that people they knew and trusted instead had acted as
vectors of interpersonalized surveillance.

Students were consistently worried about interpersonalized surveillance, including within programs. This surveillance did not document wrongdoing or rule breaking, but thoughts, attitudes, beliefs, and habits. That is, it operated and was contested not on the valence of justice and law, as policing is, but on the valence of identity. For example, even though students were informed that pre- and post-surveys were anonymous, youth often asked skeptically if they had to write their name and what would be done with the survey, expressing concern that the survey would be attached to their record. On one survey a student wrote in capital letters "I KNOW YOUR WATCHING" across the top. That student was right. Facilitators, as well as teachers and administrators, hoped to draw insights from observing student's personal responses to surveys, as well as their interactions with teachers, peers, and counselors.

Alice in Trouble

Alice, a Muslim young woman who had been through the experience of mandated reporting, confirmed many of the fears I heard about the system. Outside her school library, wearing a bright red headscarf that rippled in the wind, Alice explained how she moved to the United States in eighth grade. She felt that media representations of Muslims as terrorists had already put her "under a lot of pressure" to behave perfectly while at school and she was very isolated. She told me: "I have gotten in trouble several times with the school when I felt depressed and I actually told a friend, a teacher, that I really trust that I'm feeling like that I need to end myself or something. Then I got in trouble badly." Her parents came to school for a conference and she was assigned "a, like, counselor or psychiatrist" who "was talking to me every single Tuesday," even though Alice did not believe that she needed the counseling. "I'm just, like, 24 hours monitored, you know, I'm in trouble." Alice, as well as her mother, found that working with the counselor relieved some anxiety. But, Alice's wording is telling. She understood the interventions as "trouble" and she felt "monitored" around the clock.

From Alice's position, any formal intervention by adults designated a kind of trouble, even if those interventions were meant to be supportive. Alice explained why she saw it as monitoring:

The school organized this person to talk to me. That means they're getting records for me every single day. From the health office there are people that look at all my records, what am I doing, how my grades are, attendance, so they report it to the organization that the psychiatrist [is] from and then they communicate and I feel that I'm really watched like, you know. I feel whatever I'm doing here this and that like whatever I'm doing even if I'm just there in front of the camera over there just putting something in my backpack. I'm being watched like seriously, because I've been in trouble because they always feel like oh, I'm gonna kill myself, you know?

Although it is unlikely that this was the outcome that the school wanted to invoke with its engagement with Alice, she still felt betrayed: "I thought that whoever I spoke to would keep it to herself. But, you know, they expressed it to everyone. Now everybody's like: 'You might not hurt yourself, you might hurt someone else,' you know, I would never do that." For Alice, talking to an adult was disastrous for her social relationships and sense of self, even as everyone involved did exactly what they were supposed to do. Alice only wanted to talk to her teacher about what was going on, to share her experience and maybe get advice. In this way, she was like the vast majority of the young people I talked to who wanted, badly, to seek counsel from a trusted adult. It is worth reiterating that nothing Alice did was wrong, nor was the school's response a punitive one. Instead, it was the mandated reporting function of the school, and the way it refigured Alice's social relation with a once-trusted adult, that ultimately lead to Alice's distrust.

In response, Alice changed her behavior in order to avoid being reported again: "I try to act not myself in this school. I try to act as polite as I can, you know, not to express anger or anything. Even if I'm like mad or something I wouldn't cry or anything, you know. Don't make a drama queen out of it." Alice explained that she felt this way everywhere, and that there was nowhere she felt like she could be herself. The ramifications for Alice, then, are distinctly rooted in the realm of her behavior and selfhood. She learned that school was not a place that she could be herself, because if she did, others would be watching and taking note.

As Alice's story shows, young people, particularly young women, experienced interactions with the supportive arm of the state as "trouble," but not in the form of punitive action. Instead, the trouble was the sensation of being constantly assessed and measured, largely in relation to one's race and gender. While few young people had been pulled in by mandated reporting, Alice's experiences echo the fears I heard from many. Telling adults about one's own lived experiences was a fraught enterprise, shaped by distrust and fear. The young people I talked to about disclosing put it in personal terms—they wanted a person to "tell"—someone to talk about what they were going through—not a representative of the state.[30]

In order to understand why support could feel so distant, it is helpful to understand how young people experienced adults along a continuum between close social ties and distant institutions. Cleo, 18, who identifies as "Black with a little Cherokee," had long wavy black hair, parted in the middle. Since her dad passed away years earlier, her mother and siblings had found solace in the church. Cleo liked "helping people out" and her compassion for others was clear: "When I was in school, I always gave my counselor hugs, and everything, and it always made her feel better. And then when, like, one of my friend were crying, I guess or when someone was crying, she was, like, 'go to Cleo.'" Like many young people, particularly young women, Cleo found meaning in supporting others in the wake of trauma and loss. Inspired in part by the relationship and guidance from her counselor, Cleo planned a career in care work. She hoped to become a child psychologist; she told me, "That's my thing, children and dogs."

Although Cleo was caring and supportive to those around her, she was deeply skeptical of institutions. This was clear in Cleo's description of the government's role in her life: "So much [of the] things that's going on in the world, it's crazy, like, I just feel, like, government has a lot to do with everything . . . Like with media, with different jobs, and just the whole women and men kind of thing, but then, it goes back, way back in history. So that's where everything really started." As Cleo's description suggests, she believed that the government had far-reaching control, from the media to the economy to gendered violence. I asked Cleo to tell me more about how she believed the government enacted this power:

> They keep secrets, a lot of secrets. So I don't know what the government is really planning. I try not to really, to me I don't really try to focus on it too much, but I know the government has, like, a lot of things, like, I—I know it's some law that I heard about. It's called, it starts with an M, but supposedly, I guess, like, whoever is out at night gets shot up.

Cleo heard about this from her boyfriend, who had found out about it on the internet, along with evidence of "one-point-something billion gravesites," for those targeted by this law. As I wound down this line of questioning, Cleo's smile and sunny demeanor fell away and her posture slumped. She looked past me and trailed off: "I don't—I don't know. It's like twisted stuff." She paused and looked around the room and bit her lip. "What?" I asked. She responded in a whisper, her eyes darting around the room, "Because we're talking about the government." She was nervous.

I heard a variety of governmental conspiracy theories from many of the young people that described powerful forces operating out of view. Rather than treat these as pure myths, I suggest that they signal the fear and distrust that run through the lives of many marginalized young people. Many of the young people I talked with believed the government to be a tightly controlled and powerful force in their lives and this made them anxious. They were right, in part, but the government was also made up of many of the people she interacted with regularly. Cleo, like most of the young women I talked to, didn't think of her interactions with teachers or police as direct interaction with representatives of the government. She had a few brief interactions with police, and while the officers were slow to respond to a neighbor's call, they were neither incompetent nor malicious. She had a great deal of respect for authority figures, such as teachers, and for her elders. Ready access to conspiracy theories on the internet, coupled with distant and often inexplicable actions by institutions, created a sense of anxiety about the government and led Cleo, among others, to distrust public institutions even as she felt emotionally close to those working within them. From this angle, it is easier to understand how young women could seek out support from close adults but be put off by support that involved institutions on a larger scale. Proximity could enable trust. However, that trust could be undermined if adults reported on the personal lives of young people.

"CHOICES, IT'S ALL ABOUT CHOICES": RESPONSIBILITY

"Choices, it's all about choices," the teacher, a woman in a dark blue tracksuit, said in an aside to Joseph, a young facilitator. She sighed loudly and shook her head. She had just informed the class that if they behaved they would have fewer circuits to run later. In the short 50 minutes of the class, the teacher had called upon students to take responsibility in some form multiple times: attendance, doing their homework, listening, coming forward if you know someone who is being assaulted; these things all fell on young people alone in her telling. They were choices. At one point, she recounted a story. As a teenager, she saved up all her money and bought a bike. She rode it home from the store and tucked it by the stairs of her family's apartment while she made a sandwich. When she got back, it was gone. This, she explained, was her poor choice and there was no one to blame but herself. The same went for their homework, she told them. If someone stole it, that was your responsibility. In a couple of weeks, I thought to myself, the program will cover victim-blaming.

As Joseph started in on the day's unit, a wiry boy with a shag of black hair began to talk and turn his chair around and around. I asked what he was talking about and he shot a look toward his friend and said "rape" four times loudly and then looked to the teacher. She motioned for him to go outside. He did and she followed. When he returned, he sat in the front row, his eyes locked on Joseph. During the discussion of the cycle of abuse, a boy in the back, who "didn't think right" according to the girl next to him, called out, "Maybe people stay because they like the abuse." It was their choice. Joseph said that he has never met anyone who liked to be abused. Another boy yelled out from the back, "I do." The teacher had him stand up and went out to the hall with him. He came back a few minutes later and was quiet for the rest of the session.

Personal responsibility shadowed marginalized young people everywhere on school grounds.[31] It was threaded through school mottos, informal school contracts, loudspeaker announcements, and most of all, through the words of teachers. Teachers, aside from everything else that they do, are the most consistent representations of social policy in the lives of young people.[32] Teachers managed their classes in a variety of ways, but most of them relied on calls for responsibility in one form or another. Sometimes those calls were paired with threats of punishment or the promise of reward, but they were nearly always blunt and morally tinged appeals.[33] In particular, responsibility was used in response to a middle range of social and institutional infractions. Major breaches were met with disciplinary interventions, but for the bulk of daily infractions, personal responsibility was the central and pervasive logic for managing behavior in schools.[34] Taking responsibility, in some ritual or fleeting form, came with the promise of access to institutional support or at least shelter from scrutiny.

More than anything, it seemed, adult authorities wanted young men of color to "take responsibility"—a phrase that implies that, at the moment, it belongs to someone else. When faced with minor infractions, these adults said things like "take responsibility for your actions" or "your actions have consequences." Although it may feel like common sense, responsibility—which today most often means personal responsibility—is a political strategy (most effective political strategies feel like common sense).[35] Responsibility—for both harm and safety—has been shifted from government and communities onto individuals through a process that scholars call responsibilization.[36] Rose argues that people are not born free, but rather are

> "obliged to be free and [are] required to conduct themselves responsibly, to account for their own lives and their vicissitudes in terms of their freedom. Freedom [is] not opposed to government. On the contrary, freedom, as choice, autonomy, self-responsibility, and the obligation to maximize one's life as a kind of enterprise, [is] one of the principal strategies of . . . advanced liberal government."[37]

Young people are told repeatedly and fervently that they can make free choices as long as they make the right choices.

We can picture the politicians railing against the epidemic of irresponsibility among young people (almost always youth of color) and their proclamations that youth need to learn responsibility; that if we teach them, they will recognize inherent flaws in how they have lived, in the choices they have made, and correct their course. Those politicians may be surprised to learn that their message, repeatedly at the heart of debates in politics and academia, has won out resoundingly. In the classrooms of Los Angeles, everyone seemed to believe in personal responsibility: not only teachers and administrators, but youth.[38] Despite what politicians might claim, the young people I talked to had received the message that they should be responsible loud and clear and they agreed. Young people took responsibility for the problems in their lives and espoused their capacity to handle problems on their own. This logic made sense given the unreliable adults who represented disciplinary and supportive arms of the state. It felt reasonable to only rely on yourself when police were unpredictable and the adults responsible for your care and support might snitch on you. And there was plenty to take responsibility for, as many of the things that troubled those politicians remained, regardless of the giving and taking of responsibility.

Although it did little to combat systemic inequality, the message of personal responsibility reverberated through young people's social ties with friends and loved ones. Both young men and women projected the need for responsibility onto those around them, easily arguing that most negative consequences in the lives of their friends and peers was a result of their own bad choices. This cut off valuable avenues for support at the moments when they would need it most. I saw this clearly when I asked young people about their goals for the future and what, if anything, stood in their way. Their responses revealed how responsibility limited their connections, but also, how it was gendered. Men often said that they themselves or their friends were the risks and liabilities that kept them from a "good path." Women told me that nothing stood in their way, and that if others were not empowered, that was their own fault. Faced with unrelenting messages of responsibility from adults, young men and women developed their own ways of using responsibility to make sense of those closest to them, which had unexpected interpersonal consequences.

"My Biggest Obstacle Is Myself:" Young Men Taking and Placing Responsibility

With personal responsibility comes the promise of a "brighter future." Angel explained that school "got me focused on like, on my future . . . I'm proud of being Hispanic and young. 'Cause like, I got the chance to become what I want, not like my parents did." Angel's parents, he explained, "had no choice," they had to "work and take care of us, but . . . we can have a bright future ahead of us." Hendrix told me: "Everyone's equal. Everyone has the same opportunities. Anyone can do anything. Just 'cause I come from this doesn't mean I can't be up top like in Beverly Hills, you know?" At first, I thought Hendrix was telling me that he wanted more equality and better opportunities, but the case he was trying to make was that he already had equal opportunity and that he should not be underestimated. Or as Hendrix put it, "anyone can do anything."[39] Responsibility, seemingly, was all it took.

Many of the young men I talked to looked to be the epitome of responsibility, even in situations that made it nearly impossible to get by. Zephire took a bus one hour each way to and from his high school in South Los Angeles, so I was grateful when he agreed to stay after class to talk with me. He wore a camo zip-up with black athletic pants and had a practiced but winning confidence and a smile that came and went quickly. He spoke with an off-kilter meter that belied an imposed adulthood. He was 20 years old when we talked and identified as "mixed: my mother is from Trinidad and Tobago; my father is American from Chicago." Like many of the youth I talked with, Zephire and his family moved often as his mother struggled to make rent and to find a safe place to live. His parents divorced when he was four, and "it was one week my father, next week my mother back and forth, back and forth, back and forth" until Zephire's father moved to Chicago to take care of his ailing grandmother. He told me he disliked Compton; it was hard to fall asleep with the sirens at night: "The violence, the gangs, the life: I just really didn't like it there. Like the kids, they were rude, kind of rude to me. Like they [gave] no respect to each other." Some students bullied him and he joined the Cadet Corps: "I was trying to get away from all that." Zephire spent much of his youth plotting his escape from one bad situation after another.[40]

Always the new kid, Zephire longed to make friends. "In middle school I didn't really have many friends. Those that were my friends I didn't really consider them friends. I was kind of antisocial. I was always trying to show off, or whatever. If I got something new I'd always try to show off just to win acceptance." One year, his dad bought him a small "ninja knife," which he brought to school. One of his classmates did not believe him that the knife was real and tried to take it away from Zephire, drawing the attention of school officials. "Teachers came in, parents were called in, and I was expelled from the Compton district simply for having that at school."[41] Zephire, as he often did in our conversation, put a positive spin on a tough situation. "That was actually a good thing because if I didn't have it I would have most likely stayed in Compton up until high school, and I don't think my life would have been any better than it is now." He accepted his expulsion and he moved up to Boyle Heights, which "really changed my life," he told me. There was "no bullying, I made friends real fast and then they showed me the difference, how different life in Compton is compared to other parts of the world." While he made new friends, pressure from his family made focusing on schoolwork difficult. "I was expected to be like my dad," he told me. Zephire framed his retreat from education as a response to the standards of masculinity exemplified by his father, who wanted him to join the Marines.

> I guess everybody expected me to be carrying out my life correctly, graduating high school when I was supposed to be graduating, being in college by now. I just didn't live up to all that pressure and in sophomore year in high school I was just lazy. My teachers knew I was smart, my parents, my family knew I was smart. But I just didn't have any motivation at all.

Zephire was hard on himself for the lack of motivation he had at this point in his life, however fleeting it was. He thought little of how constant moving, bullying, expulsion, and parental pressure played a role. Zephire had been told countless times that what became of his life was up to him, and he believed it.

Zephire in fact seemed so responsible that he had time for little else. When we talked, Zephire was working most days after school and over vacations at a job paying "far below the minimum wage" shipping packages from a custom motorcycle shop. He explained that he was hoping to save up money for a trip "to Europe or Japan or somewhere," but "every time I got paid the money would go to something." He had to pay for a new phone since his old one was stolen, a bus pass, the phone bill, his nephew's plane ticket, and Christmas presents for his nieces and nephews. Between work and moving, Zephire had lost touch with his friends, the ones who had helped him when he moved away from Compton and was feeling lost. They used to get together every other weekend for movies, but now they all had jobs or were in college, "so it's very hard to like hang out. And I guess that I definitely feel a little lonely because I don't really talk to many people here." He explained that to stay safe, "I always have an umbrella even if it's sunny out so I have some sort of weapon in case I am walking home late at night and I have something with me in case somebody tries to mug me or something." Zephire, like many young men, worked hard to be responsible. He distanced himself from trouble, owned up to mistakes, took a low-paying job to support himself, gave up his earnings to friends and family, and used a makeshift weapon to defend himself. Responsibility was supposed to make life better, to guarantee rewards and privileges that come with doing things the right way. But these decisions almost never garnered the kind of support that was promised. When Zephire took responsibility, no one seemed to care about what he did.

In practice, with no limit to what could be considered their responsibility, some young men told me that the only way to truly take responsibility and stay out of trouble was to avoid friends. Ariel told me that he had stopped hanging out with his friends because they were a bad influence on him. Hendrix explained: "I stay out of trouble. I don't, I try not to talk to a lot of people. Not that I'm tryin' to be, like, you know, antisocial. It's just that I just have to be. But I know a lot of people, but I just have to, I mean, 'cause you talk to other people, they're gonna talk you into stuff." This message was vocalized by adults and codified in gang injunctions that prevent groups of young men from congregating. It was manifest in experiences of many young men being denied entry to a store with their friends. Self-imposed social isolation seemed to be the only means to avoid being seen as trouble.

As young men took the message of responsibility to heart, it triggered a split in their self-concept. When I asked Zephire, who was learning Japanese so he could travel, what might stand in the way of accomplishing his goals in life, he said, "My laziness, I have to really push myself." Hendrix, who was graduating early and starting a music studio, explained that race would not stand in his way, but his own conflicted self might. "What could stop me is myself. Like, I could be real lazy, 'cause your biggest obstacle is yourself. You could, like, really put yourself down. You could be like, nah, like, I'm really not gonna be able to do this. But you could. I think my biggest obstacle is myself." Several young men talked about themselves in this way. This split version echoed something that Ariel told me about how the administration at his school talks: "They tell us to find a path or make one, if you find a path, find a good path. Like, find a path that you want to go on, a good path or bad path. And as soon as you find [one], just make it." Similarly, Lincoln explained what life was like for a young man in Los Angeles: "If he go [on] the right path, then he going to know. But if he go [on] the wrong path, then sooner [or later] when he get to actually becoming a man, he gonna realize what he did wrong." Only young men used the "two paths" metaphor. They described a "good path" that led to a normative life of, as Ariel put it, "a good family, good car, and a good house, and don't worry about nothing else, you just have a good time," and a "bad path" that led to "the streets" and likely prison or harm. The narrative provided two choices, and the ways of acting within those were clear-cut and echoed the "street" and "decent" divides that have long been referenced in urban ethnographies of young men in marginalized urban communities coping with violence.[42]

While Zephire, Ariel, and others focused responsibility inward, other young men directed it at others. Responsibility was, in practice, a way of talking about what people deserve. And, like any discourse, it could take on new powers. Young men were told to take responsibility so often that many regularly charged others with a lack of responsibility. Hoxton, a sophomore in a crisp blue-striped shirt, explained that he felt like other students at his school failed to take responsibility: "All I know is, compared to my peers, I am very mature. All they think about, from what I've seen, is going home and doing what they feel like, ignoring any work they have to do and coming to school like they're in a prison." In one class, a group of young men wanted to talk about a story their teachers had told. A young woman had killed herself because her ex-boyfriend sent around pictures of her naked. The teachers had used it as an example of cyber-bullying, but one young man, Oscar, disagreed and argued that "it was her fault" for sending the pictures. "That is blaming the victim," Sean the facil-itator interjected. "If someone shot you is that your fault?" One young man called out from the back row, "No, because he didn't do anything." Sean amended the example to more closely parallel the story: "What if they shot him because they didn't like his Adidas shirt, would that be his fault?" he asks. One young man argued back, "It would be if he knew they didn't like the shirt." Another young man piled on, "If gangbangers get shot for wearing their colors, it's their fault." Several other men echoed this sentiment.

This scene was disconcerting, in large part because the young men so easily rationalized placing responsibility on the victim. But, it was easy to see the source of their logic. The young men were simply reiterating the messages that they or their friends or loved ones had received so many times from authorities and adults. Several times I heard adult authorities admonishing young men for wearing gang colors or sagging pants or warning them not to post things that might get them in trouble on Facebook. When young men said that everyone should take responsibility for their clothing and their actions on social media, they were repeating what adults had said to them.

Both focusing responsibility inward and outward produced social distance between young men and those closest to them. Pushing inward meant distancing themselves from friends and loved ones who could pull them away from the "right path." Pushing outward meant undermining the sources of empathy that enable caring relationships. These ways of making sense of personal responsibility were distinctly couched in the framework of masculinity. As I will show, women understood responsibility differently, seeing every decision as an empowered choice.

"To Look after Myself": Young Women on Their Own

I talked to Kashmir, a sharply dressed young African American woman in a classroom at the small charter school she attended. She sat with her posture perfect and spoke with a deliberate cadence. Early in our interview, I asked Kashmir what it meant to be an adult. "Well, letting me do what I want, like, let me spread my wings and let me go do whatever I want," she said. Susie, a Hispanic young woman, answered the same question as Kashmir similarly: "To be independent. To not rely on others, and to look after myself." While young men often told me that being an adult meant being able to fulfill their financial responsibilities to one's family, to "handle your business," young women more often framed adulthood as independence from social ties. To Kashmir, doing what she wanted did not necessarily involve being rich: "It's you having knowledge of yourself, so that's what brings you up is your knowledge of yourself, bringing yourself up. It's not money, it's what you think you're going to do." Kashmir told me that she planned to go to beauty college once she graduated high school, and when I asked her if anything might get in her way, she told me emphatically: "Nothing's going to stand in my way, because it's what I want to do, so I'm going to do it." Kashmir's response echoed what I heard from many young women, who pushed back against the dominant image of them as victims, and diverged from what the young men said.

Many of the young women I spoke to connected their self-confidence to their confidence in women as a gender category. Arianna, an enthusiastic young Latina, by way of Beyonce, put it this way: "Girls run the world."[43] When I asked her what she meant, she told me, "Well, we are what make the world go round. We run everything. Without us, what's going to happen? We are the best at everything. OK, that's kind of sexist, but it's true. Just saying." Kashmir and Arianna's confidence was inspiring and infectious. I found myself imagining Arianna's campaign for president, which she planned to run in about 30 years. At the same time, that confidence seemed to be constantly tested by sexism and racism in their daily lives. Arianna recounted a story in which she had gone to a store to try on a prom dress. Not long after she put it on and was stepping in front of the mirror, the manager began yelling and proceeded to kick her and her mother out, claiming, incorrectly, that they could not afford to buy the dress. Young men of color were constantly treated as criminals, young women of color were judged and undervalued.[44]

Scholars have argued that young women of color in schools and educational organizations are often seen as helpless, dependent, or at risk for teen pregnancy.[45] It was in stark contrast to these messages that young women used a discourse of "female empowerment."[46] One facilitator, who recounted to me her conversations with young women about avoiding unhealthy relationships, put it this way: "They were never going to be victims. I'm standing there and I'm not understanding why they're so resistant to this information and no matter what I said . . . [they said] that's not going to happen to me."

Young women of color described distrusting the police to protect them and came to believe that they could not trust anyone else to take care of them. Kashmir explained about police: "Some could help you, and some don't want [to], some just could watch you just get beat, or get snatched up." She believed that the police couldn't be trusted, even though it is their job: "It should be on the force, the police, to make sure that I'm safe on the street, because it's their job to keep people out on the street like that . . . But at the same time, I'm keeping myself safe, so it is my problem." Martha, a young Chinese American woman, explained that she felt like she could not trust anyone but herself:

> That's just how society and life really works, because you may lean on some-body, but you never know when they're going to disappear. And so yourself is really the only person you should be caring about 100 percent of the time. Someone else is maybe like 95 percent of the time. But you never know when they're going to turn. And self-defense and protecting yourself is really important, because if you fall, you're the only person who can stand up.

Both Martha and Kashmir believed deeply in their own capacity, while they distrusted most others. In turn, they often found it difficult to understand why other women would ever make decisions that they would not have. I asked Kashmir about women who stayed in unhealthy relationships: "Yes, it is their own fault, because they could get out of the relationship if they choose to, but they choose to stay in the relationship, so yes, it is their fault." Susie told me about a heated debate she had with a facilitator about whether or not it was a woman's fault if she was assaulted while drunk. According to Susie, the facilitator argued "that it's like, it's not the girl's fault when she's, like, drunk. But I said it is, because it's like, it's her responsibility whether she drinks or she doesn't." Because young women were more concerned that institutions would fail to live up to their obligations, rather than that they would actively enact harm, they were less concerned with abuses of power. Leah, a charismatic young Black woman, told me that the drug use in bathrooms at her school used to be "a big problem" but had decreased now that "there's more monitoring of, like, the bathroom and stuff. But girls used to like go in there and like do their thing or whatever." I asked Leah how she felt about the monitoring, and her response echoed something I heard often from young women about forms of criminal surveillance: "I don't mind. I mean, it's not me so I don't care." I heard several variations on this acceptance of surveillance, including "I'd never be in that situation" and "she shouldn't have done that."

While I was discouraged to hear Susie, Kashmir, Leah, and other young women take up this perspective, I was not surprised. This was the way that adults had often talked to them about what it meant to be responsible. Ciel, a "half Black half white" young woman who went to a "competitive" school, explained that she did not trust adults other than her mother. At her school, teachers seemed to never give students credit for doing well; instead they always said, "You could've done better." She explained: "So it's kind of like when they're telling you that you're not, you're like doing good, but you're not doing good enough. It still kind of makes you like, Oh, well why should I talk to you about anything If you're just going to say, like, 'Oh, that's bad, but it's still probably your fault.'"

This narrative extended out to young women's closest relationships. Leah had learned the lesson that personal responsibility meant that everyone, even close friends, are on their own. Her friend was in an abusive relationship, and while they had researched domestic violence shelters and strategies for leaving abusive relationships online, her friend consistently "made excuses down the line" for staying in the relationship. For Leah, "that just made me understand that it's up to her. Like I can't force anyone. Like they have to wake up on their own." Leah and other young women used personal responsibility to make sense of their limited choices within structural inequality and to exert agency in a world that often marginalized them.

Responsibility focused attention on a specific set of issues. Cleo told me that she was bothered by the way her peers treated each other and how they failed to live up to the school motto of "trust, respect, and responsibility." "Some people got the responsibility right. I don't know about the trust and respect. It's like, nobody really understands those two words." She continued, "Some people will make jokes about either how people are or, like, stereotypes and making jokes about people's backgrounds or whatever. And I felt, like, even though they joke about it, it like could probably hurt the person inside." She was critical of her peers for being disrespectful and wished that they would try "putting their selves in that person's shoes." Cleo's distinction is telling. The rhetoric of responsibility used by administrators and politicians ruled, and there was little consideration for trust or respect.

The confidence and responsibility signaled by many of the young women I spoke with is what mainstream discourses so often say young women lack. As young women drew on this discourse easily and freely, it became clear that this was in fact the dominant frame that women used to make sense of their circumstances. At the same time, there was a narrow arena in which women were allowed to make choices about their lives, as they repeatedly ran up against sexism, misogyny, racism, and victim-blaming and were provided few resources to combat these other than self-confidence and empowerment. For women, the discourse of personal responsibility espoused by teachers and other adults served to discourage them from engaging with supportive institutions. Unlike young men, young women looked to friends and family for support, but they were skeptical of any adult who offered help, lest they be seen as needy or a victim.

Although scholars—and in many ways school officials—view responsibilization as an approach to governing, it is better theorized as a discourse that escapes institutions and circulates through the personal relationships of individuals. Young people do not just learn to take responsibility, they also readily place it. Responsibility acted as a key way to make sense of harm, violence, and inequality and, as a result, many young people found ways to distance themselves from the friends and loved ones who could serve as vital sources of support.

To be young in the contemporary United States is to feel the brunt of myriad state and private institutions bearing down on you, making claims on your future: the threat of the legal system, the promise of education, the messages of the media. To be young and marked as at risk is to feel the added weight of daily intrusions of counselors and psychologists, of nonprofits and programs, of public health campaigns and academic tracking. For young people, the cumulative effect of the spatial and temporal fracturing of state institutions was a kind of social whiplash: disorientation and injury that comes from quick and extreme shifts in social expectations. It is the emotional and physical pain of needing to move constantly between contexts with unclear rules and responsibilities and expectations. It is the result of one's focus and attention being jerked and spun constantly. Social whiplash makes it very difficult and emotionally trying to relate to individuals in institutions. In this way, it creates distance. For the young people I met, who were neither the most criminalized nor the most deprived, but who live on the front lines of an experiment in a fractured and ephemeral state, they saw the world through the lens of the interpersonal: adults, friends, and loved ones were often fraught and dangerous. It was more responsible to try to go it alone.

EPILOGUE: The Future

Until recently, it looked like the version of the ephemeral state articulated in this book was going to be the future. That changed with the election of Donald Trump. Whereas President Obama had cultivated a constellation of short-term interventions through high-profile initiatives such as It's On Us and My Brother's Keeper, the Trump administration scaled back the public health and government funding infrastructure that made them possible, save for a few instances at the margins. One can look to the rebranding of abstinence-only education as risk avoidance to see how the echoes of change programs can be reformulated to pursue drastically different political and cultural pursuits. The culture-change apparatus of the ephemeral state, after all, can also be a propaganda apparatus. However, regardless of who occupies the White House, the same forces that gave rise to the ephemeral state continue to tear through the world of social policy, albeit in new configurations: devolution, privatization, technological advancements, a focus on culture above all. The Trump administration has hollowed out the federal government, dismantling norms and radically accelerating the pace of political discourse, pushing long-standing institutions toward clashes with ephemeral pursuits. With breakneck speed we shift our attention and narratives; social whiplash is widespread. To borrow from Ray Bradbury in *Fahrenheit 451*, we are living a "hop-scotch existence."

Change programs pull together the past and the future in novel ways, and are therefore distinct sites for thinking about time and social policy. This book has continued a scholarly project intent on capturing how time acts as a vector of state power and organization, to map the cadence of the state. I have elaborated on this from several angles, including the acute immediacy of unfolding public health campaigns, the unending grant cycle, the quieting of past traumas, the mundane repetition of run-ins with school resources officers. By bringing time into our research, we can begin to ask new kinds of questions about policy and the state.

For example, studies of mass incarceration are not just cases of physical and social exclusion, but of temporal deprivation: freedom requires time. Welfare reform, as another example, was about setting time limits on social support as much as it was about work requirements. Time also matters for policy change: I found that one difference between social movements and professional prevention work is that paid facilitators can spend more time on their cause, which may sap it of the energy of urgency.

Even as political and institutional dynamics shift in the United States, the programmatic approach that I have outlined in this book looks likely to continue, albeit quietly for now, as it is fed by big data, marketization, and globalization. Away from the increasingly hollow welfare state, curricula have remained a focus of nonprofit organizations and departments in local governments and state capitals. This process is unlikely to be reversed. New markets rarely simply disappear, especially ones that promise so much—in this case, to transform culture—at such low cost. In fact, it seems likely that the ephemeral state will be deployed to solve new problems. In the face of inert institutions, short-term programs appeal as a reasonable way to act. It also seems likely that the opening of a global marketplace for programs, implemented by NGOs, will continue as U.S. aid declines. The spread of these programs, much as it has in the United States, promises new kinds of disjuncture around the world, as well as new possibilities.

CULTURE AND POLICY

Curricula are cultural ideas about health, violence, and youth made solid, albeit temporarily. To put it another way, change programs represent the social structure of our efforts to act on culture, to change stories. Programs are made possible by a system of institutional arrangements—nonprofits, evaluations, funders, and so on—that establish a structure to promote and enact cultural change. That structure, the ephemeral state, is fleeting and head-spinning and isolating, but it is structure nonetheless. It is a form of social structure that imagines itself as culture.

With this study, I have set out to stake a claim in the middle of a simmering debate over how culture works and what it can do. On one side is public health, pushing into the public sphere on the back of data-driven claims of changing cultural norms. Despite the fact that this challenges many of sociology's core notions of how culture works, the discipline, for the most part, has been receptive, albeit halfheartedly, in response to the arguments of public health. It is appealing after all to believe that public health can transform our dangerous habits and attitudes in a matter of hours, that as far gone as society may seem, it can still be pulled back with well-placed words. On the other side of the debate about culture are scholars in the critical theoretical tradition of governmentality theory, who are largely pessimistic about the consequences of responsibilization, which is often portrayed as an inescapable and monolithic force. They are right that public health is often a kind of rebranded way to encourage personal responsibility, though they rarely acknowledge that it may be a more humane version. But this critical analysis is too often detached from the real life of culture and experience. After all, the state does not automatically produce in its subjects what it intends. Programs—like other governmental projects—create new categories and identities. But those are not unthinkingly occupied; they are contested and refined in relation to lived histories and social contexts. One goal of this book has been to build up a different framework for thinking about the fractured and indirect ways that culture works in relation to social policy, and with it, hopefully begin to see the limits of culture change.

The past lives on, among other places, in bits of narrative that chirp in the ear—or sometimes thunder—and yet individuals rarely feel that they can control the story or even follow its plot. This is always true, but trauma and violence make it starkly visible. For some young people, their histories—shot through with violence, inequality, trauma, and incongruity—were more than memories: they shaped how young people acted in the present. These stories cracked the cultural frames presented in programs and allowed unwanted parts of the picture to show through. For all of us, some things happen *to you* and they are not your choice: this is what it means to function within social structure. But the more social inequalities weigh on your social world, the more these cracks in the frame can pile up. Scholars of culture and policymakers alike must begin to grapple with the fact that sometimes violence happens not because it has become a rational choice in unrelenting circumstances, or because it is deemed socially acceptable—although it can be those things too—but because it is an old story that cannot be forgotten, even though one might try. Just as the repetitions of the past are lodged in individuals' habits, so too are past moments lodged in their narratives. Sociology and social policy have few ways to deal with this fact. Teaching new norms, it seems, is entirely inadequate. A new cultural frame can always be cracked and broken by structural harm.

THE CONSEQUENCES OF DATA

The terrain between the stories we tell about ourselves and the stories told by data is rockier and more uncertain than ever. Unprecedented quantities of data are used to hone and target the stories that drive our fears and loves, but to what end? Sociologists are only beginning to grapple with what this kind of data can do to enable new forms of identity and support, as well as to shift cultural norms, reshape social isolation, and stigmatize and exclude groups in new ways. For example, even as risk flattens our understanding of young people, it also undermines simplified categories of victim and perpetrator. Peter, a preventionist, explained to me: "When you work with 17-year-olds who grow up in homes where their mom's boyfriend is beating them up all the time and then they go and they hit another kid, you're not looking at that kid as someone who hit another kid, you're looking at them as like a whole person." As Bruce Western has argued, many perpetrators were also victims.[1] This can challenge our prevailing cultural frame that divides the world in two. Social policy would look very different if it began with the notion that there is a correlation between the events that happen to you and the ones that you happen to.

These questions will continue to multiply in the age of data. If, and I think this is apt, new forms of data are kinds of statistical ethnography, then we can think of ethnography—small data, perhaps—as an opportunity to do a kind of social life of statistics. Ethnography can reveal the connected moments that, in aggregate, add up to statistical lives. Living among statistics—and as a statistical life myself—I came to see that the ways we think about risk are flawed. It is true that social science must always balance the fullness of human experience with the necessity of collapsing those aspects into measures and concepts that can circulate through the world of theory and practice. While we cannot escape the fact that all data by its nature abstracts experience, we should constantly consider what is factored in and what is left out. Risk data is not wrong; it just picks up the story in the middle. In the course of my research, I came to recognize long-term patterns in the lives of youth marked as at risk. These patterns signal not simply the accumulation of risk over time, but the *structure of risk,* marked by uncertainty, instability, gendered violence, systemic racism, corruption, a threadbare welfare state, and an overzealous crime control system. Statistical analysis can and should begin to develop a methodological language to focus on the structural risks that beget the individual-level mechanisms that we often call risk factors. This would shift the analysis onto structures and away from individuals.

POLICY IMPLICATIONS

There was a worksheet—the power and control wheel—used in nearly every program put on by Peace Over Violence that was riddled with spelling mistakes. I saw that flawed worksheet dozens of times. I often looked at the errors and wondered why no one had fixed them. I thought about correcting them myself. It wouldn't have taken much. To some extent, this signaled a lack of investment in the formal curriculum: if facilitators believed the mistakes mattered, they would have corrected them. But the mistakes symbolized something else. For the worksheet, as is true for the wider world of programming, there is an inertia to what came before. The same flaw is reproduced, copied and copied again. It is the by-product of a system that is both perpetual and fleeting. One hope for this book is that it causes those responsible for designing, funding, and implementing programs to take pause and fix the errors that have been reproduced for too long.

In 1909, a hundred years before I began my fieldwork, social reformer Jane Addams wrote about the ways that adults avoid understanding the lives of young people:

> It is as if we ignored a wistful, over-confident creature who walked through our streets calling out, "I am the Spirit of Youth! With me, all things are pos-

sible!" We fail to understand what he wants or even to see his doings, although his acts are pregnant with meaning, and we may either translate them into a sordid chronicle of petty vice or turn them into a solemn school for civic righteousness.[2]

We have, through risk data and prevention programs, found a new way to live out Addams's concern. Young people hold countless possibilities, and we—adults—try to understand them using risk data that notes their vices—and occasionally their virtues—and programs that try to change them into the righteous. As I spent time in schools, I was disheartened to find that even the most well-intentioned efforts to build relationships with young people floundered in the context of ephemeral policies that fractured, undermined, and twisted the very possibility of those relationships. The ephemeral state stands as testament to the lengths adults will go to avoid listening to young people. A young woman I interviewed, exasperated, put it this way: "I feel like it's so stupid how society is breaking and I feel like it's so stupid that we have to make, like, programs to help people instead of just doing it. It's like, is that really hard?"

We need to do better than this. Every social metric shows that interpersonal violence is devastating for individuals, families, and communities and goes largely unchecked. And yet, our best response is prison when it spills into view, or—the subject of this book—short-term programs. This is not to say that prevention programs do not work. In the blunt end calculation, they may. Perhaps they make a one-degree change in a life, which, in the long run, sends someone on a different course. But what are we steering them toward? Their new trajectory is likely to be an isolated one, streaked across a landscape of deprived resources, racism, sexism, and distrust. Despite good people's best efforts, these programs, when viewed from the ground, fall short of their most important goals. The good that I did see coming from such programs often came in spite of the system, as a by-product of people recovering connection across a perilous social distance. We have it backwards. The problem is not that young people should change. The system should.

The alternative to the ephemeral state is stability. We should shape social institutions not as fleeting interventions in ongoing lives, nor as towering bureaucracies, but as a kind of street-level infrastructure for support and connection. Stable funding and adults in long-term, reliable roles would almost certainly bolster the well-being of young people. In addition, schools should begin to reevaluate the ways that they deal with the pasts of students. Instead of quarantining social and emotional lives, educators should work to incorporate them into school life. This would be facilitated by a revision of mandated reporting rules to allow for spaces where young people could talk openly about their lives without fear of being reported on. While many programs offered anonymity, most young people did not want it. Instead, they wanted to tell their story to someone they could trust, who was not a part of their daily life, but also who would not send their story into the precarious machine of the state. Unfortunately, the evidence-based data cannot tell us whether any of this will work. We do not have an empirical framework for understanding outcomes when we are talking about systemic and often generational inequalities. Real social change takes too long to measure on evaluations.

Tomorrow, we could start to use risk data differently. Rather than try to guess who should be provided with interventions, we might instead use risk data to funnel money to schools or even individuals. Risk is a consequence, not a cause, and it should be treated as such. Instead of money for programs, those most at risk could receive cash and services. Further, we could promote data democracy: provide the tools for people to analyze their own lives, to situate them within history and place. As long as risk data is manipulated and acted upon far from lived experience, it will tear open a gap between how the counted see their world and how the counters see them. This in and of itself is a problem. But it is one that can be ameliorated by making data available to the communities that it describes and by providing the tools to use that risk data to tell their own stories.

On the most minor scale, it is possible to enact straightforward improvements to short-term programs. Curricula should center on lived experience. They should encourage young people to make sense of their social context through structured discussions and assignments. This is, of course, not a dramatic innovation, but a return to the consciousness-raising roots of feminism and other social movements, which, a generation ago, first made the notion of cultural change possible. These new programs would be generative: they would *make* something. For this, we should build on the work of participatory action research to create programs that review institutional policy, construct youth interview projects, enable youth-led ethnographies, and more. Curricula approach youth on the ground, in the course of their daily lives, and yet, most programs treat young people like generic consumer niches to be marketed to. We must also develop new ways to gauge effectiveness. Evaluations can be helpful tools for guiding programs and allocating resources, but our current methods are too limited. All this is possible, but first we must ask young people to tell their stories.

APPENDIX: An Ephemeral Ethnography

Stories help us make sense of the world. There is a kind of plot that runs through ethnographies that Rios has called the jungle book trope.[1] An outsider, often white, comes into a wild land, often the inner city; the outsider survives with a tale to tell. But the city is not a jungle, neither are urban public schools or local nonprofits. They are social contexts, human-made ideas of how life should work that were built and cracked apart by people. They have a history that people live in. Rios argues that we need better stories. One might go like this: something happens—strange or wrenching—and people cope with it. That thing could be close-up, like a gunshot or the birth of a child, or sweeping like mass incarceration or the fracturing of the state. Mostly it will be both. In coping with that new social reality, we find its edges, test its causalities, see each other anew. For me, this is the story that goes along with the strategy of ethnographic analysis called the extended case method.[2]

At trainings and conferences, in organizations and schools, I spent a lot of my time with a tag on my chest saying who I was and why I was allowed to be there. I was at turns a graduate student from the University of Southern California and a volunteer from a nonprofit. I always had to be from somewhere. I had to sign in. I had to enter institutions through locked doors and be vouched for and account-able. I found that programs do not live in the streets and homes and civic institutions where many ethnographies occur: they exist on the far edges of institutions, where nearly everyone is a stranger. Even had I wanted to, there was no place for me to become a regular character. I was a member of a loose and shaggy network of shadow state actors.

Over the course of the first year, as I moved from context to context, I came to recognize the instability and impermanence of the endeavor of prevention. It was an endless churn. There was more stability within the organization that was my home base, but less than one might expect. Schedules were constantly shifting, funding disappeared abruptly, employees left and new ones came on. There was no time or place for settling in. In programming, by the time I learned a student's name, that student was gone. Once I got to know a teacher, we would switch schools. I often found myself searching for connection and continuity. A young person would share a story, a wrenching one, and I would want to be there, to see them again. But they would be gone or I would. That distance, and the temporary world of the program, became the focus of my research.

As the fractured social terrain made many of the anchors of ethnographic methods—stability of place and people—null, my theoretical approach kept me tethered. In line with the extended case method, I resolved to situate my work alongside and within existing theories of the state and culture. I bounced my findings off of the literature regarding the welfare state, neoliberal paternalism, and crime control. I bolstered my theoretical toolkit by drawing on feminist theory and science and technology studies. I also returned time and again to another kind of theory: the accepted dogma of public health. I set out to find ways to replicate previous findings in my method, to play a kind of cover song of risk data in an ethnography.[3]

The structure of my field of research itself, fractured and repeating, posed distinct methodological challenges, as well as surprising benefits. I found myself moving between multiple tiers of what I came to call the ephemeral state as I bounced from conference to organization to classroom to youth interview, chasing logics and discourses. In methodological design, we often prioritize the comparison of like sites, horizontally, but what we miss then is the vertical stacking and interlocking of sites and how meanings shift between them. I also found myself in looping repetitions of the same curricula over and over, which allowed for a kind of ideal type comparison case. In addition, I moved among multiple different curricula in a given day, providing constant comparison. A couple of years into my research, I stumbled on an account of the same organization from decades earlier, enabling a comparative revisit.

In the field, methodological challenges arose frequently and I found that they often signaled distortions and lapses in theory. The ephemeral state made it difficult to build the kinds of connections with young people that I had thought necessary for ethnography. But this revealed to me how the ephemeral state undermined connection broadly and it showed how connection was still possible in the right circumstances. Even though I had read the theories of neoliberalism and the fragmented state, being there, in person, was vital for grappling with phenomena in daily life. The cadence of neoliberalism was disorienting. Personal responsibility was lonely. Relentless impermanence triggered emotional disconnection. In response, I did what most facilitators learn to do: form meaningful, temporary connections and then forget about them. I learned to make connections, one hour a week over twelve weeks. This was something that the young people I met seemed to have learned long before I got there. Studies tend to pursue questions of social function and not social disjuncture and breakdown. They often ask how is it that this thing works, not why it falls apart. However, it is valuable to understand how social distance takes form despite best efforts.

Still, understanding young people only from the point of view of the program constructed them as hollow and limited. Faces and names ran together. That was a finding in and of itself. But it also pushed me to work as best I could to fill out their stories as a way to understand, or at least compel them to speak about, what the program meant to them. This also served to test my hunch that programs were constrained, at least in part, by how they came into contact with youth, not by the youth themselves, and that given a different set of mechanisms—more proximity and trust—something more impactful could arise. In the second year of fieldwork, I began conducting in-depth, semi-structured interviews with youth, ultimately conducting 32. Most of the young people that I interviewed were Latinx (19 in total) and Black (9 in total). In addition, the student interviews included two students who identified as Bangladeshi, one as Chinese American, and one as Filipino. Student interviews included 16 young men and 16 young women, ranging in age from 15–20. Although there is no formal data on the racial composition of youth participants in programming nationally, based on informal observation, these interviewee demographics roughly reflect youth targeted for programming in Los Angeles. Nineteen of them were recruited through ongoing programs at five schools and 13 from four long-term programs. Interviews were conducted in empty classrooms, breakout rooms at the nonprofit, and coffee shops. I recorded them and later transcribed them. While most of the interviews were one-on-one, later in the process I became interested in conducting focus groups to supplement my data. I conducted four small focus group–style interviews, three with two participants and one with three participants. All interviews focused on two sets of questions. The first set concerned young people's reception of the program and how they made sense of it in the context of their daily experiences. The second explored the institutional pressures they felt—at school, at home, in their community. Except for one college student, I only interviewed young people currently enrolled in high school, with most of my participants aged 16 or 17. I did spend time observing middle school programs, but I have used that data sparingly. Broadly, the findings concerning youth are associated with high school students.

When I recruited young people to be interviewed, I described my project as an opportunity for them to make their voices heard and I offered a $20 gift card as compensation for respondents' participation. I found that young people seemed to talk to me for two main reasons that went beyond compensation. The first were those who, with the promise of anonymity and confidentiality, saw an opportunity to tell their stories. I did not set out to collect stories of hurt and trauma, but as Small has argued, people will tell their struggles to those they don't know all that well. The second group told me far less about their lives.[4] They stated that they chose to participate out of curiosity, or for practice that may help them in a job interview. This told me something about how they saw me, and by extension, many of the outsiders who shuffled through their worlds. Several students I interviewed were professional, looked me straight in the eye, skillfully dodged questions about their pasts, gave smiling, vague answers. Sometimes interviews felt like dead ends. I realized that young people were trying to accomplish something too. They had given me the story they believed I wanted to hear. I came to distinguish stories that were deep and amorphous, as real stories are, from the hardened, formalized stories I also heard. When there was a connection and deep trust, where the messiness of lived experience shone through, I would work to reverse engineer how it happened, since I did not reliably know ahead of time. When a story seemed to be a dead end, I examined what patterns arose in how young people presented their lives. These two kinds of interviews sensitized me to the distinction between the narratives that appear on evaluations and the ones that shape identity and meaning. Stories, regardless of whether they are told in interviews, in curricula, or in surveys, actively construct the social world, but I saw that they do so differently.

During the third year of participant observation I conducted in-depth, semistructured interviews with 14 program facilitators. I knew the longer-term facilitators well at that point, and I took the opportunity to ask them about their experiences in the work. As I did so, I thought about the way that our closeness was just as much of a challenge to data collection as my distance from youth. They had gotten a sense or at least a working hypothesis of what I cared about that they then acted in relation to. In total, my interviews with facilitators included nine women: three Latina, two Black, three white, and one Asian American, as well as five men: two Black, two Latino, and one white. These interviews included all of the facilitators employed at the organization at the time, as well as two volunteer facilitators. Other facilitators were present during earlier participant observation research, and on several occasions, volunteers who were not interviewed conducted presentations that are part of the fieldwork—in particular one white man in his thirties and a white woman in her late twenties, both of whom were consistent volunteers. In addition, I interviewed 10 current or previous employees in various departments in the organization. I also interviewed Billie Weiss over the phone as background for the second chapter.

STANDPOINTS

Ethnographers often talk about positionality. When they do, they are often talking about two things that sometimes get treated as one: in the case at hand, how others made sense of me and how I made sense of me. Or, to put it another way, the influence of my position in the field on the social processes captured by data collection, and also how my social location shaped the ways I understood what I saw.

The first is straightforward. Everywhere I went, people tried to read me based on my appearance. I talk about this in chapter 4, but I will say more here. Race, gender, sexuality, class, age, and more were front of mind for most everyone in the ephemeral state—youth and facilitators and school personnel alike. For sure, all contexts are the product of some amount of social manufacturing, but in programs there was no moment where fading into the background felt possible, not because my embodiment meant that I could not, but because there was no background to fade into. As I moved across contexts and audiences, I experienced a barrage of intersectional dilemmas and standpoint crises. I often wondered: who am I to them today? The possibilities for building connection and empathy across social difference were constantly shifting. I was not alone in this. These dilemmas mirror the hopes and struggles of all those trying to form connection and change lives within a fractured and expansive ephemeral state.

The pieces of identity were constant topics of conversation among young people. My race, gender, relationship status, age, and occupation were all fair game for questions and comments and assessments. Young men I didn't know called me "Homey Max with the Jesus beard" or asked if I was married. Simply put: my social location mattered. The idea that it could not is a fiction only upheld if people have the privilege not to think or speak about who they are. Although social location mattered constantly, this was not a study designed to capture reliable patterns in those interactions. I did observe facilitators at a variety of social locations who had experiences that paralleled my own. The main question is this: Would the programs have looked different if I wasn't there? I do not believe so. The vast majority of the programs I observed were co-ed, and some were focused on men. There were almost always male students in the room and often male adults. There were also often other white people, as several of the staff were white, as well as many program volunteers and teachers.

The second way of talking about position concerns how my past shaped what I noticed and how I tell about it. When I was writing I thought a lot about what Donna Harraway calls the "god trick." It is the way that scientists arrange their nouns and verbs to feign objective truth. I also thought about Patricia Hill Collins and others who have articulated the fundamental limitations and benefits of our standpoints: the perches or low avenues from which we view the world. I took care to think about my standpoint as I translated the data into analysis. I strove to tell the kind of sociological story that puts on display the power of the tools of qualitative analysis as an antidote to the limitations of quantitative analysis. I tried to put theory in the room with strangers while they tried to make sense of what brought them there, and of each other. This has limited the claims I can make to causality, so I have pointed to cause and effect only when I am confident the data warrants it. Otherwise, I have done what I feel ethnography is best at: generate ideas out of lived experiences and test existing theories. That said, there are decisions I made about where to turn—and not to turn—my attention that were shaped by my social location. Specifically, it seems likely that having often had the benefit of efficient and fair interactions with the state, I was struck by the erratic character of the ephemeral state.

TALKING ABOUT HARM

At the end of the day, ethnographers create a passable facsimile of the world: they do a kind of work with narrative. Young people do the same thing in a different context: they use stories to accomplish things. When youth show up in the text, as they do often, I have tried to let them speak for themselves and I have tried to let their interpretations of the world shine. I have also tried to avoid smoothing over the contradictions and gaps that arose when talking to young people as they worked to reconcile the messy world given to them. I have tried not to obscure how challenging it was to have conversations about race and class and violence. That is part of the story I am telling.

Amanda Hess, a journalist, has described how stories about violence, particularly interpersonal violence, can take on the weight of all reality for the reader. How stories of just one moment in a life can swallow up not only the entirety of the life that surrounded it, but a whole social group. Against this weight, we need, I believe, far more stories. Nowhere is this truer, and more difficult, than when it involves violence that is close up, interpersonal, and structured by power inequalities.

One of the first things trainers teach new volunteers at Peace Over Violence is not to tell other people's stories: that stories have power, and telling someone else's is to, in a way, take their power from them and use it for yourself. I break that rule because I disagree with it. I retell the stories I heard in the field, and though I try to keep them intact, I chop and clip and frame the stories I heard to make them legible. I do not do this lightly. But I have come to believe that telling other people's stories, as long as they are told with humanity and context, is vital for the work of empathy and justice. Because the law is less likely to tread in the private spaces where this violence takes shape, the stories we tell about violence are where the meanings and the consequences are shaped. In this way, not talking about violence is to cede power.

In the universe of the university Institutional Review Board (IRB), this study did not concern human subjects. It was a study of stories and stories are not people. For the IRB, when they are concerned with humans, they are concerned with their bodies; a relic of the medical origins of the review board system. But, as I saw, stories can hurt. That, however, is not a reason for researchers to avoid them. As you have seen, trauma and violence were common in the lives of the people I talked to. This was one of the central findings of the book: a vast reservoir of experience just beneath the surface. It was something I had a sense of given the existing data, but it was not something I asked about. It bubbled up anyway. I came to recognize that the review board was much like the programs in the way they approach harm and trauma: that *asking* about trauma was a cause of trauma. And though this may at times be true, we must also take stock of what is lost. The IRB and the protections it provides are invaluable. But IRBs are also part of the same ephemeral state as programs. They chop up time into the same short chunks. They fear the same stories. The avoidance of disclosures of harm, it seems, is a recurring facet of the modern state. This likely has consequences, both for research and for social connection.

I was unprepared to navigate the trauma of youth. I struggled to manage my split roles, when I was a mandated reporter or bound to confidentiality by research ethics. When I was in the classroom, with my facilitator nametag on, I was mandated. In the other spaces and times, when I was off the clock as a facilitator, I made decisions as best I could. In interviews, however, the IRB mechanisms took over and I followed and explained them. I assessed risk; felt the program I had learned in prevention work booting up in my brain. I tried to figure out if a story was going to end poorly and give what time and care I could. I don't know if I always made the right call. I never will. I wouldn't recognize most of the young people I met. I doubt they would remember me either.

Notes

1. All names are pseudonyms, except in chapter 2.

2. Western (2018) grapples with the moral quandary presented by the fact that many or most of people who go to prison for violence experienced violence themselves.

3. The Center for Youth Wellness, drawing on data collected on 27,745 Californians, found that 61.7 percent of people in the state had experienced one Adverse Childhood Experience, while 16 percent had experienced four or more; https://centerforyouthwellness.org/wp-content/themes/cyw/build/img/building-a-movement/hidden-crisis.pdf. Also see the California Attorney General's Office 2004 report.

4. A variety of labels pre-date at risk, each denoting a particular frame of analysis: from juvenile delinquents to dropouts to at risk to opportunity youth. Placier (1993) traces the earlier history of the term using Arizona as a case study.

5. For an overview of youth violence prevention see Tharp, Simon, and Saul 2012. For evaluations see Miller et al. 2015; Ball et al. 2012; DeGue et al. 2014. For a counterargument see Popova 2016.

6. Neoliberalism means the application of market logics to expanding realms of social influence. In many ways the programs at POV are neoliberal in that they are made for the market and they cultivate personal responsibility, but such an analysis leaves out much of what takes place on the ground. In daily life, the

shifting of responsibility onto individuals is messy and sometimes it doesn't work at all. The state tries to shape the force and character of choices but does not always succeed. What it does succeed in doing, however, is redrawing the fault lines.

7. By social distance, I mean the perception of likeness—social proximity—between groups. Rios (2017) developed the concept of cultural misrecognition to describe how adults often misread the cultural symbols given off by youth. Ray (2017a) describes how upwardly mobile women enact an "identity of distance" to create space between themselves and their less mobile peers.

8. Hasenfeld (1972) describes organizations designed to manage and process people, and those intended to change them, such as schools or mental hospitals.

9. For examples of waiting as a form of state power and control, see Ayuero 2012; Reid 2013; Lara-Millan 2014; Kohler-Haussman 2013.

10. Bridges (2017) describes how data concerning the lives of poor women is taken by the state as a prerequisite for services, denying privacy rights that are afforded broadly to other citizens.

11. I draw on Haney (1996) for my analysis of the state, at the micro level, not as a single system but as conflicting systems. The term social whiplash was suggested by Saida Grundy.

12. Ferguson 2001.

13. Thorne 1994: 20. This is also a sentiment broadly articulated by critical youth studies, which foregrounds considerations of power and agency. Young people develop their own cultural world in relation to, and often against, the structure of the one that adults build for them. See Best 2007.

14. Many of these programs fall under the heading of Positive Youth Development; see Damon 2004. For examples of some of the tensions in youth empowerment programs, see Greenberg 2018; Kohfeldt et al. 2011.

15. For another example, consider New York City, where at the same time the police criminalized young men of color through a policy of "stop, question, and frisk," the city administration launched the Young Men's Initiative to empower young men of color—the same ones who were being disproportionately stopped.

16. Although I am concerned with a different set of consequences, Gilmore (2007) describes many of the aspects of the shadow state that I draw on, including a drive for efficiency, the narrowing of goals, and the abandonment of long-term investment. In addition, notably, Rose (1999) describes the decentralization of state power out to locally situated, often third sector or private organizations as "governing at a distance." Much of the research on state devolution has focused on the welfare and penal systems, and research has begun to examine health care. Some scholars have focused on the political-economic and interlocking racial dynamics of this arrangement: how services and support once doled out by state institutions are rendered in new ways, or not at all, in order to enact harsh punitive control within this framework; see Soss, Fording, and Schram 2011;

Wacquant 2009. Seim (2017) provides a street-level look at ambulance care for the urban poor in this fragmented state.

17. Eliasoph (2011) provides a compelling discussion of local, civic "empowerment projects." Globally, Krause (2014) describes the multiplication of humanitarian projects. Both of these works show how nongovernmental projects construct new social groups.

18. Milward and Provan (2000) describe a similar processes as the "hollow state." Alissa Quart, writing in the *New York Times* Opinion section, called this "the dystopian social net"; www.nytimes.com/2018/01/19/opinion/the-shadow-safety-net.html.

19. Marwell 2004; Marwell and Gullickson 2013. This seems to have been a significant shift in many urban schools, which turn to outsider organizations for an array of services.

20. www.urban.org/sites/default/files/publication/29221/412228-Human-Service-Nonprofits-and-Government-Collaboration-Findings-from-the- · National-Survey-of-Nonprofit-Government-Contracting-and-Grants.PDF.

21. www.weingartfnd.org/files/Capacity-Report-Final.pdf.

22. Several scholars have pointed to shifts in other corners of the shadow state. Haney (2010) explores some of the millions of individuals regulated by the penal system beyond prisons and jails.

23. According to my count, in total, during 2013 nearly $1.5 million in funding to POV came from government grants, while the rest was a mix of private and corporate foundations, individual donations, and program fees.

24. Scholars of the state have emphasized how the market rationality of this transformation pushes organizations to compete for grants and risks co-optation and "donor discipline."

25. Watkins and Swidler (2013), looking at NGOs and HIV prevention, describe the narrow cultural themes that arise from conflicting worldviews and goals of donors, brokers, and audiences. In their research, they find similar patterns to the ones that I describe.

26. Schudson and Baykurt (2016) provide a kind of alternative history of anti-smoking campaigns, focused on culture at the micro-sociological level.

27. The idea of changing strangers through exercises is an old one. In the 1950s, setting out against psychoanalysis, behavioral theory argued that human action was measurable, learned, and malleable through a range of techniques of self-monitoring, desensitization, and "averse" and "operant" conditioning. Famously, Pavlov's lab experiments were among the first to find that "abnormal" habits could be corrected through "conditioning" such as shock therapy and rewards for desirable behaviors. These techniques were applied to any behavior deemed abnormal—alcoholism, anorexia, phobias, obsessiveness, anxiety, and others. Abnormal was often a shorthand for not white, not straight, not wealthy.

28. See Merry (2001) for an analysis of how diverse gender violence programs deploy "technologies of the self."

29. Cruikshank (1999) describes it as a political formation, the will to empower. See Garland (1997) for a review of the themes of governmentality literature.

30. www.blueprintsprograms.com/about.

31. Finkelhor et al. 2014. Bullying was the most frequent of the five most common topics of such programs, with 55 percent of children and youth having experienced a bullying prevention program. Twenty-one percent had been exposed to sexual assault prevention programming. About a third had been exposed to dating violence prevention.

32. Barker et al. 2010: 545; Dworkin et al. 2013.

33. For sociological studies on the causes of violence, see Sharkey 2018; Anderson 1999; Irwin and Umemoto 2016; Miller 2008; Auyero, Bourgois, and Scheper-Hughes 2015; Contreras 2012.

34. Porche, Zaff, and Pan (2017) describe the unequal distribution of adverse life events. See Irwin and Umemoto (2016), who describe the lives of Hawaiian girls and boys, for the ways that long histories of violence continue to be re-contested in the present.

35. Department of Justice 2012.

36. Whitaker and Reece 2007; David-Ferdon and Simon 2014.

37. CDC 2012.

38. Puzzanchera and Adams 2011.

39. Rice 2007.

40. Niolon et al. 2015. "Of the students who had dated, 77% reported perpetrating verbal / emotional abuse, 32% reported perpetrating physical abuse, 20% reported threatening a partner, 15% reported perpetrating sexual abuse, 13% reported perpetrating relational abuse, and 6% reported stalking. Girls were more likely than boys to report perpetrating threatening behaviors, verbal / emotional abuse, and physical abuse, and boys were more likely to report perpetrating sexual abuse."

41. See Ybarra and Mitchell (2013) for more details, including race, gender, and class dynamics.

42. Rendon 2014; Chan Tack and Small 2017; Harding 2009. Exner-Cortens, Eckenrode, and Rothman (2013) show an association between experiencing dating violence and long-term health outcomes.

43. Understanding young people's stories, specifically stories about violence, puts this book in conversation with a body of literature that is concerned with how stories matter. Harding (2010) and other scholars of culture and urban violence have argued that narratives collide and conflict in people's heads. The implication is that too many stories, or weak stories, undermine action.

In Harding's telling, it is the multiplicity of narratives that causes problems. I disagree with Harding in that I believe that everyone navigates a cascade of stories.

44. I was inspired here by reading a conversation between James Baldwin and Margaret Mead that took place on stage in New York City on August 25, 1970. Baldwin said of activists, "They are acting in the past. They don't know it. It takes a long time to realize that there is a past . . . It takes a long time to understand anything at all about what we call the past—and begin to be liberated from it. Those kids are romantic, not even revolutionaries. At least not yet. They don't know what revolution entails. They think everything is happening in the present. They think they are the present. They think that nothing ever happened before in the whole history of the world" (www.brainpickings.org/2015/03/19/a-rap-on-race-margaret-mead-and-james-baldwin/).

45. Narratives are ways of taking facts of experience and hammering them into a story. Ewick and Silbey (1995) lay out a distinction between hegemonic narratives and subversive narratives (which they define as including some reference to the socio-historical forces that frame the story).

46. Polletta et al. 2011.

47. Tavory and Eliasoph (2013) provide a helpful breakdown of ways of coordinating futures. Of particular interest is their description of a variety of longer-range "trajectories" including narratives and projects.

48. Somers (1994: 614) explains: "People are guided to act in certain ways and not others on the basis of the projections, expectations, and memories derived from a multiplicity but ultimately limited repertoire of available social, public, and cultural narratives." Also see Rosen (2017), who argues that people actively pick narratives that help them make sense of their situation.

49. "Rather than being just a more or less functional bureaucratic apparatus, the state is also a powerful site of cultural and symbolic production" (Auyero 2012: 6; Cruikshank 1999). I am interested in the stories that the state tells. However, I do not assume that these stories automatically become part of subjects and identities.

50. Marriage promotion (Heath 2012), responsible fatherhood programs (Curran and Abrams 2000; Randles 2015), sex education (Fields 2008; Garcia 2012), and teen pregnancy (Barcelos and Gubrium 2014).

51. Cruikshank (1999) provides a vital articulation of the way that the state tells stories as a way to make citizen/subjects.

52. Feminist theorists have explained how silences and "missing discourses" can point us toward inequalities. See Fine 1988.

53. Merry (2016) describes the boom in social data in the 1990s and its consequences.

54. Weber et al. [1916–62] 2012: 78.

55. See Lawrence and Karim (2007) for a collection of thinking on violence.

56. Weiss 1996: 85.

57. www.who.int/violenceprevention/approach/definition/en/.

58. I study violence prevention in a "vertical slice"—see Holmes 2013—mapping flows of narrative and power across contexts from funding at the top, down to the lives of marginalized young people. This is a way of extending the case outward by using a multisited ethnography (Marcus 1998; Burawoy 2009).

59. An ethnographic approach enabled me to collect data that differed from evaluation studies based on surveys or interviews. I jotted field notes during programming when possible and otherwise narrated field notes into an audio recorder immediately after leaving the field. On the occasions that I was acting as a facilitator, I took notes during the breaks between classes. I typed detailed field notes within 24 hours (Emerson, Fretz, and Shaw 1995) and coded field notes, interviews, and content with a program called Dedoose.

60. "The technologies, discourses, and metaphors of crime and criminal justice have become more visible features of all kinds of institutions" (Simon 2007: 4; Garland 2001).

CHAPTER 2. HOW VIOLENCE BECAME PREVENTABLE

1. Walk a Mile in Her Shoes marches are designed to raise awareness about men's violence against women and often to raise money. The marches can end up reinforcing gender difference; see Bridges 2010.

2. Although I use pseudonyms in this opening vignette, throughout the rest of this chapter I use real names.

3. One implication of a market for anti-violence is that the best violence prevention should go to those who can afford it.

4. While some of the curricula are funded through foundations or government agencies, others are supported by for-profit social ventures, such as "Love is Respect," which was funded by Liz Claiborne, Inc., and later supported by Mary Kay, Inc. See Barman (2016) for an analysis of how capitalism shapes the production of social good.

5. Eikenberry and Kluver (2004) provide a review of the marketization of the nonprofit sector. Like several scholars, they are concerned with the consequences for democracy and civil society.

6. For a review of some of the concerns with evaluation in the health education field, see Popova 2016.

7. Foucault (1995) uses the notion of genealogy to unearth the ways that historical forces constructed the taken-for-granted notions of the present, such as sexuality or the prison. It is a counter-history that does not assume that the present is the result of progress or reason, but of power.

8. Max Weber was anxious over the loss of meaning and autonomy caused by bureaucratic rationalization. Eliasoph (2011) points out that the market for governmental projects has moved away from bureaucracy.

9. This analysis brings a consideration of the state to a growing body of research into the political and cultural uses of stories. Polletta (2006) describes stories as political acts and Harding (2010) considers them as cultural acts. Both are interested, to some extent, in the flexibility of stories, but provide little sense of how stories become policy. Ewick and Silbey (2003) describe how individual experiences of resistance become part of a larger social movement story. I show how they can become rationalized into programs and eventually applied to a different group.

10. Merry (2016), a legal anthropologist, has described how quantification in the world of global human rights serves to strip out social context. Harcourt (2007) has argued that actuarial data in criminal law can have unexpected consequences as they provoke responses to seemingly unjustified heightened surveillance.

11. The conceptualization of "switches in the tracks" is drawn from Weber, who contended that social change was determined in part by coincidences of history.

12. Nancy Matthews studied the collective and LACAAW, the organization it became, as well as several other groups navigating the transition from movement to local organization between 1972 and 1990 in Los Angeles County. Her book, *Confronting Rape* (1994), draws on case studies of six local crisis hotlines and interviews with officials and documents from the Office of Criminal Justice Planning (OCJP), which oversaw the Sexual Assault Program in the state.

13. For a history of anti-rape activism and public policy, see Bevacqua 2000.

14. Polletta (2006) argues that stories are politically effective when they are complex and morally ambiguous.

15. For a history of rape crisis centers, see Martin and Schmitt 2007; Martin 2005. Scholars have pointed to a variety of "paradoxes of professionalization" in feminist organizations—the trade-off between stability, funding, and legitimacy on one hand and stagnation, depoliticization, and donor discipline on the other (Staggenborg 1988; Markowitz and Tice 2002; Fried 1994). More broadly, Hwang and Powell (2009) describe how, across nonprofits, professionalization not only leads to full-time careers and expertise, but more professional ideals.

16. Urban sociologists have called for increased attention to historical context (Katz 2010) and collective action (Auyero, Bourgois, and Scheper-Hughes 2015). A focus on the role of place in social movements begins to fulfill both calls. Several scholars have explored how a variety of organizations' functions shift alongside historical changes (Katz 2010; Small 2004).

17. Drawing on Matthews 1994.

18. *Healthy People: The Surgeon General's Report on Health Promotion and Disease Prevention*, U.S. Department of Health, Education, and Welfare

(Washington, DC: U.S. Government Printing Office, 1979); https://profiles.nlm.nih.gov/ps/access/NNBBGK.pdf.

19. Faludi (1991) describes this backlash. Marwell (2004) provides a helpful overview of the processes of privatization and devolution.

20. Reger 2012. This required balancing internal feminist values against "environmental" pressures such as public opinion and by aligning with standardized organizational forms (Faludi 1991; Staggenborg and Taylor 2005; Thomas 1999).

21. Marwell 2009; McQuarrie and Marwell 2009.

22. For the panic around urban violence, see Cuklanz (1996) and Glassner (1999).

23. Anderson (1999), Rios (2011), and Goffman (2014) all chronicle the way that policing constrains and reshapes daily life in poor urban communities of color. Merry (2008) describes the spatial segregation of the policing of gender violence in cities. There is a long history in urban sociology and criminology of investigating urban violence; interpersonal violence is rarely included in these studies. I have set out to bring together feminist thinking on violence with urban sociology to lay the groundwork for a sociology of interpersonal violence and place.

24. Richie 2012.

25. See Manning (2011) for the ways that technology has changed policing.

26. Simon 2007; Kohler-Hausmann 2013; Western 2006. Roughly 2.2 million people are in jails and prisons and roughly 5 million people are under some form of correctional supervision. Out of all the Black men born since the late 1970s, a quarter have been to prison by their mid-thirties. Of those who dropped out of high school, seven in ten have been to prison.

27. Criminalization is often racialized, as police officers and third-party police attach notions of criminality to specific kinds of racial bodies; see Rios 2011.

28. The Juvenile Crime Challenge. Retrieved from www.lhc.ca.gov/sites/lhc.ca.gov/files/Reports/127/Report127.pdf.

29. Flores (2013) describes how Homeboy Industries uses religious gang rehabilitation to transform former gang members' masculinities.

30. Hartmann (2016) chronicles Midnight Basketball, which arose during this same time and reflects many facets of the ephemeral state.

31. The twentieth century marked the rise of "surveillance medicine" that tracked and measured individuals against the normal rates of whole healthy populations. The population came into view as an object, with patterns—births, deaths, suicides, violence, disease—consistent beyond the subjects comprising it. Babies were charted along the normal curve of the height and weight chart, and hygiene came to schools, paired with regular checkups, daily exercise, and mental health (Armstrong 1995).

32. For Prothrow-Stith's work (with Michaele Weissman), see *Deadly Consequences: How Violence Is Destroying Our Teenage Population and a Plan to Begin Solving the Problem* (1991).

33. Cohen and Swift (1993) lay out the public health approach to violence.

34. "The Prevention of Youth Violence: A Framework for Community Action." Retrieved from https://wonder.cdc.gov/wonder/prevguid/p0000026/p0000026 .asp#head001000000000000.

35. Armstrong 2009.

36. For the history of the violence-prevention program Mentors in Violence Prevention, see Katz, Heisterkamp, and Fleming 2011.

37. In an intriguing parallel, Green and Kolar (2015) describe the disjuncture between biomedical science of HIV / AIDS and the social science epistemology of behavioral intervention.

38. On June 17, 1994, the same year as VAWA, the O. J. Simpson case caused sharp rises in reports of domestic violence in cities across the country, but perhaps nowhere more than in Los Angeles, where news reports stated that crisis calls had increased by 80 percent. Cathy Friedman, in the June 26, 1994 *New York Times* article "Calls to Spouse-Abuse Hot Lines on the Rise," is quoted explaining that men began calling too, stating: 'I don't want it to turn into what happened with O. J.'" (www.nytimes.com/1994/06/26/us/calls-to-spouse-abuse-hot-lines-on-the-rise.html). An organization that launched in response to the O. J. case, Victory Over Violence, prefigured Peace Over Violence.

39. Richie (2012) describes "carceral feminism" as the strategy used by some feminists whereby they encourage increased policing, which ends up hurting Black communities, and Black women in particular. Also see Corrigan (2013) for an analysis of the unexpected consequences of anti-rape laws.

40. Purvin 2007.

41. Soss, Schram, and Fording (2011) in particular have described the rise of what they call neoliberal paternalism, the approach of the state to disciplining and constraining the choices of the poor. Hays (2003) describes welfare reform and the immense pressure to work and marry that it carried with it.

42. For more on the historical tensions between post- and pre-violence policies, as well as distinctions between victim and perpetrator orientations, see Greenberg and Messner 2014.

43. Sharkey (2018) describes the impact of local citizens and organizations— as well as increases in policing—in bringing about the crime decline.

44. In particular, it seems that public health researchers focused on forms of violence that the criminal justice system often failed to control, such as sexual assault, sexual harassment, bullying, interpersonal violence, teen dating violence, and emotional abuse.

45. www.lhc.ca.gov/sites/lhc.ca.gov/files/Reports/159/ExecutiveSummary159 .pdf.

46. Pan and Bai (2009), drawing on a meta-analysis of 20 controlled studies, found that teens enrolled in the program were just as likely to use drugs as were those who received no intervention. See also Lynam et al. 1999.

47. Messner, Greenberg, and Peretz 2015. The name change represented a trend toward bringing multiple forms of violence prevention together. "The Contagion of Violence" explains, "researchers have recognized the tendency for violent acts to cluster, to spread from place to place, and to mutate from one type to another" (IOM 2012: 1.2). Created by epidemiologist Gary Slutkin, Project Cease-Fire in Chicago was built on the premise that "the spread of violence mimics the spread of infectious diseases, and so the treatment should be similar: go after the most infected and stop the infection at its source" (Kotlowitz 2008). Project CeaseFire became CureViolence.

48. Murphy (2009) analyzed the MyStrength public media campaign and argues that it sends contradictory messages to young men about their role in contesting violence.

49. A commentary by Schubert (2015) lays out Robert Wood Johnson's approach to healthy relationships and a culture of health more broadly.

50. Several other healthcare companies have also begun to fund violence prevention through their foundation arms as well, including for the California Endowment, which was founded by Blue Cross of California.

51. For more on positive youth development, see Catalano et al. 2004.

52. See Mounk 2017. The language here implies that violence is a choice, but not a choice that one should make. It frames choice not as a moral value aligned with freedom, but a responsibility.

53. Prevention by this point had shifted almost entirely to a focus on youth. In 2015, of the nine programs under the umbrella of the CDC's Division of Violence Prevention, five were focused on youth programs, two were data collection mechanisms, and the final two, which focused on domestic violence and rape prevention, both contained significant youth elements.

54. Law enforcement agencies "weed out" violent criminals and drug abusers, and public agencies and community-based private organizations collaborate to "seed" human services, including prevention, intervention, treatment, and neighborhood restoration programs.

55. Fineberg 2013: 85.

56. This proliferation of "programs in a box" has meant less professionalized facilitators and more of what Lichterman (2006) describes as "plug-in" work.

57. In theorizing this process, I drew on the research on medicalization, the process whereby social problems—alcoholism for example—come to be seen as medical problems and thus are met with the tools of medical intervention: doctors and hospitals and pharmaceuticals among them. Scholars argued that medicalization narrowed institutions' focus to treating individual pathologies and obscured the role of social structures in producing health and disease. See Conrad and Schneider 1980; Zola 1972; McKinlay 1979.

58. While this chapter concerns interpersonal violence in particular, curricularization appears to have occurred with other social ills, such as poverty, gang

violence, drug use, teen pregnancy, smoking, obesity, anorexia, homelessness, AIDS, and drunk driving.

CHAPTER 3. STATISTICAL LIVES

1. Feinberg 2013. Degutis (2012: 232) also describes the relationship between statistics and lived experience: "From language comes the ability to tell stories—to put a face on the data and make it real for people who do not live in a world of p values, confidence intervals and standard deviations."

2. My analysis draws on scholarship in the social studies of science and technology, which explores how seemingly objective science is made within and shaped by distinct social contexts. See, for example, the foundational book by Latour and Woolgar (1986) that describes the social production of laboratory science. Also see Merry (2016), an ethnographic study of the production of indicators.

3. Records data can tell us how many people called the police because of a violent partner or who showed up at the emergency room with an injury. In this way, it reveals how people interact with institutions. Survey data collects information directly from a representative sample of individuals through questionnaires. Examples include the National Violence Against Women Survey or the National Intimate Partner and Sexual Violence Survey. Survey data often show higher rates of violence when compared with records data, pointing to a gap between the violence that is reported to authorities and people's self-reported experiences.

4. Perhaps the most widely used application of this logic is what is called the Adverse Childhood Experiences Study, or ACES, which examined the long-term impacts of 12 types of childhood trauma, including abuse, sexual assault, death of a parent, and parental drug abuse. The study found that the more ACEs one has, the worse his or her mental and physical health as an adult. See more at www.cdc.gov/violenceprevention/acestudy/index.html.

5. Rose 2001: 7. In their histories of risk and probabilistic thinking, Hacking (1990) and Rose (2006) trace the genealogy of this logic and orientation toward power.

6. With the rise of "preventive strategies," the dangerous subject was replaced as the object of inquiry by a pool of risk factors solidified in a "case file" and discovered through a shifting array of experts and surveillance pursuing "risk reduction" (Castel et al. 1991: 281). Kelly (2000) analyzes the youth at-risk discourse as a form of governmentality that enables unprecedented regulation of young people's lives and their identities. Kelly (2007) builds a theoretical argument about the process through which risks are abstracted from young people. That argument parallels some of what I say here.

7. Mills 1959.

8. De Santos 2009: 468. See also Foucault et al. 1991; Hacking 1990; Law 2009.

9. Espeland and Sauder (2007) on college rankings and Igo (2008) on public opinion polls both describe some of the ways that new forms of data have cultural consequences for groups and identities.

10. Allen (2017: 150) points to a similar dynamic in how statistics shaped crime policy: "The legislators who voted to try as adults sixteen-year-olds, and then fourteen-year-olds, were not interested in retribution. They had become deterrence theorists. They were designing sentences not for people but for a thing: the aggregate level of crime. They wanted to reduce that level, regardless of what constituted justice for any individual involved. The target of Michael's sentence was not a bright fifteen-year-old boy with a mild proclivity for theft but the thousands of carjackings that occurred in Los Angeles. Deterrence dehumanizes. It directs at the individual the full hatred that society understandably has for an aggregate phenomenon. But no individual should bear that kind of responsibility."

11. See Harcourt (2006) for a discussion of actuarial policing. Some statistical analysis seeks to capture additional facets of individuals' lives to explain this variation within high-risk groups. Problem Behavior Theory (Jessor 1992) is one example.

12. Ray (2017b) describes how upwardly mobile marginalized youth deploy risk narratives in order to distance themselves from other marginalized youth.

13. Dworkin 1983.

14. Shim (2014) describes how the variable of race works as a blunt measure of a diverse array of factors: place, stress, culture, diet, racism, socioeconomic status. Molina (2006) describes how public health agencies in Los Angeles had once explicitly constructed racial categories. Now, place obscures the function of racial inequality.

15. For example, Duck (2009) describes how law enforcement can construct narratives of violent incidents that are starkly different from community members' accounts.

16. The CDC highlights eight risk factors for teen dating violence—whether youth: believe that dating violence is acceptable; are depressed, anxious, or have other symptoms of trauma; display aggression toward peers or display other aggressive behaviors; use drugs or illegal substances; engage in early sexual activity and have multiple sexual partners; have a friend involved in dating violence; have conflicts with a partner; witness or experience violence in the home. In a review of the research, Vagi et al. (2013) found 53 risk factors for teen dating violence across 20 studies. Also see Higgins et al. 2017.

17. Rios 2011.

18. Ferguson 2001.

19. Laursen and Henriksen (2018) describe how different understandings of violence between audiences and facilitators, in their case in Danish prisons, lead to disputes and misunderstandings.

20. Blume 2014. This number includes alternative school programs.

21. Sum et al. 2014.

22. Ray (2017b) notes that analyses often miss the "less sensational pain and suffering" that is everyday in the lives of marginalized individuals, such as hunger, unstable homes, bodily discomfort, relationships burdened by too many responsibilities, and long hours traveling to work and school.

23. Morris 2012.

24. Los Angeles has the highest concentration of garment industry workers in the country. According to one study by the U.S. Department of Labor, 85 percent of garment industry employers studied were violating federal minimum wage and record-keeping laws, and some workers took home as little as $3 an hour.

25. Today, the average trucker in America makes about $40,000 per year, considerably less than the $110,000 they would have been making in comparable dollars in 1980, and they often work more and have less job security. See www.theatlantic.com/business/archive/2016/05/truck-stop/481926/.

26. According to Rumberger and Losen (2016), suspensions caused a 6.5 percentage point drop in graduation rates.

27. www2.ed.gov/policy/gen/guid/school-discipline/data.html: Of the 49 million students enrolled in public schools in 2011–12: 3.5 million students were suspended in-school; 3.45 million students were suspended out-of-school; 130,000 students were expelled.

28. www.childtrends.org/indicators/physical-fighting-by-youth: About one in four high school students report having been in a physical fight in the past year.

29. www.edweek.org/ew/issues/student-mobility/index.html: More than 6.5 million students nationwide experience school mobility, which has negative consequences for learning and social relationships.

30. The Los Angeles Unified School District student body in 2010 was majority-minority: 74 percent Latinx and 9 percent white. The ratio differed significantly from the largely white Beverly Hills Unified School District (5 percent Latinx and 74 percent white).

31. Loneliness causes a raft of health problems: https://www.nytimes.com/2017/12/11/well/mind/how-loneliness-affects-our-health.html.

32. https://www.publicintegrity.org/2012/12/27/11984/los-angeles-school-police-still-ticketing-thousands-young-students: In 2013, Los Angeles issued nearly half of all of its student tickets to minors under the age of 14.

33. Somers (1994) describes how identity is constructed through narrative.

34. See Rios (2017) for a description of how Latinx youth are criminalized and culturally misrecognized.

35. Scholars have pointed to "missing discourses" in the way we talk to youth. Fine (1988) described the missing discourse of desire in sexual education. Bettie (2003) pointed to a missing discourse of class.

CHAPTER 4. FAMILIAR STRANGERS

1. As Haney (1996: 759) argues, the state is not a single monolithic entity, but a "network of differentiated institutions layered with conflicting and competing messages."

2. Eliasoph (2011) also documents how unclear funding guidelines strained connections between youth marked at risk and civic project volunteers.

3. Haney (1996) draws on ethnographic data to develop a theoretical analysis of the state at the level of micro-processes of power. See also Lipsky 1980; Watkins-Hays 2009.

4. Seim (2017) and Lara-Millan (2014) describe how poverty governance works by alternately slowing and rushing care to the poor.

5. Auyero (2012) describes the institutionalized waiting forced on poor people as a means of domination, as does Reid (2013). We also can see the slow state in the factory logic of the school and the warehousing logic of the prison.

6. Rose, O'Malley, and Valverde (2006: 89) have argued that the supportive arm of the state has not retreated from the lives of citizens, but rather has become increasingly engaged in "governing at a distance"—"acting from a center of calculation such as a government office or the headquarters of a nongovernmental organization on the desires and activities of others who [are] spatially and organizationally distinct." Soss, Fording, and Schram (2011) describe the rise of programs aimed at transforming the poor as neoliberal paternalism.

7. In a 2018 article in *Sociological Perspectives*, I describe how facilitators attempted to cultivate empowerment within the disciplinary context of the school. See Ball et al. (2015) for a more formal assessment of the experiences of facilitators.

8. Throughout the 1990s, school-based health and safety programs were largely implemented by institutional insiders, such as health teachers or, in the case of D. A. R. E., by representatives of other state institutions, such as police officers.

9. In some ways, the connections formed between youth and facilitators resembled the "disposable ties" that Desmond (2012) found between the urban poor: brief and filled with intensity.

10. Rios (2017) describes cultural misrecognition as the way that adult authorities make incorrect assumptions about the behaviors and motivations of Latinx youth. In Rios's case the consequences were unjustified policing and surveillance.

11. See Rios 2011; Ferguson 2001; Becker 1963.

12. The way that Lauren used the term "at risk" was distinct from its technical statistical application.

13. In Seim's (2017) study of ambulance care, he describes how, in a fragmented state, the burden of caring for the poor—and the poor themselves—are shuffled between institutions. Something similar happens within the school.

14. At risk can be used as a code word for Black and Brown youth. In the schools with prevention programs, where the vast majority of the students were students of color, the label did not function that way. Hughey and Jackson (2017) describe how "inner-city school" has been used to obscure and constitute race. As inner cities are gentrified and the schools in inner cities are increasingly populated by white students, it seems possible that at risk may replace inner-city as the code word for Black and Brown students.

15. Timmermans and Berg 2003.

16. Latour and Woolgar (1986) describe laboratories as social contexts subject to the same social dynamics as other groups, rather than as bastions of objective science.

17. Burawoy 1979.

18. For a history of child maltreatment policy, including mandated reporting, see Nelson 1984.

19. "Report of the Attorney General's National Task Force on Children Exposed to Violence," December 12, 2012, at www.justice.gov/defendingchildhood /cev-rpt-full.pdf.

20. Social movement theorists use the term "free spaces" to describe settings—such as the consciousness-raising groups of the feminist movement— that are set aside from the direct observation of authorities, which allow interactions among those who would resist or advocate reform (Kellogg 2009; Polletta 1999).

CHAPTER 5. STORIES COME APART

1. Program development involves creating a logic model: list potential risk and protective factors and map the causal pathways and how they relate to perpetration or victimization; see Hawkins et al. 2009.

2. Hlavka (2014) describes how young women make sense of widespread and commonplace gendered violence in ways that can prevent it from being reported.

3. Prevention programs often draw on social psychological theories of behavioral change, such as Bandura 1986; Janz and Becker 1984; Ajzen 1991. For an overview of health promotion theories, see U.S. Department of Health and Human Services 2005.

4. Health promotion has produced a "moral imperative of health" extending into the realms of habits, diet, marketing, sex, and more. Health, as a collection

of "technologies of the self," shapes the way we "understand, think and talk about and live our bodies" in ways that reinforce gender difference, class status, and productive citizenship (Lupton 1995: 6). See also Dworkin and Wachs 2009; Rose 1990.

5. Feminist scholars have shown that gendered narratives are built in to state welfare policies. See Randles 2015; Curran and Abrams 2000; Hays 2003.

6. Polletta et al. (2011) describe three key aspects of narrative: First, power inheres in storytelling rights that are unevenly distributed. Second, stories often unfold over repeated interactions rather than being told in an uninterrupted fashion. Third, the meaning of the story is often negotiated by teller and audience.

7. These quotes are drawn from the 2004 edition of Safe Dates.

8. Foshee et al. 1998; Foshee et al. 2005; Foshee et al. 2014; Tharp 2012.

9. Foshee et al. 1998.

10. See, for example, Pascoe 2007.

11. Plummer 1994. Stories are mechanisms through which we create coherent narratives of our experience, and, at the same time, they are negotiations we undertake with others over what is true and possible (Ewick and Silbey 2003; Somers 1994). Rosen (2017) has argued that the failure of a narrative, called "narrative rupture," triggers action.

12. Harding (2010) describes three patterns of attachment to cultural narratives: model shifting (weak commitments to cultural models); dilution (lack of knowledge about models); and simultaneity (conflicts between competing models).

13. Drawing on the case of young women in Malawi, Frye (2012) describes how "future goals" are shaped not just by rational choices, but by the social meaning of stated aspirations. In this case, Frye finds that young women draw on the public campaigns aimed at them to make their claims to a virtuous identity. Ralph (2014) describes how marginalized young men look to "renegade dreams" to organize their efforts to overcome obstacles.

14. Orlando Patterson, a sociologist at the heart of the debate around culture, suggested in a 2014 essay in the *Chronicle of Higher Education* that "cultural values, norms, beliefs, and habitual practices may be easier to change than structural ones." In many ways, social policies have bounded past these theoretical debates and made cultural change a focal point of prevention programs.

15. My interest is not in effectiveness per se, or in distinctions between programs, but rather in the shared aspects of curricula. For this reason, I do not always distinguish which curriculum was being used.

16. Scholars of youth and education have long argued that students are not simply passive receptacles of school processes (Willis 1977). Instead, young people actively engage in learning and, at times, oppose cultural forms (Rios 2011; Nolan 2011; McLeod 1987).

17. Lewis and Russell (2012) argue that public health campaigns are insufficient to overcome the structural forces within which people engage in "unhealthy" and "risky" behaviors.

18. Personal narratives and policy narratives differ. For example, Fine (1988) notes that sex education lacked the discourse that young women used about sexual agency. However, scholars have not adequately explored how personal narratives and policy narratives intersect and influence each other.

19. The *New York Times* wrote a story on a similar exercise; www.nytimes.com/2012/06/04/us/middle-school-students-focus-of-anti-violence-effort.html.

20. Bettie (2003) describes the missing discourse of class among young women in a California high school.

21. Polletta et al. (2013) draw on a survey and focus-group study to argue that, though plot lines may be adapted to shifting circumstances, audiences' expectations of characters are rigid.

22. See, for example, the scene that precedes this chapter, which is pulled from Safe Dates.

23. Institutions generate "cultural commonsense" as repeated interactions can make patterns of belief and action feel normal and logical. See Swidler 2001; Armstrong and Hamilton 2006.

24. See Shedd (2015) and Nolan (2011) for discussions of the enactment of power and control in schools. As several scholars have noted, urban public schools in particular have been subsumed under what Garland (2001) called a "culture of control."

25. McFarland (2004) develops an interactional understanding of student resistance, which points both to the way that classrooms are contested spaces and how an interactional-level analysis provides distinct insights.

26. Harding et al. (2016) explore how narratives change, or sometimes do not, in response to structural constraints.

27. Certainly, training and skill matter for the effectiveness of facilitators. However, beyond that, there is a disjuncture between how the curriculum is constructed and the dynamics of social interaction.

28. I draw on Goffman (1983) to think about the interactions that occur during programs. See Anderson (1990) and Duneier (1999) for analyses of how interactions between strangers can go wrong in public contexts.

29. In my analysis of the after-effects of programs, I draw on research into audience reception. In particular, I was inspired by Radway (1991), who explores how women take unexpected meanings away from romance novels.

30. Evaluations, I found, were unable to capture this nuance. Rather than look to survey responses, I pursued three related questions in depth in interviews: First, I examined how young people rearticulated the narrative of the

program. Second, I explored how they felt that they applied what they learned in the program to their lives. Lastly, I assessed whether or not young people felt that they had changed because of the program and how.

31. See Polletta et al. (2013) for a discussion of plot and character in narratives of interpersonal violence. See Best (2011) and Abrams and Hyun (2008) for a discussion of the way young people construct identities. Trimbur (2011) describes how discourses of responsibility shift meaning as they move across contexts.

32. Ewick and Silbey (2003) draw on narratives of interactions with the law to show how stories are used to give acts of resistance life beyond their direct consequences.

33. Collins 2000. This is one reason why violence prevention programs represent a valuable case study in understanding narrative projects.

34. Narratives are best conceptualized as processes, not distinct entities: "A story draws upon the well of past stories and flows into future stories" (Ewick and Silbey 2003). Change programs provide a distinct opportunity to understand narratives under construction. Tavory and Eliasoph (2013) describe somewhat different definitions of narratives and projects.

35. Ray 2017a. For how postfeminism undermines the messages of sexual violence prevention, see Burkett and Hamilton 2012.

36. Messner 2011.

37. Scholars have described a pattern of "contrived carelessness" among young men in schools (Morris 2012). This pattern of behavior entails downplaying investment in education. While I saw some of this, it was not echoed in my conversations, nor was it the most common response from men, perhaps because educational content was not my focus.

38. Here, Alex echoes what sociologists have found about labeling (Becker 1963).

39. See Ray (2017b) for a description of how upwardly mobile young women navigate the challenges of relationships in the context of a powerful risk discourse.

40. Chan Tack and Small (2017) describe how navigating violence in childhood shaped friendships and physical movements.

41. Maticka-Tyndale (1992) makes a similar point about the distinctions between the way that scientific discourses construct the risk of HIV/AIDS and the way that individuals construct risk in their daily lives.

42. Finkelhor et al. 2014.

CHAPTER 6. THE STATE OF ADULTS

1. See Varga and Zaff 2017; Resnick et al. 1997.

2. Murphey et al. 2013; Spencer et al. 2016; National Scientific Council on the Developing Child 2004; Meltzer, Muir, and Craig 2018.

3. According to Murphey et al. (2013), about one in ten youth did not have close relationships with adults outside the home (as reported by parents). But this number is higher for those where English was not the primary language at home, less affluent families, and those families in which the mother had less than a high school degree.

4. Edin and Nelson (2013), who documented the lives of unwed fathers, provide an example of this.

5. There is a body of research in public health and education on "school climate." Although I am concerned with similar questions, I apply a critical, social-structural analysis. Rather than think of schools as possessing a diffuse culture, I concentrate on specific social ties and how they are situated within systems of power and authority. Rios (2017) takes a similar approach to understanding adults in the lives of marginalized youth.

6. There are, of course, other angles from which to view the state. Most significantly, the men and women caught up in the system of mass incarceration experience the state as a total institution. Those who work for the state—such as politicians, street-level bureaucrats, and military personnel—also see the state from a different angle.

7. Justice and Meares 2013.

8. Haney (1996) developed a theoretical approach to understanding the contested terrain of the state in practice. Haney is focused on gender and women in particular, while I am interested in the contested meanings of the state in the lives of marginalized young people.

9. In contrast to prevailing formulations of neighborhoods as having singular cultures, Harding (2010) describes how neighborhoods contain multiple, often contradictory cultural frames.

10. Kulkarni (2017) describes the dissonant disciplinary responses from adults that become evident in response to major breaches of discipline, such as a fight.

11. Much of the existing research on interactions between citizens and the state focuses on clear and bounded interactions such as police stops or welfare orientations; see Epp, Maynard-Mooney, and Haider-Markel 2014; Watkins-Hays 2009. However, schools are one of the few places outside of incarceration where interactions with the state are sustained and open ended.

12. Lipsky (1980) points out that the state "teaches political lessons contributing to future political expectations" by way of street-level interactions between citizens and state representatives. Here, I am riffing on C. Wright Mills's (1959) description of the way that public issues can often feel like personal problems.

13. Soss, Fording, and Schram 2011.

14. See Garland 2001; Simon 2007; Goffman 2009.

15. Freeman, Kim, and Rawson 2013.

16. Nolan 2011; Kupchick 2012.

17. Urban schools in particular have been reshaped by a heightened police presence, multiple forms of surveillance, and exclusionary punishment (Shedd 2015; Lyons and Drew 2006). Escalating crime control approaches in urban schools are transforming urban education for youth of color in ways that differ from and outpace those at majority-white schools (Welch and Payne 2010; Hirschfield 2008; Kupchik and Ward 2014). Excluded and punished youth, most significantly young men of color, suffer directly in terms of education, grades, and dropout rates (Kang-Brown et al. 2013).

18. The "ubiquity of the threat" of punishment dominates the daily life in schools to such an extent that students who are not punished directly still experience the symbols and technologies of disciplinary control, as well as its consequences: alienation, distrust of authority, and anxiety (Nolan 2011: 68; Perry and Morris 2014). Such contexts promote "legal cynicism," the view of law enforcement as illegitimate, and create a sense of injustice and "shared skepticism of a range of governmental institutions" (Hagan, Shedd, and Payne 2005: 398). Brayne (2014) has found that contact with the criminal justice system can lead individuals to avoid institutions that carry out surveillance.

19. Shedd (2015) found that in Chicago, nearly half of all students had interactions with police officers at some point, while significant proportions had been searched and arrested.

20. The inconsistent application of the law is one cause of legal cynicism. In my research, it was not just that law enforcement seemed unfair, but that police don't seem like law at all.

21. Shedd 2015.

22. Garcia 2012; Miller 2008.

23. For more on young women and violence, see Jones 2009; Miller 2008.

24. See Holland (2015) for a discussion of the dynamics underlying trust between students and counselors.

25. Freeman, Kim, and Rawson 2013: 16.

26. Foucault 1995: 189.

27. Morris 2010.

28. For a robust consideration of surveillance, see Marx 2016; Lyon 1994.

29. Personalized surveillance is different from Brayne's (2017) "big data surveillance," which is largely crime focused.

30. In fact, school-based adults could be valuable resources for youth. Small (2017) argues that people are more often to talk through issues and concerns with someone on the outside edges of their social network, rather than risk their personal life becoming fodder for discussion.

31. Much of the ethnographic literature on governmentality has explored how state and private programs aim to reshape the behavior of troublesome populations through responsibilization (Fox 1999; Franzén 2014). Ethnographic studies have shown that in such programming a "discourse of freedom" can reinforce

disciplinary control (Haney 2010; Gengler 2012). Silva (2012) describes how similar social forces impact working-class people in their 20s and 30s.

32. Schooling enacts a hidden curriculum alongside the formal curriculum; see Meighan and Harber 2007. For an analysis of the hidden gender and sexuality curriculum, see Pascoe 2007.

33. Anderson (1999) discusses how a cultural system arises in urban neighborhoods to navigate interpersonal violence when the rule of law is absent. He states that this code "emerges where the influence of the police ends and personal responsibility for one's safety is felt to begin" (p. 10). I set out to include how personal responsibility is also constructed by the state in the context of schools.

34. Kwon (2013) draws on ethnographic data in after-school and community-based youth organizing projects to examine the workings of power in the development of self-empowered and responsible citizens, particularly youth of color. Similar to the prevention programs that I researched, the organizing projects that Kwon studied are mobilized to prevent potentially "at-risk" youth from turning to "juvenile delinquency" and focuses on the tensions between meaningful personal change and the ramifications of large-scale entrenchment of nonprofits in the logic of a neoliberal state. Kwon reaches similar conclusions about the role of neoliberalism in shifting approaches to youth, but is oriented toward the theoretical implications for the production of neoliberal subjects.

35. Mounk (2017) describes how the concept of responsibility in the United States has been narrowed over the last 40 years, from a conception of shared social responsibility to personal responsibility.

36. Rose 1999.

37. Rose, O'Malley, and Valverde 2006: 90.

38. The young people in this study were different from the youth chronicled in the work of scholars like Rios (2011), who describe young men resisting "the system" of structural inequality rather than placing responsibility on themselves.

39. Oeur (2016) argues for a reframing of the language we use to describe criminalized young men of color, away from respect and toward dignities.

40. In this way, Zephire was constantly choosing from an array of cultural strategies to get by (Harding 2010; Carter 2005).

41. Duck (2017) recounts a stunningly similar story of a young Black man bringing a Japanese weapon to school to show to friends and being met with zero-tolerance policies.

42. Anderson 1999.

43. See Pomerantz, Raby, and Stefanik (2013) for a discussion of the contradictions between sexism and postfeminism in schools.

44. The threat of violence is particularly stark for women of color and poor or working-class women, who encounter sexual and domestic violence without a robust institutional support network (Miller 2008; Sokoloff and Dupont 2005). A distrust of the criminal justice system along with a cultural focus on

compulsory heterosexuality and personal responsibility leads young women to rarely report sexual violence (Hlavka 2014).

45. Garcia 2012; Miller 2008.

46. Ray (2017a) describes how upwardly mobile young women of color in poor neighborhoods used empowerment language to symbolically distance themselves from peers. I found something similar.

EPILOGUE: THE FUTURE

1. Western 2018.
2. Addams [1909] 2010: 161.

APPENDIX. AN EPHEMERAL ETHNOGRAPHY

1. Rios 2011.
2. Burawoy 2009.
3. See Griffith et al. 2017.
4. Small 2017.

References

Abrams, L.S., and A. Hyun. 2008. "Mapping a Process of Negotiated Identity among Incarcerated Male Juvenile Offenders." *Youth & Society* 41(1): 26–52.

Addams, J. [1909] 2010. *The Spirit of Youth and the City Streets*. ReadaClassic .com.

Ajzen, I. 1991. "The Theory of Planned Behavior." *Organizational Behavior and Human Decision Processes* 50: 179–211.

Allen, D.S. 2017. *Cuz: The Life and Times of Michael A*. New York: Liveright.

Anderson, E. 1990. *Streetwise: Race, Class, and Change in an Urban Community*. Chicago: University of Chicago Press.

———. 1999. *Code of the Street: Decency, Violence, and the Moral Life of the Inner City*. New York: W.W. Norton.

Armstrong, D. 1995. "The Rise of Surveillance Medicine." *Sociology of Health & Illness* 17(3): 393–404.

———. 2009. "Origins of the Problem of Health-Related Behaviours." *Social Studies of Science* 39(6): 909–26.

Armstrong, E.A., L. Hamilton, and B. Sweeney. 2006. "Sexual Assault on Campus: A Multilevel, Integrative Approach to Party Rape." *Social Problems* 53(4): 483–99.

Auyero, J. 2012. *Patients of the State: The Politics of Waiting in Argentina*. Durham, NC: Duke University Press.

——— and K. Jensen. 2015. "For Political Ethnographies of Urban Marginality." *City & Community* 14(4): 359–63.

———, P. Bourgois, and N. Scheper-Hughes, eds. 2015. *Violence at the Urban Margins*. New York: Oxford University Press.

Ball, B., K. M. Holland, K. J. Marshall, C. Lippy, S. Jain, et al. 2015. "Implementing a Targeted Teen Dating Abuse Prevention Program: Challenges and Successes Experienced by Expect Respect Facilitators." *Journal of Adolescent Health* 56(2): S40–46.

Ball, B., A. T. Tharp, R. K. Noonan, L. A. Valle, M. E. Hamburger, and B. Rosenbluth. 2012. "Expect Respect Support Groups: Preliminary Evaluation of a Dating Violence Prevention Program for At-Risk Youth." *Violence Against Women* 18(7): 746–62.

Bandura, A. 1985. *Social Foundations of Thought and Action: A Social Cognitive Theory*. Englewood Cliffs, NJ: Prentice Hall.

Barcelos, C. A., and A. C. Gubrium. 2014. "Reproducing Stories: Strategic Narratives of Teen Pregnancy and Motherhood." *Social Problems* 61(3): 466–81.

Barker, G., C. Ricardo, M. Nascimento, A. Olukoya, and C. Santos. 2010. "Questioning Gender Norms with Men to Improve Health Outcomes: Evidence of Impact." *Global Public Health* 5(5): 539–53.

Barman, E. 2016. *Caring Capitalism: The Meaning and Measure of Social Value*. Cambridge: Cambridge University Press.

Becker, H. S. 1963. *Outsiders: Studies in the Sociology of Deviance*. New York: Free Press.

Best, A. 2011. "Youth Identity Formation: Contemporary Identity Work: Youth Identity Formation." *Sociology Compass* 5(10): 908–22.

Best, A. L., ed. 2007. *Representing Youth: Methodological Issues in Critical Youth Studies*. New York: NYU Press.

Bettie, J. 2003. *Women without Class: Girls, Race, and Identity*. Berkeley: University of California Press.

Bevacqua, M. 2000. *Rape on the Public Agenda: Feminism and the Politics of Sexual Assault*. Boston: Northeastern University Press.

Blume, H. 2014. "L. A. Unified Reports Big Rise in Its Graduation Rate." *Los Angeles Times*, October 3. www.latimes.com/local/education/la-me-1004-lausd-grad-rates-20141003-story.html.

Brayne, S. 2014. "Surveillance and System Avoidance: Criminal Justice Contact and Institutional Attachment." *American Sociological Review* 79(3): 367–91.

———. 2017. "Big Data Surveillance: The Case of Policing." *American Sociological Review* 82(5): 977–1008.

Bridges, K. M. 2017. *The Poverty of Privacy Rights*. Stanford, CA: Stanford Law Books.

Bridges, T. S. 2010. "Men Just Weren't Made to Do This: Performances of Drag at 'Walk a Mile in Her Shoes' Marches." *Gender & Society* 24(1): 5–30.

Burawoy, M. 1979. *Manufacturing Consent: Changes in the Labor Process under Monopoly Capitalism*. Chicago: University of Chicago Press.

———. 2009. *The Extended Case Method: Four Countries, Four Decades, Four Great Transformations, and One Theoretical Tradition.* Berkeley: University of California Press.

Burkett, M., and K. Hamilton. 2012. "Postfeminist Sexual Agency: Young Women's Negotiations of Sexual Consent." *Sexualities* 15(7): 815–33.

California Attorney General's Office and the California Department of Education. 2004. *A Preventable Epidemic: Teen Dating Violence.* Sacramento: Author.

Carter, P. L. 2005. *Keepin' It Real: School Success beyond Black and White.* New York: Oxford University Press.

Castel, R., M. Foucault, G. Burchell, and C. Gordon. 1991. "From Dangerousness to Risk." In *The Foucault Effect: Studies in Governmentality: With Two Lectures by and an Interview with Michel Foucault,* edited by G. Burchell, C. Gordon, and P. Miller. Chicago: University of Chicago Press.

Catalano, R. F., M. L. Berglund, J. A. M. Ryan, H. S. Lonczak, and J. D. Hawkins. 2004. "Positive Youth Development in the United States: Research Findings on Evaluations of Positive Youth Development Programs." *Annals of the American Academy of Political and Social Science* 591(1): 98–124.

Center for Youth Wellness. 2013. *A Hidden Crisis: Findings on Adverse Childhood Experiences in California.* https://centerforyouthwellness.org/wp-content/themes/cyw/build/img/building-a-movement/hidden-crisis.pdf.

Centers for Disease Control. 2012. *Youth Violence: Facts at a Glance.* www.cdc.gov/violenceprevention/pdf/yv-datasheet-a.pdf.

Chan Tack, A. M., and M. Small. 2017. "Making Friends in Violent Neighborhoods: Strategies among Elementary School Children." *Sociological Science* 4: 224–48.

Clear, E. R., A. L. Coker, P. G. Cook-Craig, H. M. Bush, L. S. Garcia, et al. 2014. "Sexual Harassment Victimization and Perpetration among High School Students." *Violence Against Women* 20(10): 1203–19.

Cohen, C. 2010. *Democracy Remixed: Black Youth and the Future of American Politics.* New York: Oxford University Press.

Cohen, L., and S. Swift. 1993. "A Public Health Approach to the Violence Epidemic in the United States." *Environment and Urbanization* 5(2): 50–66.

Collins, P. H. 2000. *Black Feminist Thought: Knowledge, Consciousness, and the Politics of Empowerment.* New York: Routledge.

Conrad, P., and J. W. Schneider. 1980. *Deviance and Medicalization: From Badness to Sickness.* Philadelphia: Temple University Press.

Contreras, R. 2012. *The Stickup Kids: Race, Drugs, Violence, and the American Dream.* Berkeley: University of California Press.

Corrigan, R. 2013. *Up against a Wall: Rape Reform and the Failure of Success.* New York: NYU Press.

Cruikshank, B. 1999. *The Will to Empower: Democratic Citizens and Other Subjects.* Ithaca, NY: Cornell University Press.

Cuklanz, L. M. 1996. *Rape on Trial: How the Mass Media Construct Legal Reform and Social Change.* Philadelphia: University of Pennsylvania Press.

Curran, L., and L. S. Abrams. 2000. "Making Men into Dads." *Gender & Society* 14(5): 662–78.

Dahlberg, L. L., and J. A. Mercy. 2009. "History of Violence as a Public Health Problem." *Virtual Mentor* 11(2): 167–72.

Damon, W. 2004. "What Is Positive Youth Development?" *Annals of the American Academy of Political and Social Science* 591(1): 13–24.

David-Ferdon, C., and T. Simon. 2014. "Preventing Youth Violence: Opportunities for Action." National Center for Injury Prevention and Control, Centers for Disease Control and Prevention, Atlanta, GA.

De Santos, M. 2009. "Fact-Totems and the Statistical Imagination: The Public Life of a Statistic in Argentina 2001." *Sociological Theory* 27(4): 466–89.

DeGue, S., L. A. Valle, M. K. Holt, G. M. Massetti, J. L. Matjasko, and A. T. Tharp. 2014. "A Systematic Review of Primary Prevention Strategies for Sexual Violence Perpetration." *Aggression and Violent Behavior* 19(4): 346–62.

Degutis, L. C. 2012. "The Future of Injury and Violence Prevention: Where Are We Going?" *Journal of Safety Research* 43(4): 231–32.

Desmond, M. 2012. "Disposable Ties and the Urban Poor." *American Journal of Sociology* 117(5): 1295–335.

Duck, W. 2009. "'Senseless' Violence: Making Sense of Murder." *Ethnography* 10(4): 417–34.

———. 2017. "The Complex Dynamics of Trust and Legitimacy: Understanding Interactions between the Police and Poor Black Neighborhood Residents." *Annals of the American Academy of Political and Social Science* 673(1): 132–49.

Duneier, M. 1999. *Sidewalk.* New York: Farrar Straus & Giroux.

Dworkin, A. 1983. "I Want a 24-Hour-Truce during which There Is No Rape." Speech given at the Midwest Regional Conference of the National Organization for Changing Men, St. Paul, Minnesota. www.nostatusquo.com/ACLU /dworkin/WarZoneChaptIIIE.html.

Dworkin, S. L., A. M. Hatcher, C. Colvin, and D. Peacock. 2013. "Impact of a Gender-Transformative HIV and Antiviolence Program on Gender Ideologies and Masculinities in Two Rural, South African Communities." *Men and Masculinities* 16(2): 181–202.

Dworkin, S. L., and F. L. Wachs. 2009. *Body Panic: Gender, Health, and the Selling of Fitness.* New York: NYU Press.

Edin, K., and T. J. Nelson. 2013. *Doing the Best I Can: Fatherhood in the Inner City.* Berkeley: University of California Press.

Eikenberry, A. M., and J. D. Kluver. 2004. "The Marketization of the Nonprofit Sector: Civil Society at Risk?" *Public Administration Review* 64(2): 132–40.

Eliasoph, N. 2011. *Making Volunteers: Civic Life after Welfare's End*. Princeton, NJ: Princeton University Press.

Emerson, R. M., R. I. Fretz, and L. L. Shaw. 1995. *Writing Ethnographic Fieldnotes*. Chicago: University of Chicago Press.

Epp, C. R., S. Maynard-Moody, and D. P. Haider-Markel. 2014. *Pulled Over: How Police Stops Define Race and Citizenship*. Chicago and London: University of Chicago Press.

Espeland, W. N., and M. Sauder. 2007. "Rankings and Reactivity: How Public Measures Recreate Social Worlds." *American Journal of Sociology* 113(1): 1–40.

Ewick, P., and S. Silbey. 2003. "Narrating Social Structure: Stories of Resistance to Legal Authority." *American Journal of Sociology* 108(6): 1328–72.

Exner-Cortens, D., J. Eckenrode, and E. Rothman. 2013. "Longitudinal Association between Teen Dating Violence Victimization and Adverse Health Outcomes." *Pediatrics* 131(1): 71–78.

Faludi, S. 1991. *Backlash: The Undeclared War against American Women*. New York: Three Rivers Press.

Ferguson, A. A. 2001. *Bad Boys: Public Schools in the Making of Black Masculinity*. Ann Arbor: University of Michigan Press.

Fields, J. 2008. *Risky Lessons: Sex Education and Social Inequality*. New Brunswick, NJ: Rutgers University Press.

Fine, M. 1988. "Sexuality, Schooling, and Adolescent Females: The Missing Discourse of Desire." *Harvard Educational Review* 58(1): 29–54.

———, and S. I. McClelland. 2006. "Sexuality Education and Desire: Still Missing after All These Years." *Harvard Educational Review* 76(3): 297–338.

Fineberg, H. V. 2013. "The Paradox of Disease Prevention: Celebrated in Principle, Resisted in Practice." *JAMA* 310(1): 85–90.

Finkelhor, D., J. Vanderminden, H. Turner, A. Shattuck, and S. Hamby. 2014. "Youth Exposure to Violence Prevention Programs in a National Sample." *Child Abuse & Neglect* 38(4): 677–86.

Flores, E. 2013. *God's Gangs: Barrio Ministry, Masculinity, and Gang Recovery*. New York: NYU Press.

Foshee, V. A., K. E. Bauman, X. B. Arriaga, R. W. Helms, G. G. Koch, and G. F. Linder. 1998. "An Evaluation of Safe Dates, an Adolescent Dating Violence Prevention Program." *American Journal of Public Health* 88(1): 45–50.

Foshee, V. A., K. E. Bauman, S. T. Ennett, C. Suchindran, T. Benefield, and G. F. Linder. 2005. "Assessing the Effects of the Dating Violence Prevention Program 'Safe Dates' Using Random Coefficient Regression Modeling." *Prevention Science* 6(3): 245–58.

Foshee, V. A., L. M. Reyes, C. B. Agnew-Brune, T. R. Simon, K. J. Vagi, et al. 2014. "The Effects of the Evidence-Based Safe Dates Dating Abuse Prevention Program on Other Youth Violence Outcomes." *Prevention Science* 15(6): 907–16.

Foucault, M. 1995. *Discipline & Punish: The Birth of the Prison*. New York: Vintage Books.

———, M. Bertani, A. Fontana, F. Ewald, and D. Macey. 2003. *Society Must Be Defended: Lectures at the Collège de France, 1975–76*, vol. 1. New York: Picador USA.

———, G. Burchell, C. Gordon, and P. Miller. 1991. *The Foucault Effect: Studies in Governmentality: With Two Lectures by and an Interview with Michel Foucault*. Chicago: University of Chicago Press.

Fox, K. J. 1999. "Changing Violent Minds: Discursive Correction and Resistance in the Cognitive Treatment of Violent Offenders in Prison." *Social Problems* 46: 88.

Franzén, A. G. 2014. "Responsibilization and Discipline: Subject Positioning at a Youth Detention Home." *Journal of Contemporary Ethnography* 44(3): 251–79.

Freeman, J., D. Kim, and Z. Rawson. 2013. "Black, Brown, and Over-Policed in L. A. Schools." Community Rights Campaign of the Labor / Community Strategy Center, Los Angeles, CA.

Fried, A. 1994. "It's Hard to Change What We Want to Change." *Gender & Society* 8(4): 562–83.

Frye, M. 2012. "Bright Futures in Malawi's New Dawn: Educational Aspirations as Assertions of Identity." *American Journal of Sociology* 117(6): 1565–624.

———. 2017. "Cultural Meanings and the Aggregation of Actions: The Case of Sex and Schooling in Malawi." *American Sociological Review* 82(5): 945–76.

Garcia, L. 2012. *Respect Yourself, Protect Yourself: Latina Girls and Sexual Identity*. New York: NYU Press.

Garland, D. 1997. "'Governmentality' and the Problem Of Crime: Foucault, Criminology, Sociology." *Theoretical Criminology* 1(2): 173–214.

———. 2001. *The Culture of Control: Crime and Social Order in Contemporary Society*. New York: Oxford University Press.

Geertz, C. 1973. *The Interpretation of Cultures: Selected Essays*, vol. 5043. New York: Basic Books.

Gengler, A. M. 2012. "Defying (Dis)Empowerment in a Battered Women's Shelter: Moral Rhetorics, Intersectionality, and Processes of Control and Resistance." *Social Problems* 59(4): 501–21.

Gilmore, R. W. 2007. "In the Shadow of the Shadow State." In *The Revolution Will Not Be Funded: Beyond the Non-Profit Industrial Complex*, edited by INCITE! Women of Color against Violence, pp. 41–52. Cambridge, MA: South End Press.

Glassner, B. 1999. *The Culture of Fear: Why Americans Are Afraid of the Wrong Things*. New York: Basic Books.

Go, J. 2008. *American Empire and the Politics of Meaning: Elite Political Cultures in the Philippines and Puerto Rico during U.S. Colonialism*. Durham: Duke University Press Books.

Goffman, A. 2009. "On the Run: Wanted Men in a Philadelphia Ghetto."
    American Sociological Review 74(3): 339–57.
———. 2014. *On the Run: Fugitive Life in an American City.* Chicago and
    London: University of Chicago Press.
Goffman, E. 1983. "The Interaction Order: American Sociological Association,
    1982 Presidential Address." *American Sociological Review* 48(1): 1–17.
Green, A., and K. Kolar. 2015. "Engineering Behaviour Change in an Epidemic:
    The Epistemology of NIH-Funded HIV Prevention Science." *Sociology of
    Health & Illness* 37(4): 561–77.
Greenberg, M.A. 2018. "Empowerment in a Controlling Place: Youth Program
    Facilitators and Resistance to School Discipline." *Sociological Perspectives*
    61(4): 610–25.
———, and M.A. Messner. 2014. "Before Prevention: The Trajectory and
    Tensions of Feminist Antiviolence." In *Gendered Perspectives on Conflict and
    Violence: Part B,* vol. 18, edited by M.T. Segal and V. Demos, pp. 225–49.
    Bingley, West Yorkshire, UK: Emerald Group.
Griffith, D.M., R.C. Shelton, and M. Kegler. 2017. "Advancing the Science of
    Qualitative Research to Promote Health Equity." *Health Education &
    Behavior* 44(5): 673–76.
Hacking, I. 1990. *The Taming of Chance.* Cambridge: Cambridge University Press.
Hagan, J., C. Shedd, and M.R. Payne. 2005. "Race, Ethnicity, and Youth
    Perceptions of Criminal Justice." *American Sociological Review* 70(3):
    381–407.
Haney, L.A. 1996. "Homeboys, Babies, Men in Suits: The State and the
    Reproduction of Male Dominance." *American Sociological Review* 61(5):
    759–78.
———. 2010. *Offending Women: Power, Punishment, and the Regulation of
    Desire.* Berkeley: University of California Press.
Harcourt, B.E. 2007. *Against Prediction: Profiling, Policing, and Punishing in
    an Actuarial Age.* Chicago: University of Chicago Press.
Harding D.J. 2009. "Violence, Older Peers, and the Socialization of Adolescent
    Boys in Disadvantaged Neighborhoods." *American Sociological Review*
    74(3): 445–64.
———. 2010. *Living the Drama: Community, Conflict, and Culture among
    Inner-City Boys.* Chicago: University of Chicago Press.
———, C.C. Dobson, J.J. Wyse, and J.D. Morenoff. 2016. "Narrative Change,
    Narrative Stability, and Structural Constraint: The Case of Prisoner Reentry
    Narratives." *American Journal of Cultural Sociology* 5(1–2): 261–304.
Hartmann, D. 2016. *Midnight Basketball: Race, Sports, and Neoliberal Social
    Policy.* Chicago and London: University of Chicago Press.
Hasenfeld, Y. 1972. "People Processing Organizations: An Exchange Approach."
    American Sociological Review 37(3): 256.

Hawkins, S. R., A. M. Clinton-Sherrod, N. Irvin, L. Hart, and S. J. Russell. 2009. "Logic Models as a Tool for Sexual Violence Prevention Program Development." *Health Promotion Practice* 10(1): S29–37.

Hays, S. 2003. *Flat Broke with Children: Women in the Age of Welfare Reform.* New York: Oxford University Press.

Higgins, G. E., C. D. Marcum, J. Nicholson, and P. Weiner. 2017. "Predictors of Physical and Dating Violence in Middle and High School Students in the United States." *Crime & Delinquency* 64(5).

Hirschfield, P. J. 2008. "Preparing for Prison?: The Criminalization of School Discipline in the USA." *Theoretical Criminology* 12(1): 79–101.

Hlavka, H. R. 2014. "Normalizing Sexual Violence: Young Women Account for Harassment and Abuse." *Gender & Society* 28(3): 337–58.

Holland, M. M. 2015. "Trusting Each Other: Student-Counselor Relationships in Diverse High Schools." *Sociology of Education* 88(3): 244–62.

Holmes, S., and P. Bourgois. 2013. *Fresh Fruit, Broken Bodies: Migrant Farmworkers in the United States.* Berkeley: University of California Press.

Hughey, M. W., and C. A. Jackson. 2017. "The Dimensions of Racialization and the Inner-City School." *Annals of the American Academy of Political and Social Science* 673(1): 312–29.

Hwang, H., and W. W. Powell. 2009. "The Rationalization of Charity: The Influences of Professionalism in the Nonprofit Sector." *Administrative Science Quarterly* 54: 268–98.

Igo, S. E. 2008. *The Averaged American: Surveys, Citizens, and the Making of a Mass Public.* Cambridge, MA: Harvard University Press.

INCITE! Women of Color against Violence, ed. 2007. *The Revolution Will Not Be Funded: Beyond the Non-Profit Industrial Complex.* Cambridge, MA: South End Press.

Institute of Medicine (IOM). 2012. *The Contagion of Violence.* Washington, DC: National Academies Press.

Irwin, K., and K. Umemoto. 2016. *Jacked Up and Unjust: Pacific Islander Teens Confront Violent Legacies.* Oakland: University of California Press.

Janz, N. K., and M. H. Becker. 1984. "The Health Belief Model: A Decade Later." *Health Education Quarterly* 11(1): 1–47.

Jessor, R. 1992. "Risk Behavior in Adolescence: A Psychosocial Framework for Understanding and Action." *Developmental Review* 12(4): 374–90.

Jones, N. 2009. *Between Good and Ghetto: African American Girls and Inner-City Violence.* New Brunswick, NJ: Rutgers University Press.

Justice, B., and T. L. Meares. 2013. "How the Criminal Justice System Educates Citizens." *Annals of the American Academy of Political and Social Science* 651(1): 159–77.

Kang-Brown, J., J. Trone, J. Fratello, and T. Daftary-Kapur. 2013. *A Generation Later: What We've Learned about Zero Tolerance in Schools.* Vera Institute of

Justice.www.vera.org/publications/a-generation-later-what-weve-learned-about-zero-tolerance-in-schools.

Katz, J. 2010. "Time for New Urban Ethnographies." *Ethnography* 11(1): 25–44.

———, H. A. Heisterkamp, and W. M Fleming. 2011. "The Social Justice Roots of the Mentors in Violence Prevention Model and Its Application in a High School Setting." *Violence Against Women* 17(6): 684–702.

Kellogg, K. C. 2009. "Operating Room: Relational Spaces and Microinstitutional Change in Surgery." *American Journal of Sociology* 115(3): 657–711.

Kelly, P. 2000. "The Dangerousness of Youth-at-Risk: The Possibilities of Surveillance and Intervention in Uncertain Times." *Journal of Adolescence* 23(4): 463–76.

———. 2007. "Governing Individualized Risk Biographies: New Class Intellectuals and the Problem of Youth At-Risk." *British Journal of Sociology of Education* 28(1): 39–53.

Klinenberg, E. 2003. *Heat Wave: A Social Autopsy of Disaster in Chicago.* Chicago: University of Chicago Press.

Kohfeldt, D., L. Chun, S. Grace, and R. D. Langhout. 2011. "Youth Empowerment in Context: Exploring Tensions in School-Based yPAR." *American Journal of Community Psychology* 47(1–2): 28–45.

Kohler-Hausmann, I. 2013. "Misdemeanor Justice: Control without Conviction." *American Journal of Sociology* 119(2): 351–93.

Kotlowitz, A. 2008. "Blocking the Transmission of Violence." *New York Times,* May 4. www.nytimes.com/2008/05/04/magazine/04health-t.html.

Krause, M. 2014. *The Good Project: Humanitarian Relief NGOs and the Fragmentation of Reason.* Chicago and London: University of Chicago Press.

Kulkarni, V. S. 2017. "The Fight: Discipline and Race in an Inner-City Public Charter High School." *Annals of the American Academy of Political and Social Science* 673(1): 150–68.

Kupchik, A. 2012. *Homeroom Security: School Discipline in an Age of Fear.* New York: NYU Press.

——— and G. Ward. 2014. "Race, Poverty, and Exclusionary School Security: An Empirical Analysis of U. S. Elementary, Middle, and High Schools." *Youth Violence and Juvenile Justice* 12(4): 332–54.

Kwon, S. A. 2013. *Uncivil Youth: Race, Activism, and Affirmative Governmentality.* Durham, NC, and London: Duke University Press.

Lara-Millan, A. 2014. "Public Emergency Room Overcrowding in the Era of Mass Imprisonment." *American Sociological Review* 79(5): 866–87.

Latour, B., and S. Woolgar. 1986. *Laboratory Life: The Construction of Scientific Facts.* Princeton, NJ: Princeton University Press.

Laursen, J., and A-K Henriksen. 2018. "Altering Violent Repertoires: Perspectives on Violence in the Prison-Based Cognitive-Behavioral Program Anger Management." *Journal of Contemporary Ethnography* 26.

Law, J. 2009. "Seeing Like a Survey." *Cultural Sociology* 3(2): 239–56.

Lawrence, B. B., and A. Karim, eds. 2007. *On Violence: A Reader.* Durham, NC: Duke University Press.

Lewis, S., and A. Russell. 2012. "Young Smokers' Narratives: Public Health, Disadvantage and Structural Violence." *Sociology of Health & Illness* 35(5): 746–60.

Lichterman, P. 2006. "Social Capital or Group Style? Rescuing Tocqueville's Insights on Civic Engagement." *Theory and Society* 35(5–6): 529–63.

Lipsky, M. 1980. *Street-Level Bureaucracy: Dilemmas of the Individual in Public Services.* New York: Russell Sage Foundation.

Listenbee, R. L., J. Torre, G. Boyle, S. W. Cooper, S. Deer, et al. 2012. *Report of the Attorney General's National Task Force on Children Exposed to Violence,* December 12. www.justice.gov/defendingchildhood/cev-rpt-full.pdf.

Lupton, D. 1995. *The Imperative of Health: Public Health and the Regulated Body.* London: Sage.

Lynam, D. R., R. Milich, R. Zimmerman, S. P. Novak, T. K. Logan, et al. 1999. "Project DARE: No Effects at 10-Year Follow-Up." *Journal of Consulting and Clinical Psychology* 67(4): 590–93.

Lyon, D. 1994. *Electronic Eye: The Rise of Surveillance Society.* Minneapolis: University of Minnesota Press.

Lyons, W., and J. Drew. 2006. *Punishing Schools: Fear and Citizenship in American Public Education.* Ann Arbor: University of Michigan Press.

MacLeod, J. 1987. *Ain't No Making It: Leveled Aspirations in a Low-Income Neighbourhood.* Boulder, CO: Westview Press.

Manning, P. K. 2011. *The Technology of Policing: Crime Mapping, Information Technology, and the Rationality of Crime Control.* New York and Chesham: New York University Press.

Marcus, G. E. 1998. *Ethnography through Thick and Thin.* Princeton, NJ: Princeton University Press.

Markowitz, L., and K. W. Tice. 2002. "Paradoxes of Professionalization." *Gender & Society* 16(6): 941–58.

Martin, P. Y. 2005. *Rape Work: Victims, Gender and Emotions in Organization and Community Context.* New York: Routledge.

——— and E. E. Schmitt. 2007. "The History of the Anti-Rape and Rape Crisis Center Movements." In *Encyclopedia of Interpersonal Violence,* edited by C. M. Renezetti and J. Edleson. Thousand Oaks, CA: Sage.

Marwell, N. P. 2004. "Privatizing the Welfare State: Nonprofit Community-Based Organizations as Political Actors." *American Sociological Review* 69(2): 265–91.

———. 2009. *Bargaining for Brooklyn: Community Organizations in the Entrepreneurial City.* Chicago: University of Chicago Press.

———— and A. Gullickson. 2013. "Inequality in the Spatial Allocation of Social Services: Government Contracts to Nonprofit Organizations in New York City." *Social Service Review* 87(2): 319–53.

Marx, G. T. 2016. *Windows into the Soul: Surveillance and Society in an Age of High Technology*. Chicago and London: University of Chicago Press.

Maticka-Tyndale, E. 1992. "Social Construction of HIV Transmission and Prevention among Heterosexual Young Adults." *Social Problems* 39(3): 238–52.

Matthews, N. A. 1994. *Confronting Rape: The Feminist Anti-Rape Movement and the State*. London and New York: Routledge.

McDonnell, T. E. 2010. "Cultural Objects as Objects: Materiality, Urban Space, and the Interpretation of AIDS Campaigns in Accra, Ghana." *American Journal of Sociology* 115(6): 1800–52.

McFarland, D. A. 2004. "Resistance as a Social Drama: A Study of Change-Oriented Encounters." *American Journal of Sociology* 109(6): 1249–318.

McKinlay, J. B. 1979. "A Case for Refocusing Upstream: The Political Economy of Illness." In *Patients, Physicians, and Illness*, pp. 9–25. New York: Free Press.

McQuarrie, M., and N. P. Marwell. 2009. "The Missing Organizational Dimension in Urban Sociology." *City & Community* 8(3): 247–68.

Meighan, R., and C. Harber. 2007. *A Sociology of Educating*, Fifth ed. New York: Continuum.

Meltzer, A., K. Muir, and L. Craig. 2018. "The Role of Trusted Adults in Young People's Social and Economic Lives." *Youth & Society* 50(5): 575–92.

Merry, S. E. 2001. "Rights, Religion, and Community: Approaches to Violence against Women in the Context of Globalization." *Law & Society Review* 35(1): 39–88.

————. 2008. "Spatial Governmentality and the New Urban Social Order: Controlling Gender Violence through Law." *American Anthropologist* 103(1): 16–29.

————. 2016. *The Seductions of Quantification: Measuring Human Rights, Gender Violence, and Sex Trafficking*. Chicago: University of Chicago Press.

Messner, M. 2011. "Gender Ideologies, Youth Sports, and the Production of Soft Essentialism." *Sociology of Sport Journal* 28(2): 151–70.

————, M. A. Greenberg, and T. Peretz. 2015. *Some Men: Feminist Allies and the Movement to End Violence against Women*. New York: Oxford University Press.

Miller, J. 2008. *Getting Played: African American Girls, Urban Inequality, and Gendered Violence*. New York: New York University Press

Miller, S., J. Williams, S. Cutbush, D. Gibbs, M. Clinton-Sherrod, and S. Jones. 2015. "Evaluation of the Start Strong Initiative: Preventing Teen Dating

Violence and Promoting Healthy Relationships among Middle School Students." *Journal of Adolescent Health* 56(2): S14–19.

Miller S.A. 2016. "'How You Bully a Girl': Sexual Drama and the Negotiation of Gendered Sexuality in High School." *Gender & Society*. 30(5): 721–44.

Mills, C.W. 1959. *The Sociological Imagination*. Oxford: Oxford University Press.

Milward H.B., and K.G. Provan. 2000. "Governing the Hollow State." *Journal of Public Administration Research and Theory: J-PART* 10(2): 359–80.

Molina, N. 2006. *Fit to Be Citizens?: Public Health and Race in Los Angeles, 1879–1939*. Berkeley: University of California Press.

Morris, E.W. 2010. "'Snitches End Up in Ditches' and Other Cautionary Tales." *Journal of Contemporary Criminal Justice* 26(3): 254–72.

———. 2012. *Learning the Hard Way: Masculinity, Place, and the Gender Gap in Education*. New Brunswick, NJ: Rutgers University Press.

Mounk, Y. 2017. *The Age of Responsibility: Luck, Choice, and the Welfare State*. Cambridge, MA: Harvard University Press.

Murphey, D., T. Bandy, H. Schmitz, and K.A. Moore. 2013. *Caring Adults: Important for Positive Child Well-Being*. Child Trends. www.childtrends.org/wp-content/uploads/2013/12/2013-54CaringAdults.pdf.

Murphy, M.J. 2009. "Can 'Men' Stop Rape?: Visualizing Gender in the 'My Strength Is Not for Hurting' Rape Prevention Campaign." *Men and Masculinities* 12(1): 113–30.

Musto, J. 2016. *Control and Protect: Collaboration, Carceral Protection, and Domestic Sex Trafficking in the United States*. Oakland: University of California Press.

National Scientific Council on the Developing Child. 2004. "Young Children Develop in an Environment of Relationships." *Working Paper No. 1*. Retrieved from www.developingchild.net:12.

Nelson, B.J. 1984. *Making an Issue of Child Abuse: Political Agenda Setting for Social Problems*. Chicago: University of Chicago Press

Niolon, P.H, A.M. Vivolo-Kantor, N.E. Latzman, L.A. Valle, H. Kuoh H, et al. 2015. "Prevalence of Teen Dating Violence and Co-occurring Risk Factors among Middle School Youth in High-Risk Urban Communities." *Journal of Adolescent Health* 56(2): S5–13.

Nolan, K. 2011. *Police in the Hallways: Discipline in an Urban High School*. Minneapolis: University of Minnesota Press.

Oeur, F. 2016. "Recognizing Dignity Young Black Men Growing Up in an Era of Surveillance." *Socius: Sociological Research for a Dynamic World* 2: 1–15.

Pager, D. 2003. "The Mark of a Criminal Record." *American Journal of Sociology* 108(5): 937–75.

Pan, W., and H. Bai. 2009. "A Multivariate Approach to a Meta-Analytic Review of the Effectiveness of the D.A.R.E. Program." *International Journal of Environmental Research and Public Health* 6(1): 267–77.

Pascoe, C. J. 2007. *Dude, You're a Fag: Masculinity and Sexuality in High School*. Berkeley: University of California Press.

Patterson, O. 2014. "How Sociologists Made Themselves Irrelevant." *Chronicle of Higher Education*, December 1. www.chronicle.com/article/How-Sociologists-Made/150249.

Perry, B. L., and E. W. Morris. 2014. "Suspending Progress: Collateral Consequences of Exclusionary Punishment in Public Schools." *American Sociological Review* 79(6): 1067–87.

Placier, M. L. 1993. "The Semantics of State Policy Making: The Case of 'At Risk.'" *Educational Evaluation and Policy Analysis* 15(4): 380.

Plummer, K. 1994. *Telling Sexual Stories: Power, Change and Social Worlds*. London and New York: Routledge.

Polletta, F. 1999. "'Free Spaces' in Collective Action." *Theory and Society* 28(1): 1–38.

———. 2006. *It Was Like a Fever: Storytelling in Protest and Politics*. Chicago: University of Chicago Press.

———, P. C. B. Chen, B. G. Gardner, and A. Motes. 2011. "The Sociology of Storytelling." *Annual Review of Sociology* 37(1): 109–30.

———, M. Trigoso, B. Adams, and A. Ebner. 2013. "The Limits of Plot: Accounting for How Women Interpret Stories of Sexual Assault." *American Journal of Cultural Sociology* 1(3): 289–320.

Pomerantz, S., R. Raby, and A. Stefanik. 2013. "Girls Run the World?: Caught between Sexism and Postfeminism in School." *Gender & Society* 27(2): 185–207.

Popova, L. 2016. "Can We Resolve the Disconnect between How Communication Interventions Work and How We Evaluate Them?" *Health Education & Behavior* 43(2).

Porche, M. V., J. F. Zaff, and J. Pan. 2017. *Barriers to Success: Moving Towards a Deeper Understanding of Adversity's Effects on Adolescents*. America's Promise Alliance, Washington, DC.

Pugh, A. 2015. *The Tumbleweed Society: Working and Caring in an Age of Insecurity*. New York: Oxford University Press.

Purvin, D. M. 2007. "At the Crossroads and in the Crosshairs: Social Welfare Policy and Low-Income Women's Vulnerability to Domestic Violence." *Social Problems* 54(2): 188–210.

Puzzanchera, C., and B. Adams. 2011. *Juvenile Arrests 2009*. Juvenile Offenders and Victims National Report Series Bulletin. www.ojjdp.gov/pubs/236477.pdf.

Radwa, J. A. 1991. *Reading the Romance: Women, Patriarchy, and Popular Literature*. Chapel Hill: University of North Carolina Press

Ralph, L. 2014. *Renegade Dreams: Living through Injury in Gangland Chicago*. Chicago and London: University of Chicago Press.

Randles, J. M. 2015. "Redefining the Marital Power Struggle through Relationship Skills: How US Marriage Education Programs Challenge and Reproduce Gender Inequality." *Gender & Society* 30(2): 240–64.

Ray, R. 2017a. "Identity of Distance: How Economically Marginalized Black and Latina Women Navigate Risk Discourse and Employ Feminist Ideals." *Social Problems*.

———. 2017b. *The Making of a Teenage Service Class: Poverty and Mobility in an American City.* Oakland: University of California Press.

Reger, J. 2012. *Everywhere and Nowhere: Contemporary Feminism in the United States.* New York and Oxford: Oxford University Press.

Reid, M. 2013. "Social Policy, 'Deservingness,' and Sociotemporal Marginalization: Katrina Survivors and FEMA." *Sociological Forum* 28(4): 742–63.

Rendon, M. G. 2014. "'Caught Up': How Urban Violence and Peer Ties Contribute to High School Noncompletion." *Social Problems* 61(1): 61–82.

Resnick, M. D. 1997. "Protecting Adolescents from Harm: Findings from the National Longitudinal Study on Adolescent Health." *JAMA* 278(10): 823–32.

Rice, C., S. Lee, M. Meza, and C. Fraser. 2007. *A Call to Action: Los Angeles' Quest to Achieve Community Safety.* Advancement Project: Closing the Opportunity Gap. http://advancementprojectca.org.

Richie, B. E. 2012. *Arrested Justice: Black Women, Violence, and America's Prison Nation.* New York: NYU Press.

Rios, V. M. 2011. *Punished: Policing the Lives of Black and Latino Boys.* New York: NYU Press.

———. 2017. *Human Targets: Schools, Police, and the Criminalization of Latino Youth.* Chicago: University of Chicago Press

Rose, N. 1990. *Governing the Soul: The Shaping of the Private Self.* London: Routledge.

———. 1999. *Powers of Freedom: Reframing Political Thought.* Cambridge: Cambridge University Press.

———. 2001. "The Politics of Life Itself." *Theory, Culture, and Society* 18(6): 1–30.

———. 2006. *The Politics of Life Itself: Biomedicine, Power, and Subjectivity in the Twenty-First Century.* Princeton, NJ: Princeton University Press.

———, P. O'Malley, and M. Valverde. 2006. "Governmentality." *Annual Review of Law and Social Science* 2: 83–104.

Rosen, E. 2017. "Horizontal Immobility: How Narratives of Neighborhood Violence Shape Housing Decisions." *American Sociological Review* 82(2): 270–96.

Rumberger R. W., and D. J. Losen. 2016. "The Hidden Cost of California's Harsh School Discipline." Center for Civil Rights Remedies. www.civilrightsproject.ucla.edu/resources/projects/center-for-civil-rights-remedies/school-to-prison-folder/summary-reports/the-hidden-cost-of-californias-harsh-discipline.

Schubert, K. 2015. "Building a Culture of Health: Promoting Healthy Relationships and Reducing Teen Dating Violence." *Journal of Adolescent Health*
56(2): S3–4.

Schudson, M., and B. Baykurt. 2016. "How Does a Culture of Health Change?
Lessons from the War on Cigarettes." *Social Science & Medicine* 165:
289–96.

Seim, J. 2017. "The Ambulance: Toward a Labor Theory of Poverty Governance." *American Sociological Review* 82(3): 451–75.

Sharkey, P. 2018. *Uneasy Peace: The Great Crime Decline, the Renewal of City
Life, and the Next War on Violence.* New York: W. W. Norton.

Shedd, C. 2015. *Unequal City: Race, Schools, and Perceptions of Injustice.*
New York: Russell Sage Foundation.

Shim, J. K. 2014. *Heart-Sick: The Politics of Risk, Inequality, and Heart
Disease.* New York: NYU Press.

Silva, J. M. 2012. "Constructing Adulthood in an Age of Uncertainty." *American
Sociological Review* 77(4): 505–22.

Simon, J. 2007. *Governing through Crime: How the War on Crime Transformed
American Democracy and Created a Culture of Fear.* Oxford and New York:
Oxford University Press.

Small, M. 2004. *Villa Victoria: The Transformation of Social Capital in a
Boston Barrio.* Chicago: University of Chicago Press

Small, M. L. 2017. *Someone To Talk To.* New York: Oxford University Press.

———, D. J. Harding, and M. Lamont. 2010. "Reconsidering Culture and
Poverty." *Annals of the American Academy of Political and Social Science*
629(1): 6–27.

Smith, S. R., and M. Lipsky. 1993. *Nonprofits for Hire: The Welfare State in the
Age of Contracting.* Cambridge, MA: Harvard University Press.

Sokoloff, N. J., and I. Dupont. 2005. "Domestic Violence at the Intersections of
Race, Class, and Gender: Challenges and Contributions to Understanding
Violence against Marginalized Women in Diverse Communities." *Violence
Against Women* 11(1): 38–64.

Somers, M. R. 1994. "The Narrative Constitution of Identity: A Relational and
Network Approach." *Theory and Society* 23(5): 605–49.

Soss, J., R. C. Fording, and S. F. Schram. 2011. *Disciplining the Poor: Neoliberal
Paternalism and the Persistent Power of Race.* Chicago: University of
Chicago Press.

Spencer, R., T. Tugenberg, M. Ocean, S. E. Schwartz, and J. E. Rhodes. 2016.
"'Somebody Who Was on My Side': A Qualitative Examination of Youth-
Initiated Mentoring." *Youth & Society* 48(3): 402–24.

Staggenborg, S. 1988. "The Consequences of Professionalization and Formalization in the Pro-Choice Movement." *American Sociological Review* 53(4):
585–605.

————— and V. Taylor. 2005. "Whatever Happened to the Women's Movement?" *Mobilization: An International Quarterly* 10(1): 37–52.

Sum, A., I. Khatiwada, M. Trubskyy, and S. Palma. 2014. *The Plummeting Labor Market Fortunes of Teens and Young Adults*. Brookings Institution. https://assets.rockefellerfoundation.org/app/uploads/20150310143832/The-Plummeting-Labor-Market-Fortunes-of-Teends-and-Young-Adults1.pdf.

Swidler, A. 2001. *Talk of Love: How Culture Matters*. Chicago and London: University of Chicago Press.

Tavory, I., and N. Eliasoph. 2013. "Coordinating Futures: Toward a Theory of Anticipation." *American Journal of Sociology* 118(4): 908–42.

Tharp, A. T. 2012. "Dating Matters™: The Next Generation of Teen Dating Violence Prevention." *Prevention Science* 13.

—————, T. R. Simon, and J. Saul J. 2012. "Preventing Violence against Children and Youth." *Journal of Safety Research* 43(4): 291–98.

Thomas, J. E. 1999. "Everything about Us Is Feminist." *Gender & Society* 13(1): 101–19.

Thorne, B. 1993. *Gender Play: Girls and Boys in School*. New Brunswick, NJ: Rutgers University Press.

Timmermans, S., and M. Berg. 2003. *The Gold Standard: The Challenge of Evidence-Based Medicine*. Philadelphia: Temple University Press.

Trimbur, L. 2011. "'Tough Love': Mediation and Articulation in the Urban Boxing Gym." *Ethnography* 12(3): 334–55.

U.S. Department of Health and Human Services. 2005. *Theory at a Glance: A Guide for Health Promotion Practice*. National Institutes of Health Publication no. 05–3896.

Vagi, K. J., E. F. Rothman, N. E. Latzman, A. T. Tharp, D. M. Hall, and M. J. Breiding. 2013. "Beyond Correlates: A Review of Risk and Protective Factors for Adolescent Dating Violence Perpetration." *Journal of Youth and Adolescence* 42(4): 633–49.

Varga, S. M., and J. F. Zaff. 2017. *Defining Webs of Support: A New Framework to Advance Understanding of Relationships and Youth Development*. America's Promise Alliance, Washington, DC. www.americaspromise.org/sites/default/files/d8/WebsSupport_ResearchBrief_v2.pdf.

Wacquant, L. 2009. *Punishing the Poor: The Neoliberal Government of Social Insecurity*. Durham, NC: Duke University Press.

Watkins, S. C., and A. Swidler. 2013. "Working Misunderstandings: Donors, Brokers, and Villagers in Africa's AIDS Industry." *Population and Development Review* 38(s1): 197–218.

Watkins-Hayes, C. 2009. *The New Welfare Bureaucrats: Entanglements of Race, Class, and Policy Reform*. Chicago: University Of Chicago Press.

Weber, M., H. H. Gerth, and C. W. Mills. [1916–62] 2012. *From Max Weber: Essays in Sociology*. Ulan Press.

Weiss, B. P. 1996. "Violence in the United States." In *Defining Violence: Understanding the Causes and Effects of Violence,* edited by Hannah Bradley, 83–99. Brookfield, VT: Averbury Ashgate.

Welch, K., and A. A. Payne. 2010. "Racial Threat and Punitive School Discipline." *Social Problems* 57(1): 25–48.

Western, B. 2006. *Punishment and Inequality in America.* New York: Russell Sage Foundation.

———. 2018. *Homeward: Life in the Year after Prison.* New York: Russell Sage Foundation.

Whitaker, D. J., and L. Reese. 2007. *Preventing Intimate Partner Violence and Sexual Violence in Racial/Ethnic Minority Communities.* CDC's Demonstration Projects. Atlanta: Centers for Disease Control and Prevention.

Willis, P. E. 1977. *Learning to Labor: How Working Class Kids Get Working Class Jobs.* New York: Columbia University Press.

Wolch, J. R. 1990. *The Shadow State: Government and Voluntary Sector in Transition.* New York: Foundation Center.

Ybarra, M. L., and K. J. Mitchell. 2013. "Prevalence Rates of Male and Female Sexual Violence Perpetrators in a National Sample of Adolescents." *JAMA Pediatrics* 167(12): 1125.

Zola, I. K. 1972. "Medicine as an Institution of Social Control." *Sociological Review* 20(4): 487–504.

Index

ABCDE Method, 12
abuse, 15–16, 38, 198n40
activism, 9–10, 29–31
Addams, Jane, 1, 182–83
administrators, 155–58.
adolescence. *See* youth
adults, 78, 144–46, 148–51, 164, 182–84, 213n3
Adverse Childhood Experience Study (ACES), 195n3, 205n5
agency, 8–9, 67–68, 102, 142–43. *See also* empowerment
aggression, 52, 57–59, 62–64
Aldridge, Leah, 33, 37–39, 43–44, 129
anti-rape squad, 29–30
at-risk youth. *See* youth
authority, 18–19, 73–74, 159–61

behavior: and change programs, 12, 97, 111, 113–14, 209n3; and public health, 36, 47; and risk factors, 55
behavioral theory, 13, 97, 197n27
BeStrong, 43, 129–30
Black youth: criminalization of, 34–36; and health disparities, 32; and risk factors, 71–72; and social support, 40. *See also* youth of color

Blueprints for Healthy Youth Development, 13
Blue Shield of California, 45, 204n50
branding, 27, 44, 85
bullying, 41, 61–62, 157, 198n31
bureaucracies: and change programs, 95–97; and ephemeral state, 6; and institutional relationships, 145–46; and intervention, 92–93; and nonprofits, 10–11

California Coalition Against Sexual Assault, 44
California Endowment, 46
California Office of Criminal Justice Planning (OCJP), 31
Campbell's Law, 99
capitalism, 10–13, 25–27, 96–97, 179, 200n4
Castel, Robert, 54
Centers for Disease Control (CDC), 32, 36–37, 40
change. *See* personal change
change programs: and bureaucracy, 97; as commodities, 27–28; and cultural change, 12–14, 98–99, 179–80; and curricula, 110–13, 209n1; and empowerment, 130–32; and ephemeral state, 108–9; ethnographic studies of, 21–22; and financial concerns, 25–26; and narrative, 16, 114–15, 142; and narrative projects, 128–29, 138–41; and

Mills, C. Wright, 54, 213n12
morality, 13, 19
MyStrength, 45, 129–30, 204n48

narrative: and abuse, 15–17, 198n43; and
change programs, 115–16, 127–28; and
counters, 122–24; and cultural entropy,
119–20; and curricula, 118–19; and disclosure, 108; and ephemeral state, 21–22;
and identity, 75–78, 180; and lived experience, 120–21, 138–41; and playback, 124–
27; political uses of, 201n9; and responsibility, 171–72; and risk factors, 55–57; and
social policy, 114; and sparks, 120–22; and
statistics, 52–53; and violence prevention,
23, 28–30, 33–34, 39, 111–13, 210n6,11
narrative projects: and change programs,
138–41; and empowerment, 128–32; and
lived experience, 142–43; and personal
change, 133–37
National Institute for Mental Health, 31
National Violent Death Reporting System
(NVDRS), 42
neoliberalism: and change programs, 195–
96n6; and ephemeral state, 3; and paternalism, 203n41, 208n6; and responsibility, 215n34
nonprofit sector: and change programs, 22;
and effectiveness measures, 97–98; and
funding, 11; marketization of, 27–28,
200n5; and privatization, 32–33; and
shadow state, 9–10; and the state, 82–83,
208n1; and upper-income schools, 94–95;
and violence prevention, 42

Obama, Barack, 178
Office of Child Abuse Prevention (OCAP), 33
Office of Criminal Justice Planning (OCJP), 37

Peace Over Violence: and change programs,
3; and Choose Peace, 45–46; and curricula, 113; and definitions of violence, 20;
evaluations of, 95–102; and facilitators,
83–87; and financial concerns, 25–27;
and funding, 197n23; and intervention,
92–93; and marketing, 44, 204n47;
and slow state, 6; and violence prevention, 20–22. See also Los Angeles Commission on Assaults Against Women
(LACAAW)
personal change 133–37, 140
personal choice: and empowerment, 129–32;
and public health, 45–47; and responsi-

bility, 165–68, 204n52; and risk data,
66–67; and violence, 58
personal responsibility. See responsibility
Personal Responsibility and Work Opportunity Act, 40
Plummer, Ken, 113
policing. See crime control; law enforcement
policy in person, 146
post-traumatic stress disorder, 1. See also
trauma
preventionists, 54–55
Prevention of Youth Violence, The, 36
primary prevention, 13, 41–46
principals, 73–74, 92–93, 147–48, 151
prison-industrial complex, 10
prisons, 149–50, 214n7
privatization, 32
process-based evidence, 97–98
Prothrow-Smith, Deborah, 36
public health: and change programs, 12–13,
33, 211n17; and cultural change, 179–80;
and curricularization, 48–50; and data
collection, 41; and funding, 178; and narrative entropy, 119; and personal change,
134; and risk data, 202n31; and Safe
Dates, 112; and the state, 29; and statistical analysis, 53; and VAWA, 39–40; and
violence, 19; and violence prevention,
24–25, 31–37, 39, 43–44, 46–47

race, 88–90, 94, 209n14. See also Black
youth; Latinx youth; youth of color
rape, 29–31
rape crisis centers, 29–30
Rape Prevention Education (RPE) grant, 26
Ravitz, Judy, 31
red flags, 64–69, 98
relationships: and change programs, 139–40;
and curricula, 115–17; and institutions,
7–8; interpersonal vs. institutional, 146,
152–55; and personal change, 134–36;
and youth, 121
Report of the Secretary's Task Force on Black
and Minority Health, 32
responsibility: and behavior, 66–68; and
choice, 165–69, 204n52; and institutional
relationships, 146–47; and public health,
180; and young men, 169–73; and young
women, 175–76
risk data: critiques of, 55, 206n11; and interpretation, 62–64; vs. lived experiences,
64–68; and the past, 75–78; and predict-
ability, 53; and statistical lives, 78, 181–

violence *(continued)*
198n43; and narrative projects, 142–43;
and personal change, 140–41; and public
health, 31–32, 39; and risk, 35–36; and
at-risk youth, 2; and the state, 17–20,
28–29; and trauma, 59–60; understanding of, 69–70, 207n19; and young women,
215–16n44
Violence Against Women Act (VAWA), 39–40
Violence Prevention Coalition (VPC): and
definitions of violence, 19; formation of,
37; and public health, 10, 46; and violence prevention, 24–25
violence prevention programs: and abuse, 38;
and agency, 8–9; and change programs,
13–14; and curricularization, 48–50; evaluations of, 36–37, 42–44, 132–33; and
facilitator burnout, 95–97; and facilitators, 11, 79–80; and feminism, 29–34,
38–39; and financial concerns, 25–27;
and funding, 33; history of, 29; and ideas
of violence, 17–18; and law enforcement,
34–35, 40–42; and mandated reporting,
103–8; and nonprofits, 10; and Peace
Over Violence, 21–22; and personal
change, 133–37; and public health,
46–48; and risk, 54; and "at risk" label,
90–93; and at-risk youth, 3–4; and
social policy, 111–12; and student
engagement, 82–83; and trauma, 4–5;
and upper-income schools, 94–95; and
urban crime, 35–36. *See also* change
programs

Weber, Max, 17, 201n8
Weiss, Billie, 35–37, 42, 46–47
welfare. *See* social support
welfare state, 10, 34
Western, Bruce, 181
Wolch, Jennifer, 10
World Health Organization, 19

Young Men's Initiative, 196n15
youth: adultification of, 65–68, 76–78; and
adults, 144–46, 164, 182–84, 213n3; and
agency, 8–9; and change programs, 45,
127–28; and curricula, 119; and discipline,
148–51; and disclosure, 104–8; effects of
violence on, 14–15; and empowerment,
129–32; and evaluation, 99–102; and facilitators, 83–90; and growing up, 76–68;
and lived experience, 118; and narrative,
114–17, 120; and personal change, 133–37;
and responsibility, 165–68; as at-risk, 55,
69–70, 90–93; and risk factors, 3, 177
youth of color: and administrators, 155–58;
adultification of, 65–66, 68, 76–78; and
aggression, 62; and crime control, 152–55;
criminalization of, 151; and empowerment, 173–77; and law enforcement, 74,
149–50, 152–55; and responsibility, 167–
73; and risk factors, 71–72; and surveillance, 160–62. *See also* Black youth; Latinx youth
Youth Risk Behavior Surveillance System, 36
*Youth Violence: A Report of The Surgeon
General*, 42